David A White

Mecha Zone 1.5

www.mechazone.com

Written and illustrated by David A. White

ISBN: 978-0-9845495-1-1

Proudly printed in the USA by Taylor Specialty Books
www.taylorspecialtybooks.com

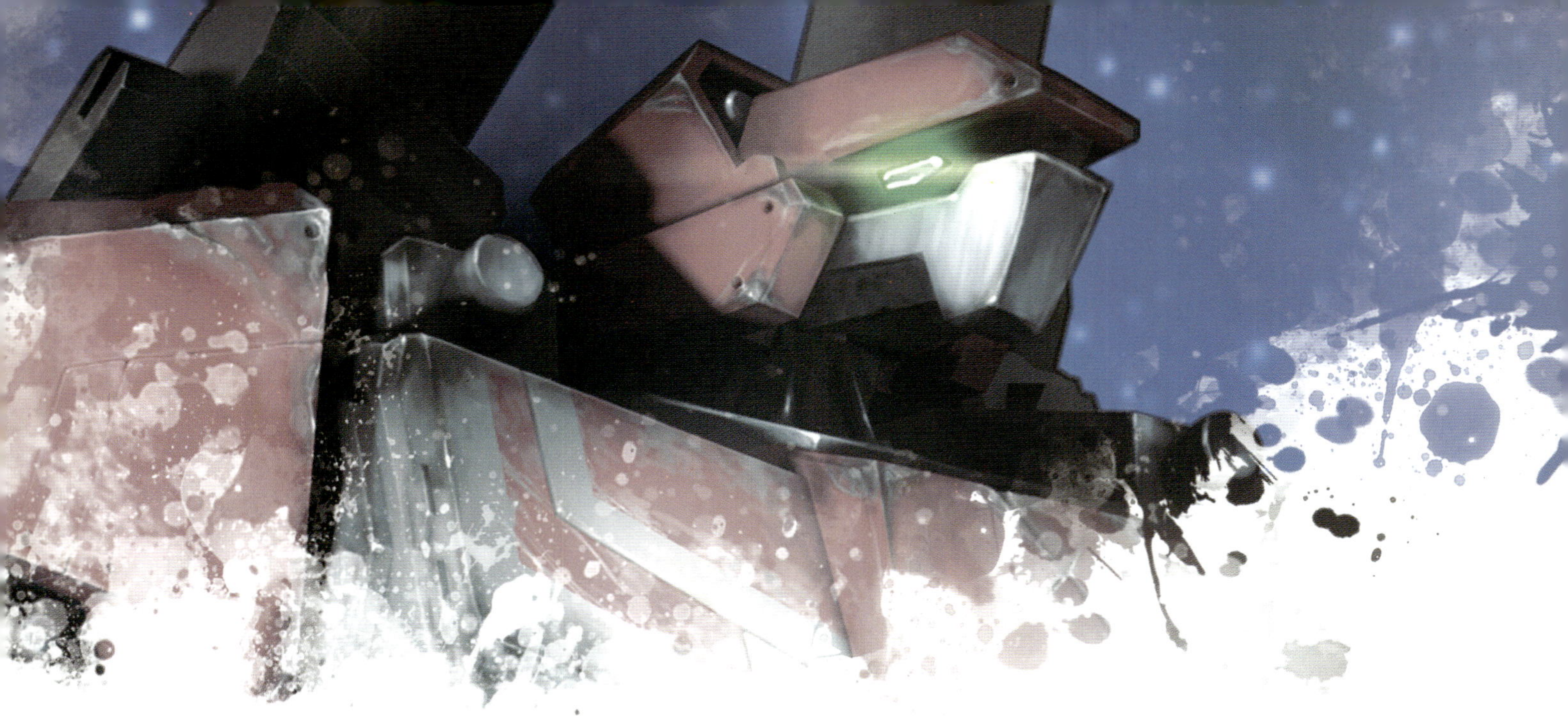

Mecha Zone 1.5

Introduction

Welcome! *Mecha Zone 1.5* is a revised and enhanced second edition of my original art book, *Mecha Zone 1*. This new edition features a larger format with 32 additional pages and even more robots than the first edition! The layout has also been modernized to fit the paradigm set in Mecha Zone 2.

I created the *Mecha Zone* in 1997 as a web page to share my robot designs. The web page has had several face-lifts over the years and has featured a lot of cool content. *Mecha Zone* has inspired hundreds of fellow mecha fans to contact me and has also helped me find many terrific freelance art jobs.

The mecha art showcased within represents a time span of almost 15 years and I'm sure you will notice changes in style, technique, and ability. Designing mecha is a very challenging and time-consuming hobby. Like all artists, I continually strive to improve. I sincerely hope that everyone who looks through this book will be inspired just as I am when I see new and intriguing artwork.

Thanks for your support and have fun!

David White

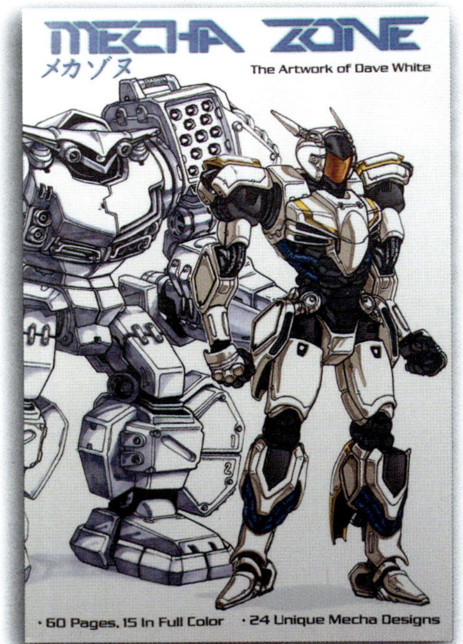

The original *Mecha Zone 1*.

A special thank you to my wife Melissa, The Western Mass Illustrators Guild, and the deviantART.com mecha community, for all of their wisdom and support.

Meet the artist

Hi everyone, I'm David White! Here's a photo of me at the 2010 New York Comic Con where I premiered my other art book, *Mecha Zone 2*.

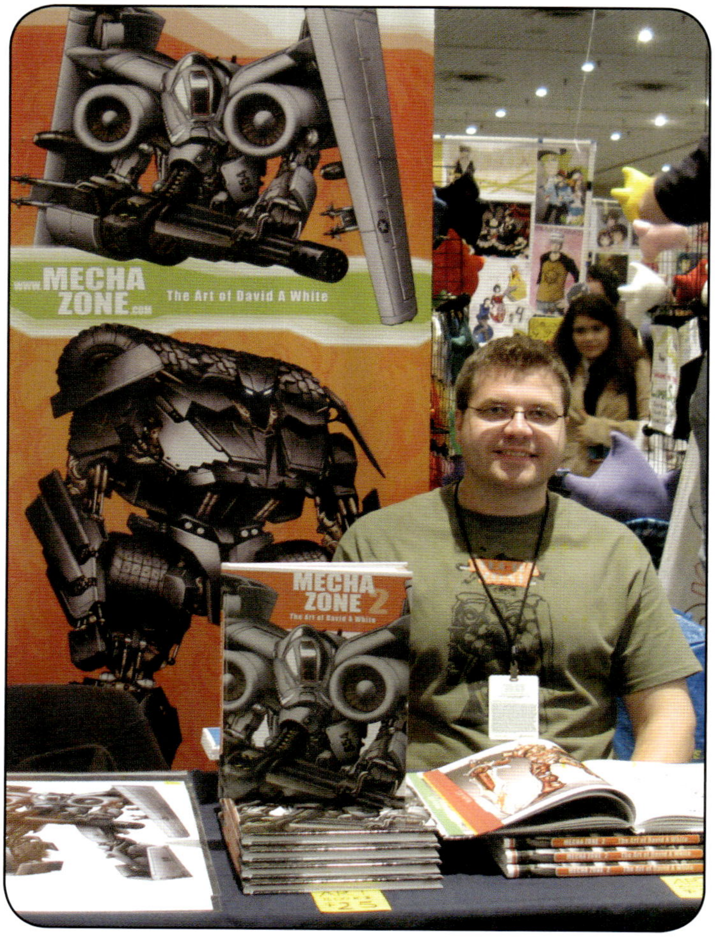

I am an illustrator who likes to design and draw machines of all sorts, but especially giant robots. I have contributed robot drawings to many books and video games over the last 10 years. I also enjoy creating artwork for comics, animation, and toys.

If my work looks familiar then you may have seen it in some of these books and games...

- *Mecha Mania* (Watson-Guptill)
- *Anime Mania* (Watson-Guptill)
- *50 Robots to Draw and Paint* (Barrons)
- *MechWarrior4™ : Mercenaries* (Microsoft Games)
- *MechWarrior4™ : Black Knight* (Microsoft Games)
- *MechWarrior Dark Age®* (Wizkids)
- *Battletech: TRO 3085* (Catalyst Game Labs)
- *Battletech: TRO Prototypes* (Catalyst Game Labs)
- Transformers: War for Cybertron (NDS versions)

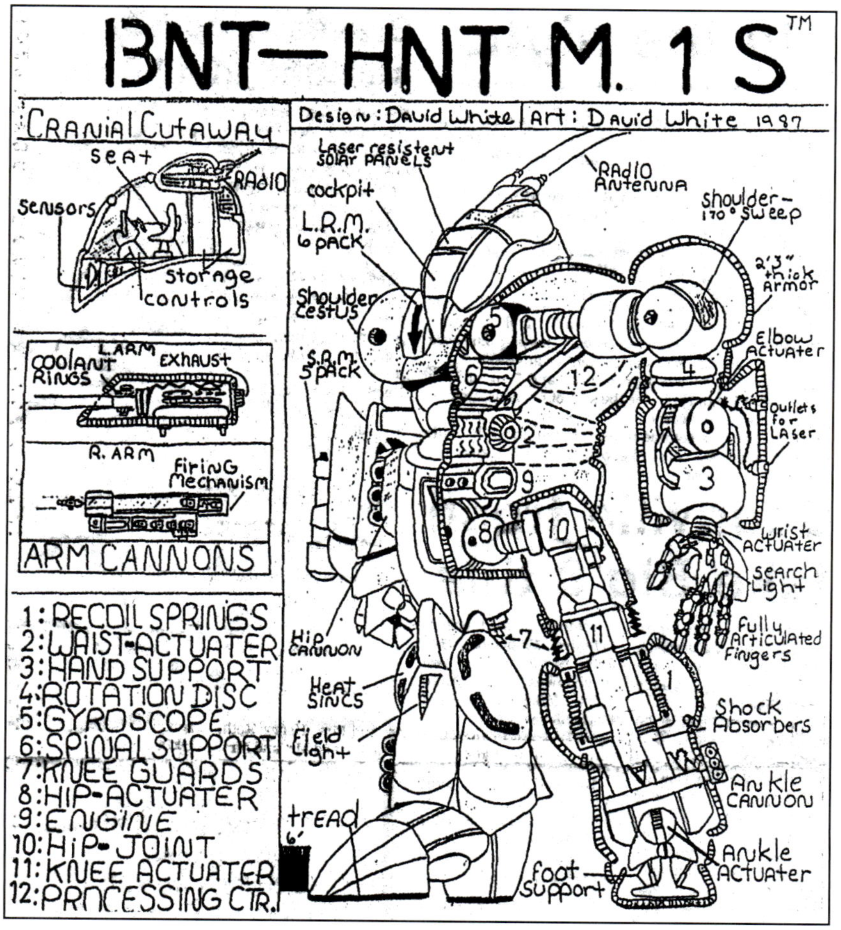

I started drawing robots in the early 80's. I was inspired by toys, comics, and Japanese cartoons that I saw on TV. My favorites were *Shogun Warriors*, *Starblazers*, *Battle of the Planets*, *Voltron*, *Transformers*, *Robotech*, and *Battletech*.

I am still a fan of all robots, or "mecha" as I call them. Mecha is slang for mechanical so it can be used for robots, tanks, jets, etc...

Check out this robot I made when I was 14. I had a lot of fun making this *Battletech* inspired image and it was a sign of things to come. Now, I actually draw robots for the real *Battletech* game as a freelancer. I am always excited to get a new assignment and I feel blessed to be so fortunate.

I hope you have fun looking at this book. Who knows, maybe you'll be inspired to draw some mecha of your own!

July 19th, 2011 David A. White

MECHA ZONE 1.5

KICKSTARTER THANKS

Thank you to everyone who donated to my Kickstarter.com fundraising project. This book would only be 33% as awesome without your support! Your generosity allowed me to add 32 pages, print the entire book in color, and even add some special cover treatments such as the embossing.

What is Kickstarter? Kickstarter is a new way to fund creative projects using an all-or-nothing pledge system. People who make pledges receive something in return, such as a copy of the final product. Anyone who pledged $25 or more to my project received a copy of this book along with a limited edition print.

As an extra token of my appreciation, everyone who pledged $100 or more got their name printed in my book. I received a total of 77 backers for this project. Thank you to everyone for his and her support!

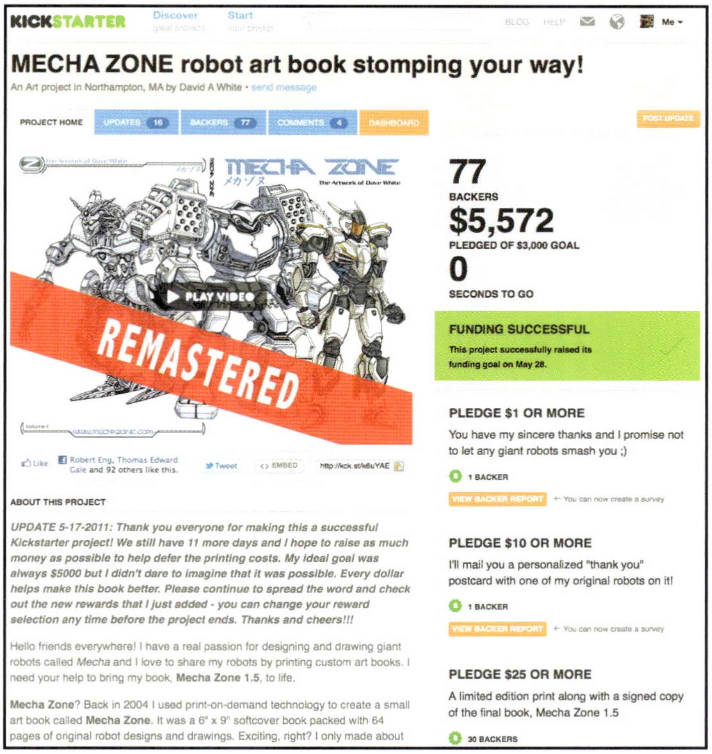

Stephen Cordova	CollectionDX
David Silverman	Wordman
Jim Peterson	Captain Kevin Tribe
Alex Taylor	Thomas Jakob
Richard Parker	Stephan Szabo
Charles Raney	The Youngblood family
Darren Popik	Sean Wang & Peggy Twardowski
Ken Grey	Eric Marcoullier
Hallam Lowmass	The Hutchinson Family
Julian Orr	DS99

CHAPTER 1

Chapter 1 showcases 4 of my newest designs. Three of the designs were created just for this book and a long-time fan commissioned the other.

These designs represent my current style of drawing and coloring. I enjoy intricate line work, rich colors, translucent details, and a hint of texture.

Most of my freelance robot designs focus on military themes with a lot of missiles, guns, and lasers. For my personal works, I prefer to focus primarily on the beauty of the overall form and less on weapons or secondary components.

NEW MECHA

LIBELLE AKA DRAGONFLY

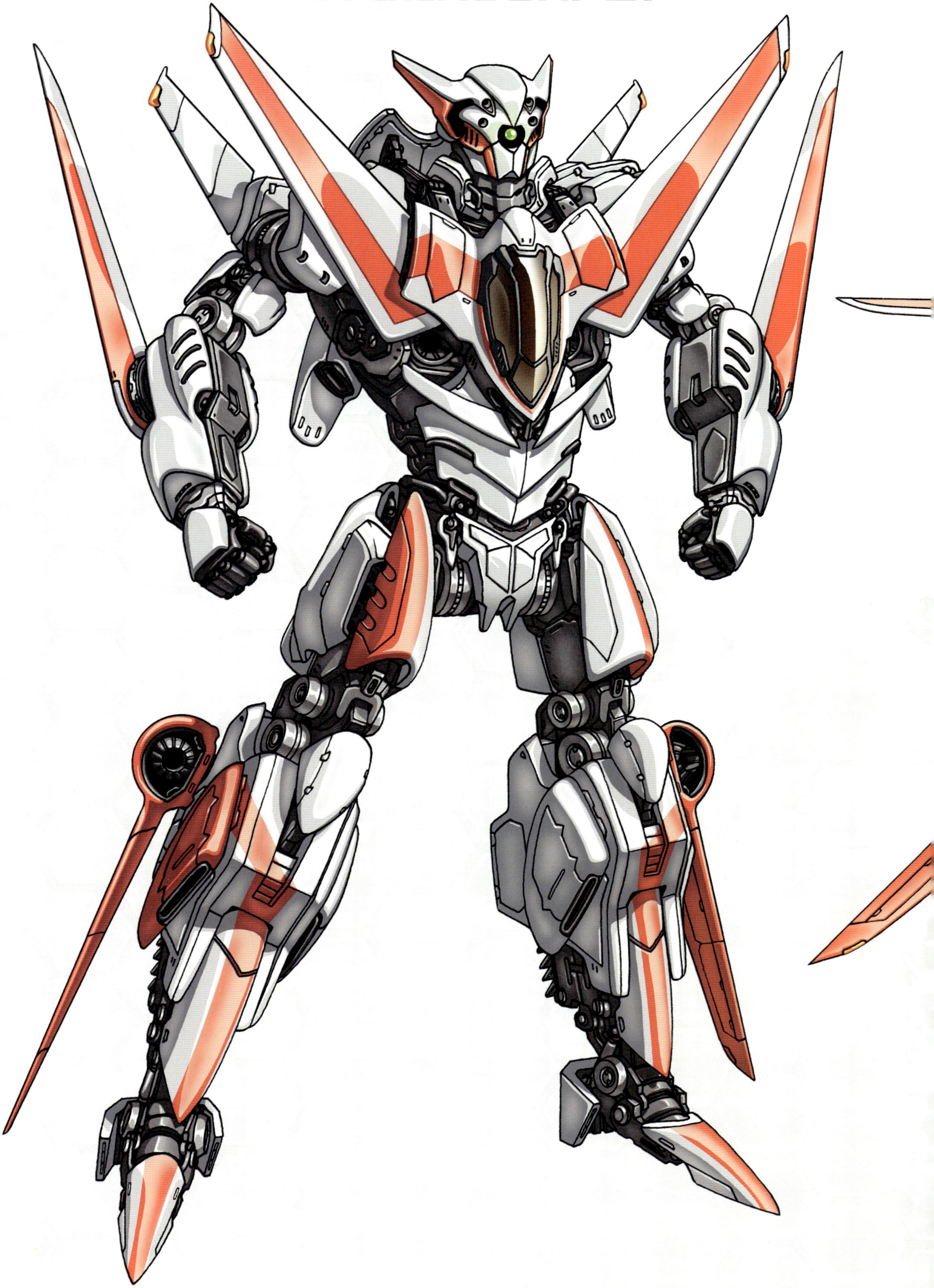

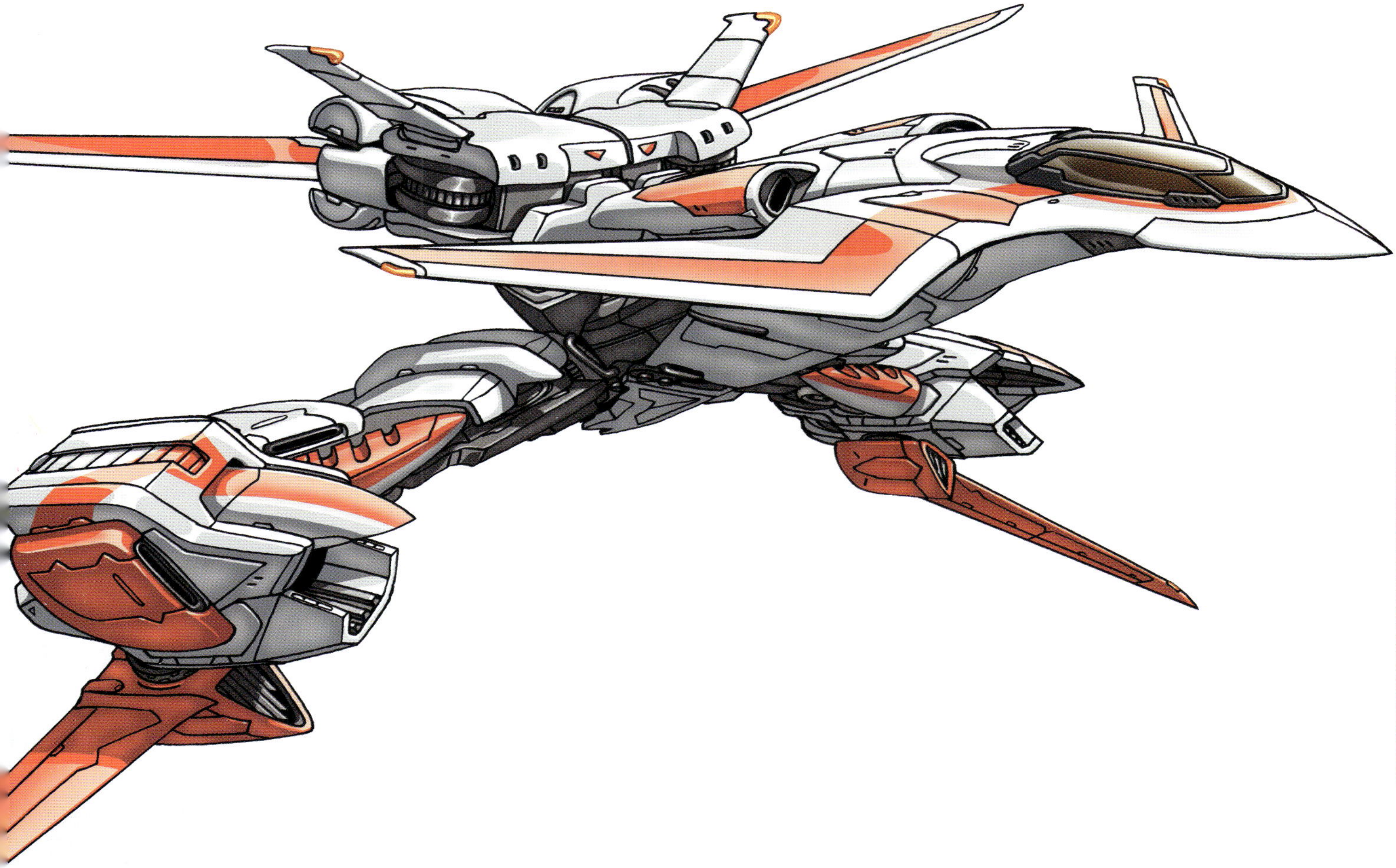

The Libelle is a transforming mecha that changes from a robot to an advanced space fighter.

This design was inspired by many of the transforming robots you see so often in Japanese animation. It has an air of familiarity, but I worked hard to infuse it with my own ideas and flair.

The cockpit and front wings can detach as a smaller fighter and escape craft.

LIBELLE AKA DRAGONFLY

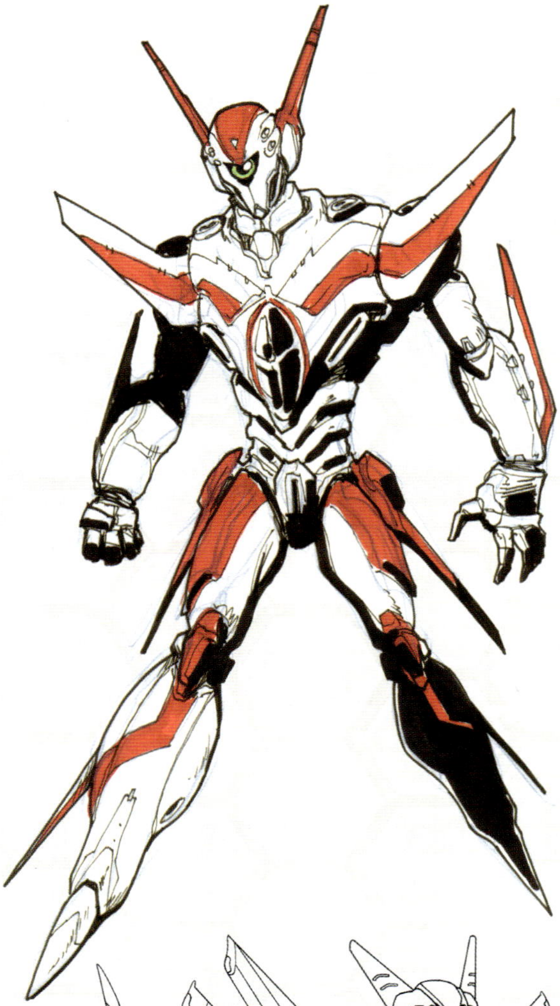

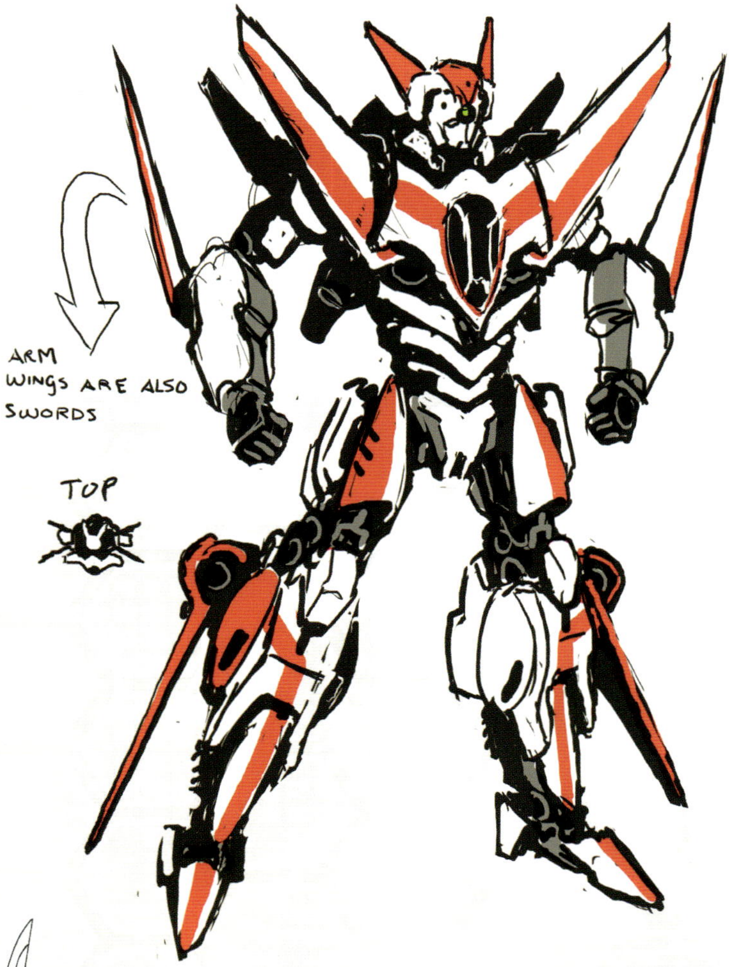

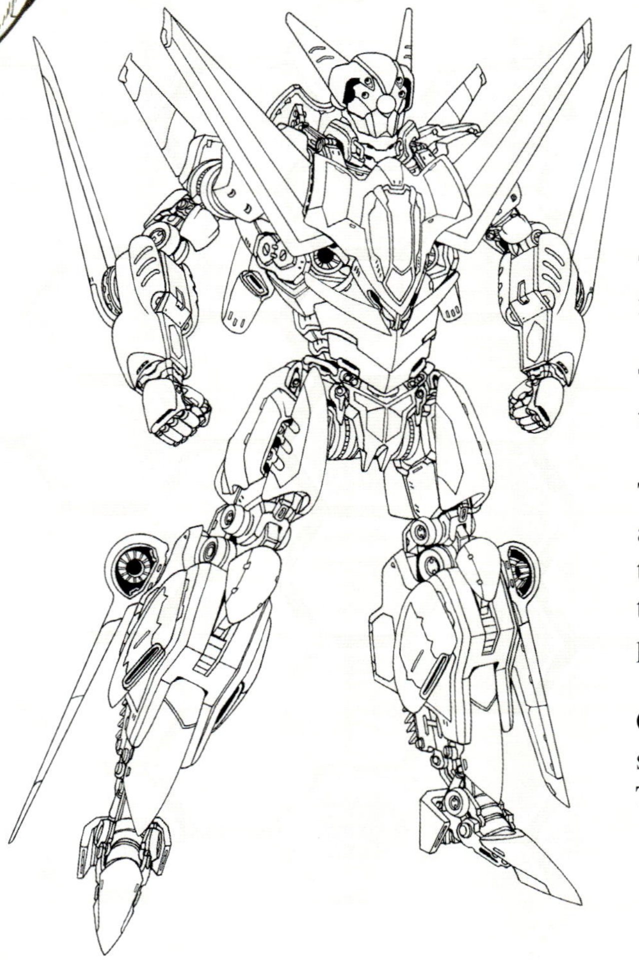

The upper left sketch served as the initial inspiration for the final design.

The image directly above has all of the major parts of the final design, but is still lacking the fine details.

The lower left image is the final inked design. It has all of the details, but there are still some minor parts that need work. If you look closely, you will notice that the head is slightly different in the final version on page 8.

Opposite page: These are concept sketches for the space fighter mode. They progress from top to bottom. The last image is the final inked design.

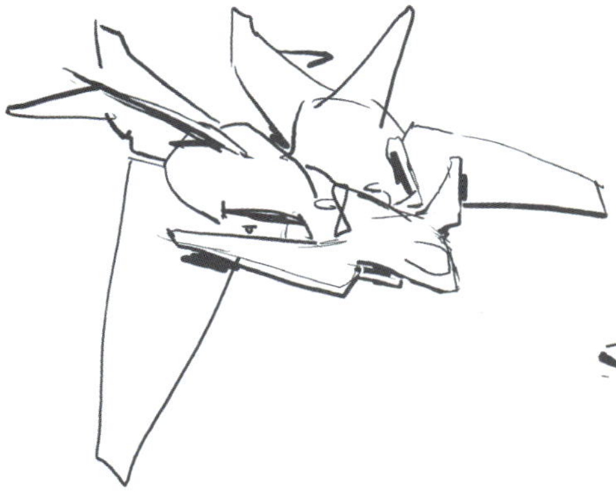
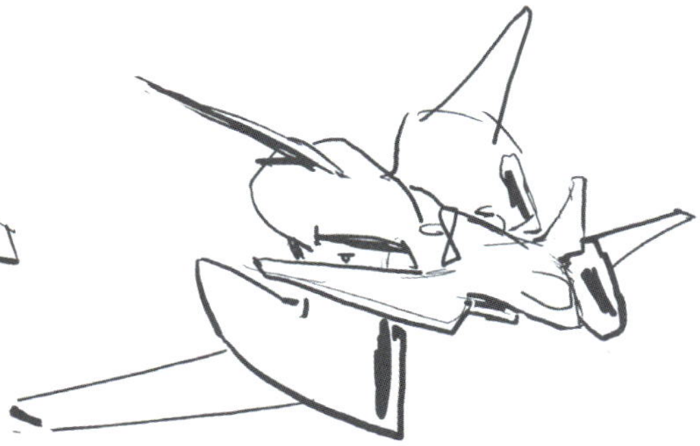
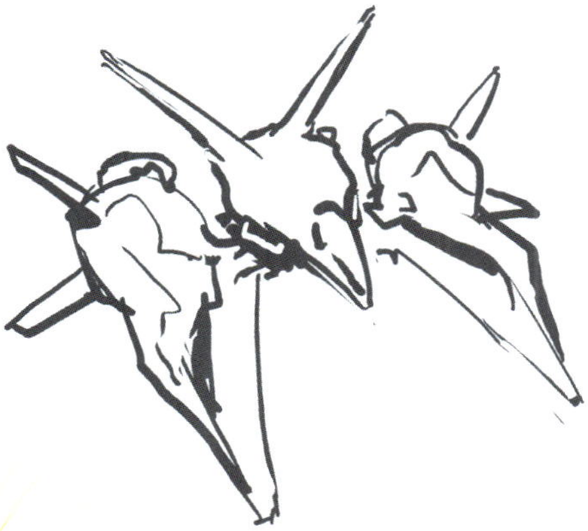
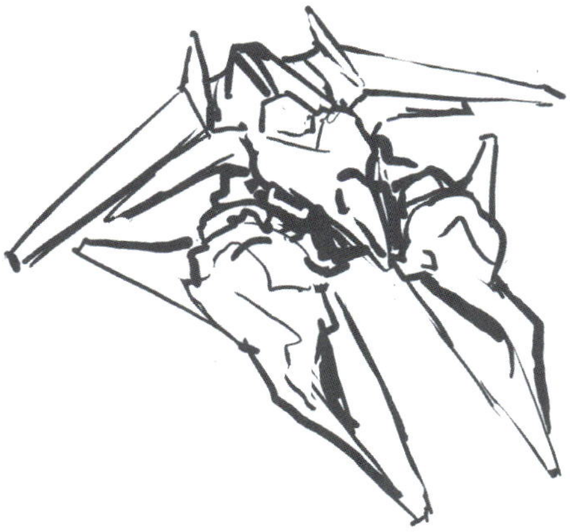
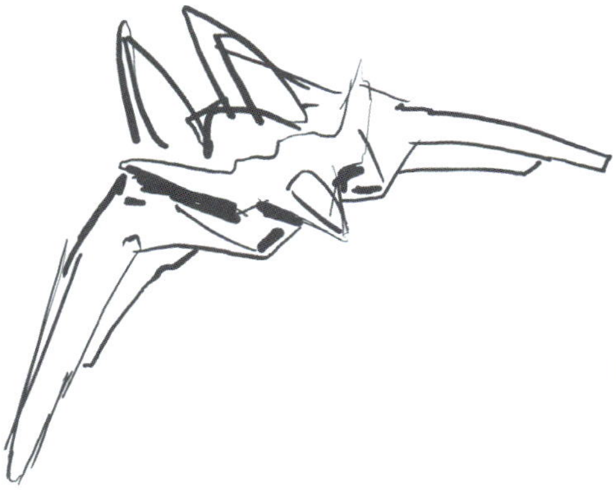
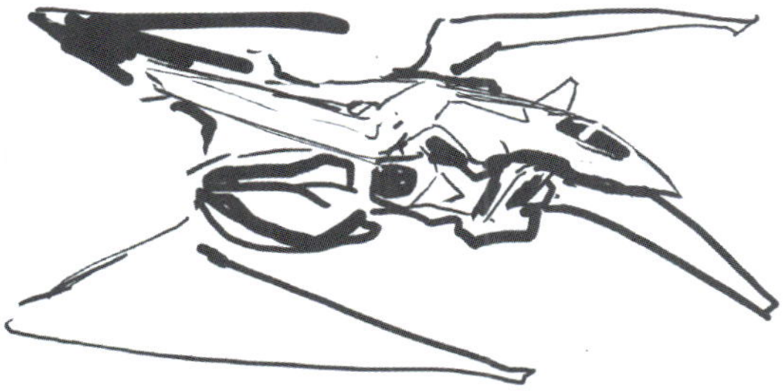
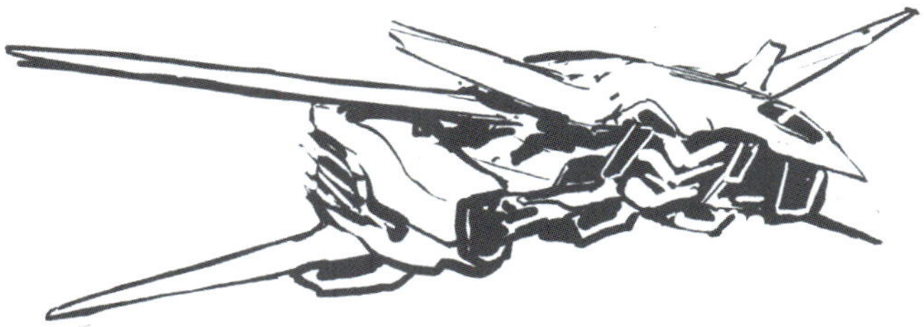
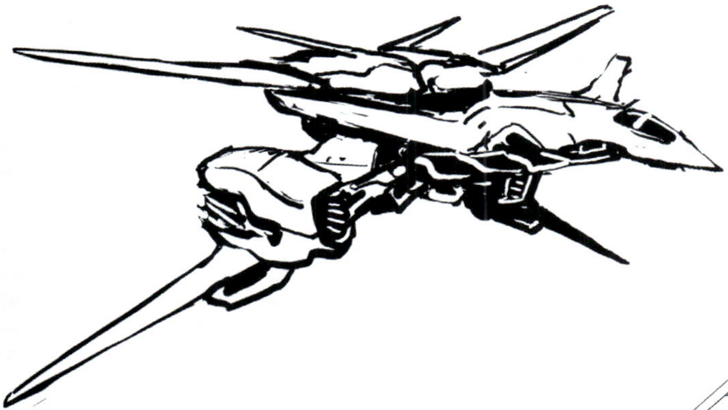
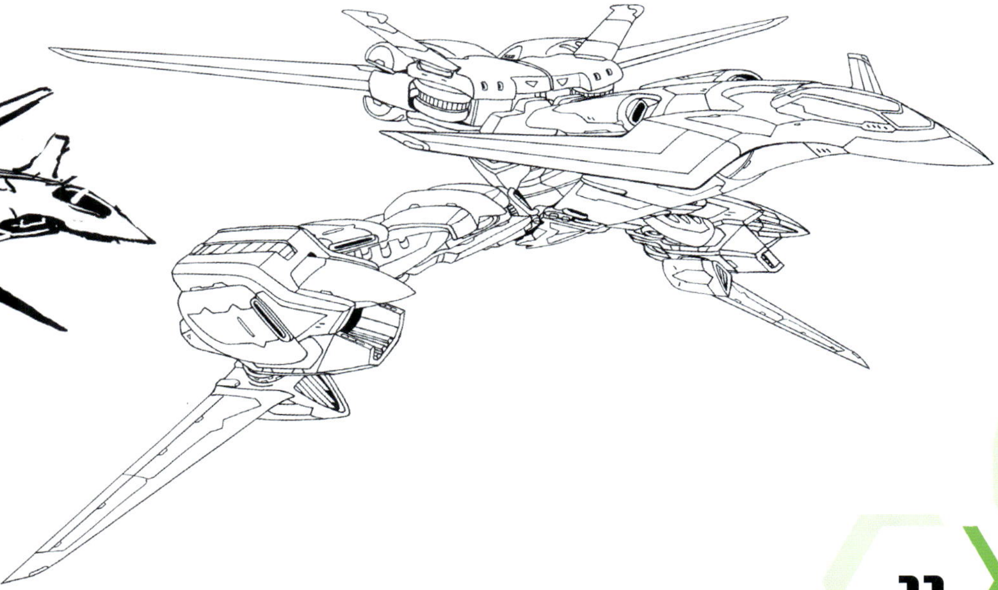

AEGIS PROTOTYPE

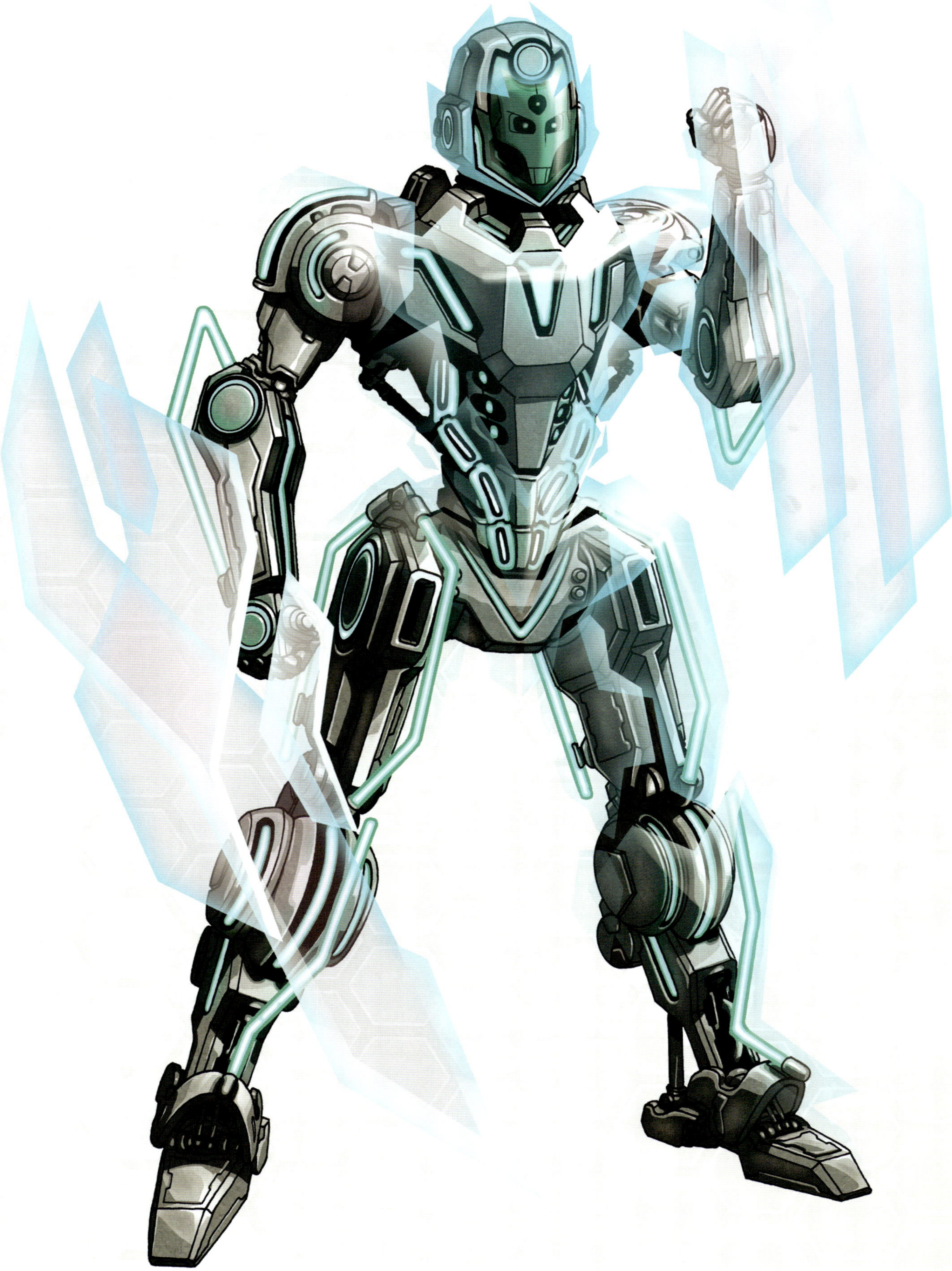

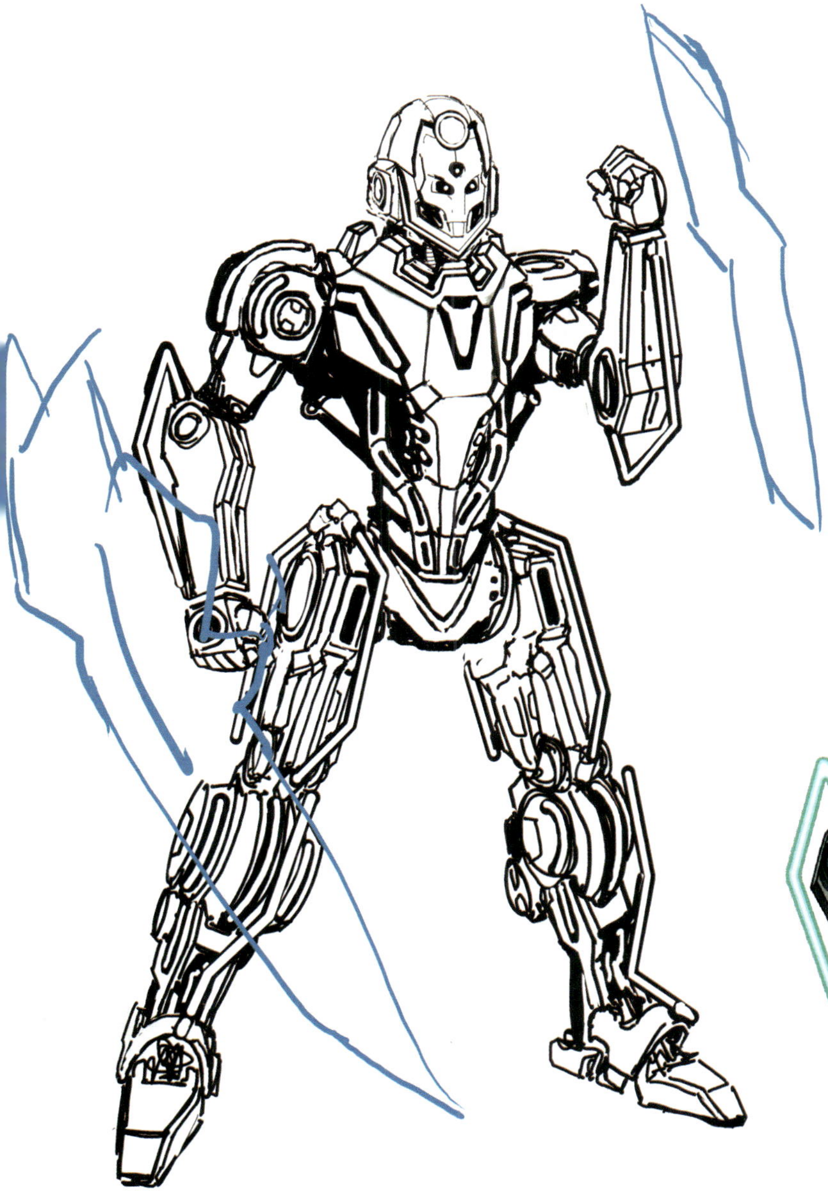

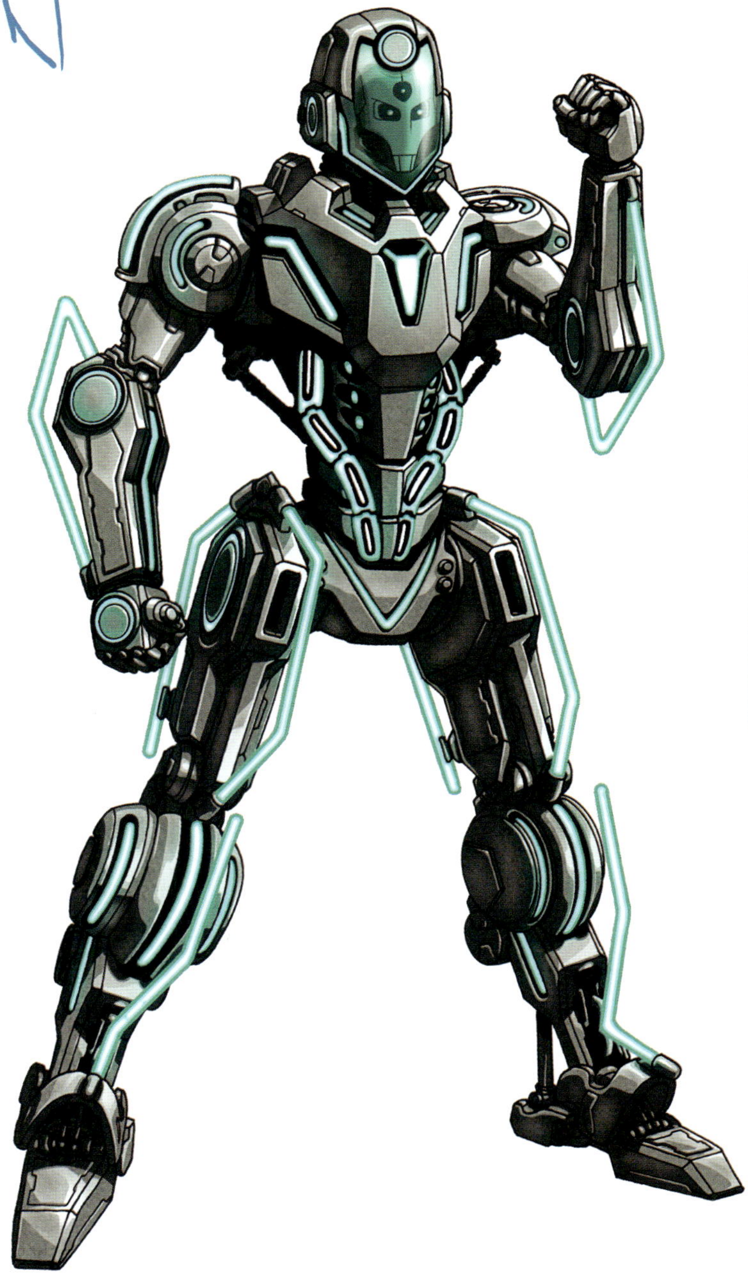

As a reward for his charitable donation to the funding of mecha zone 1.5, Stephen Cordova collaborated with me to design this mecha. Thank you, Stephen!

The Aegis prototype has an advanced inner frame that can generate focused energy shields for defense and offence.

The glowing shield projector bars tie into a central power generator, located in the chest.

Aegis Prototype

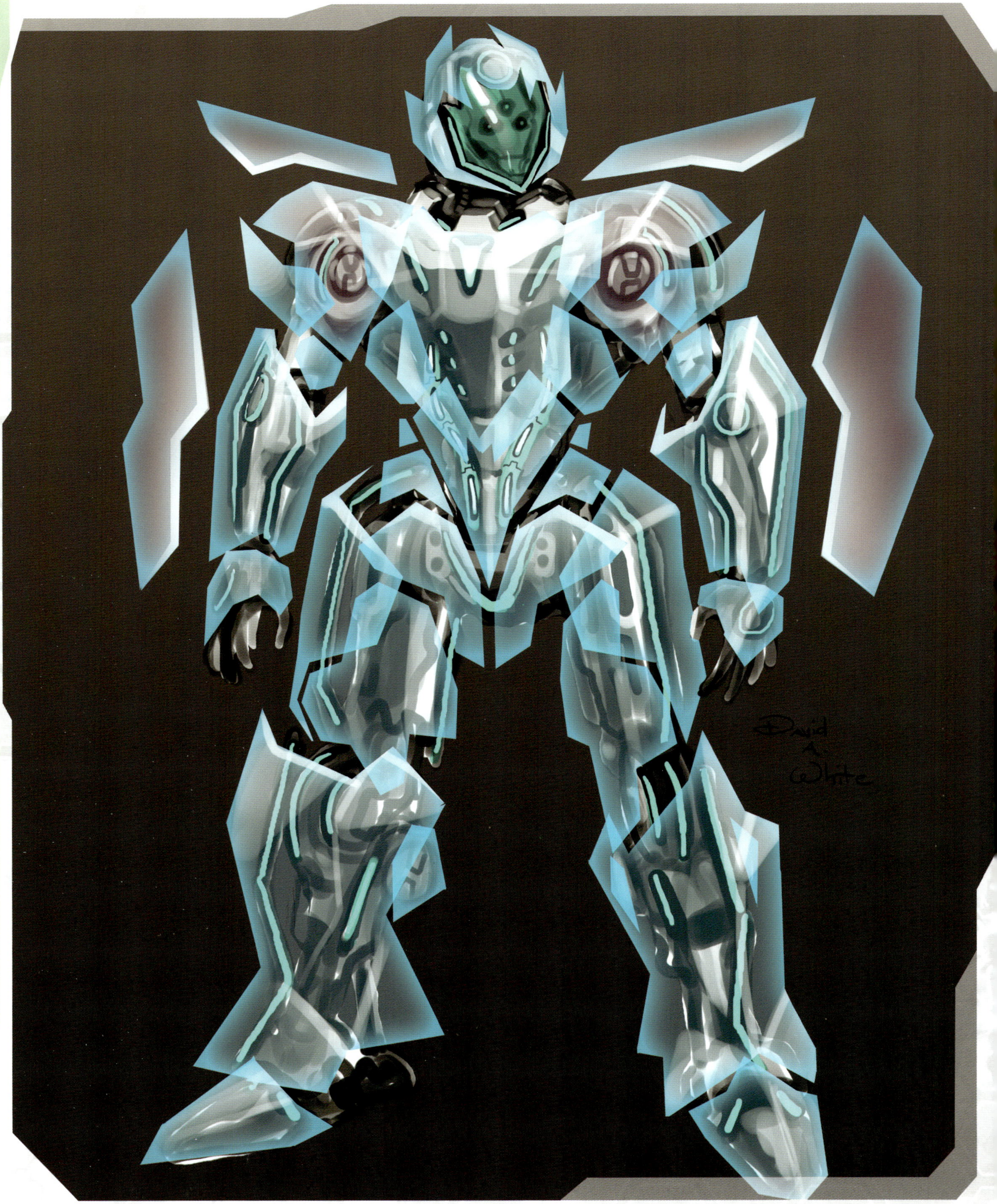

Opposite page: Concept art showing the Aegis unit with all shield units active.

The shields are only projected when and where needed to conserve energy. There is an inner layer of shields that conform to the general shape of the skeleton and an outer layer of shields that can be used as blades.

The images to the right show the beginning of the concepting process. I had to find a good pose and overall form, and then I began to add the details.

The bottom image is the final concept art for the inner skeleton.

The lower right image was my first design for the energy shields.

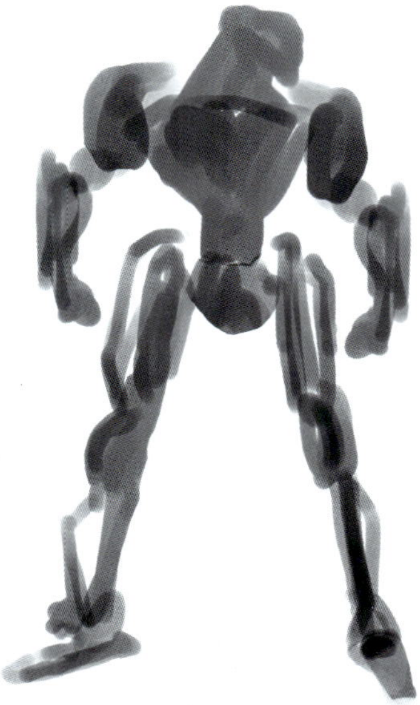

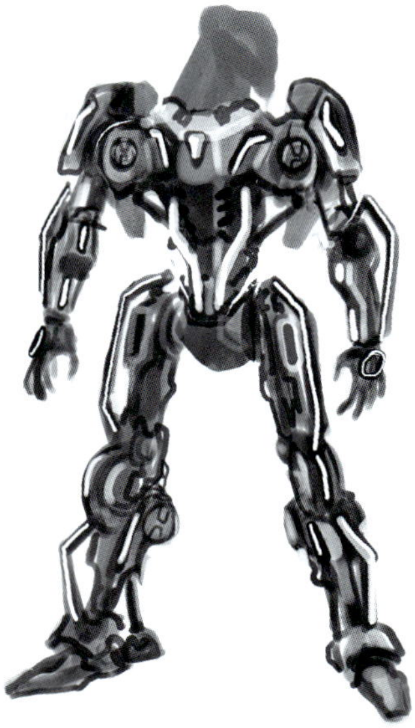

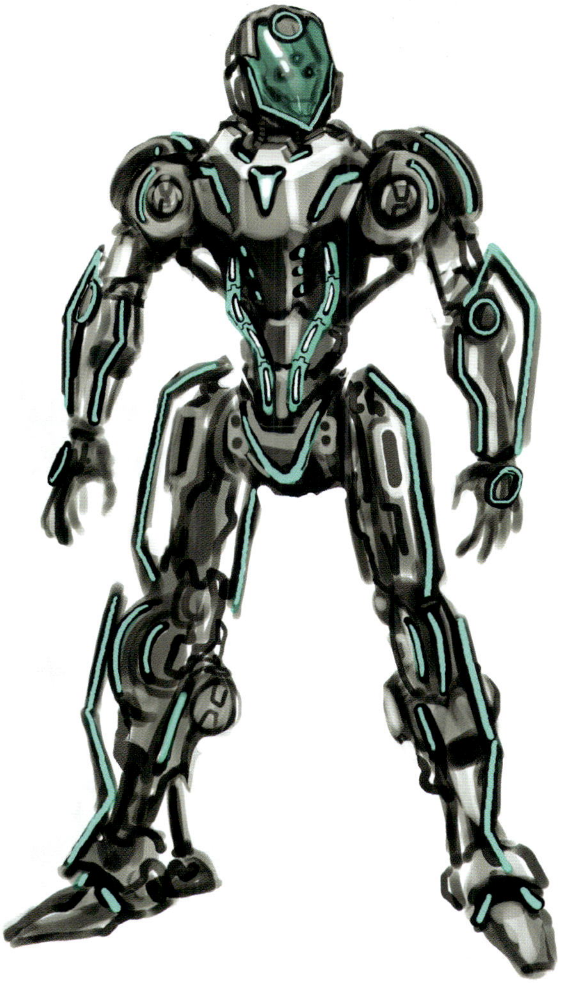

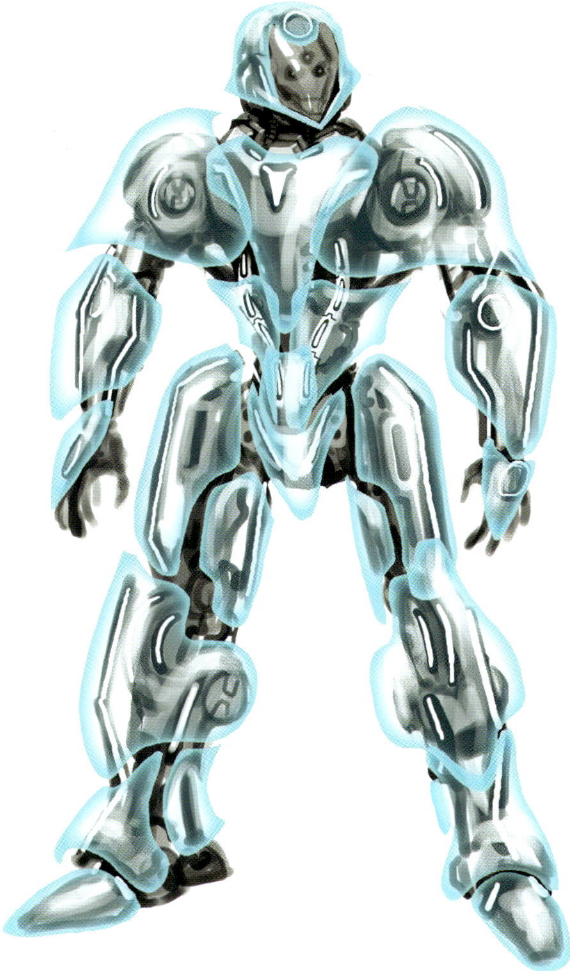

MOTO ARMOR JB-K1000

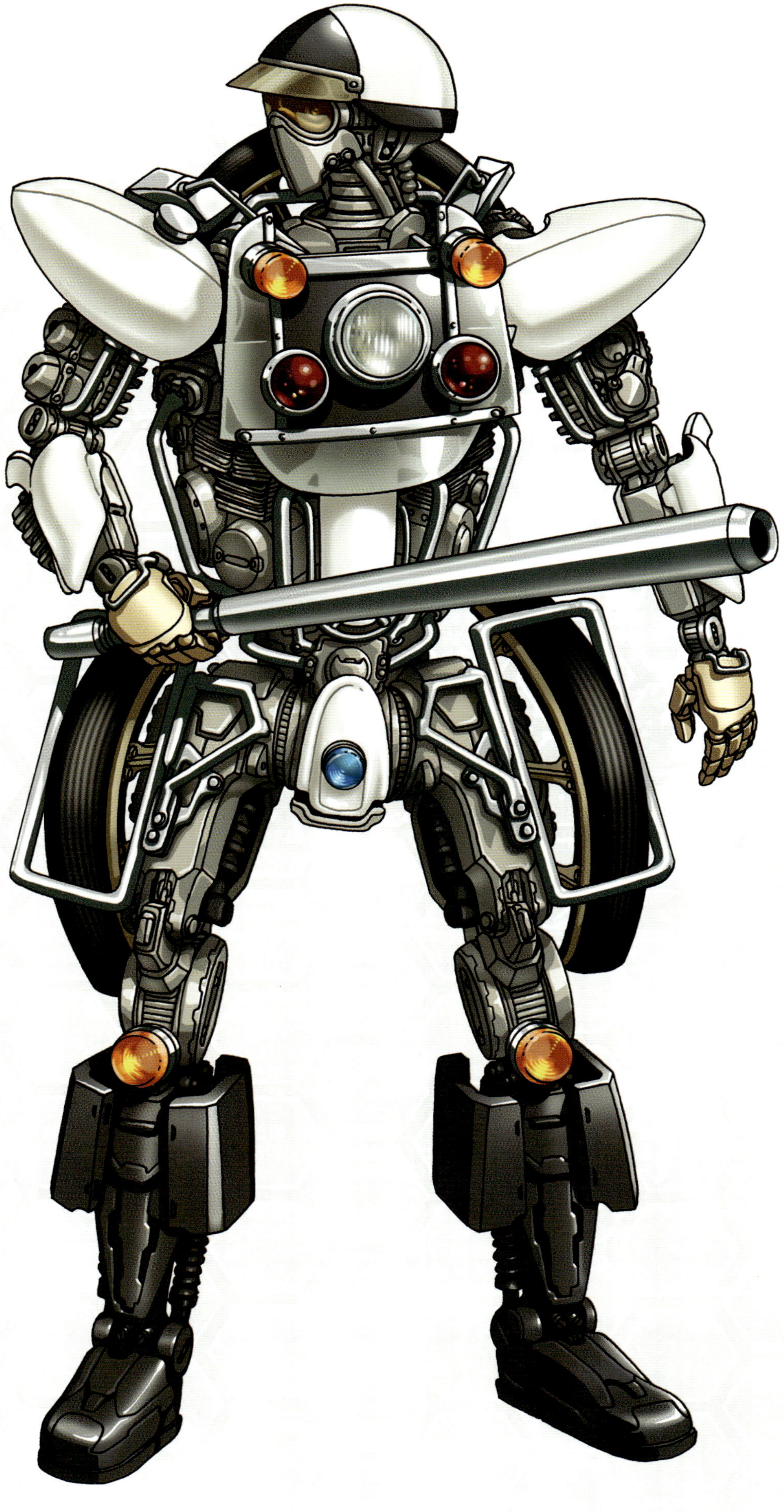

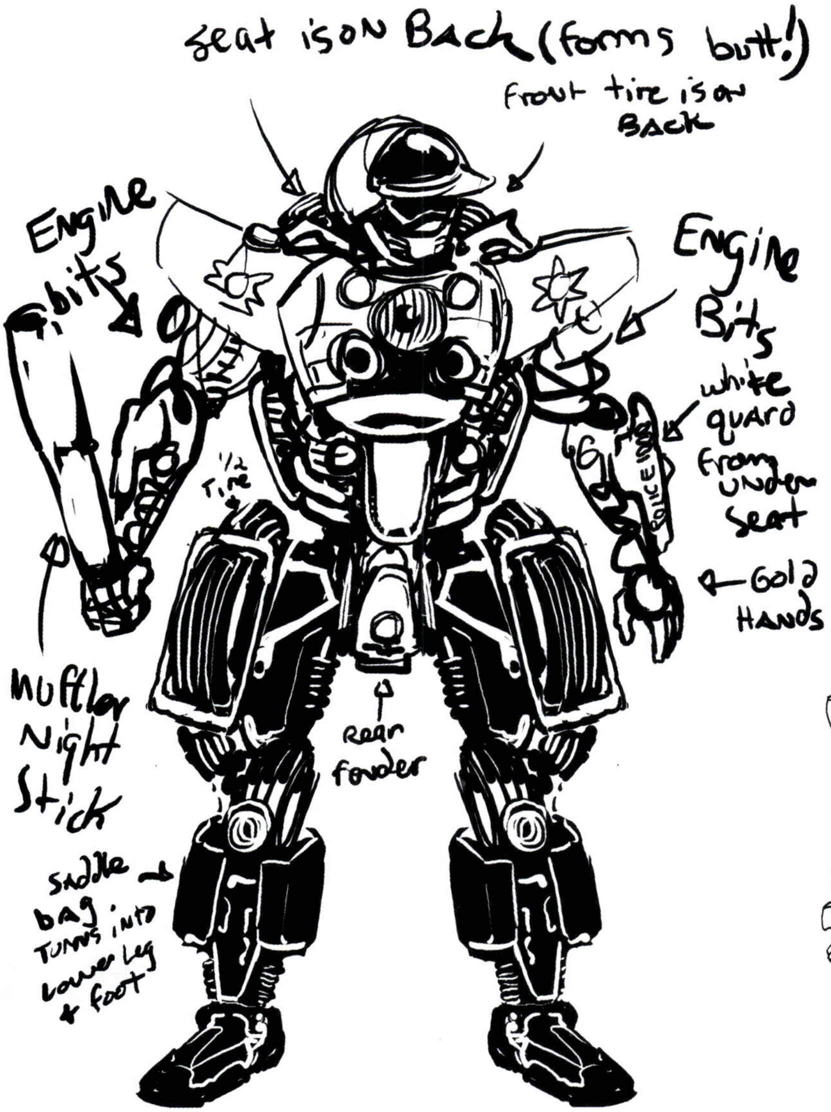

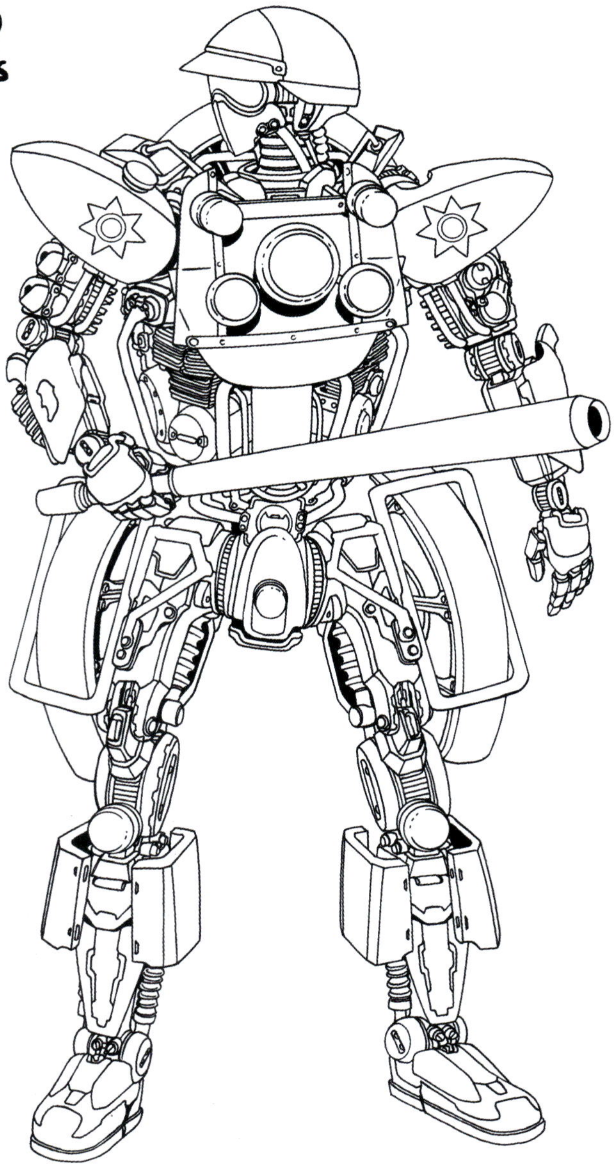

The Moto Armor JB-K1000 was commissioned by a fan and was very fun to create. The job was to take an old Kawasaki 1000 police motorcycle and transform it into a mecha.

The top image has some of the parts labeled so you can see where different parts of the motorcycle went.

The overall height of this mecha is about 7 feet.

Police Assault Drone II

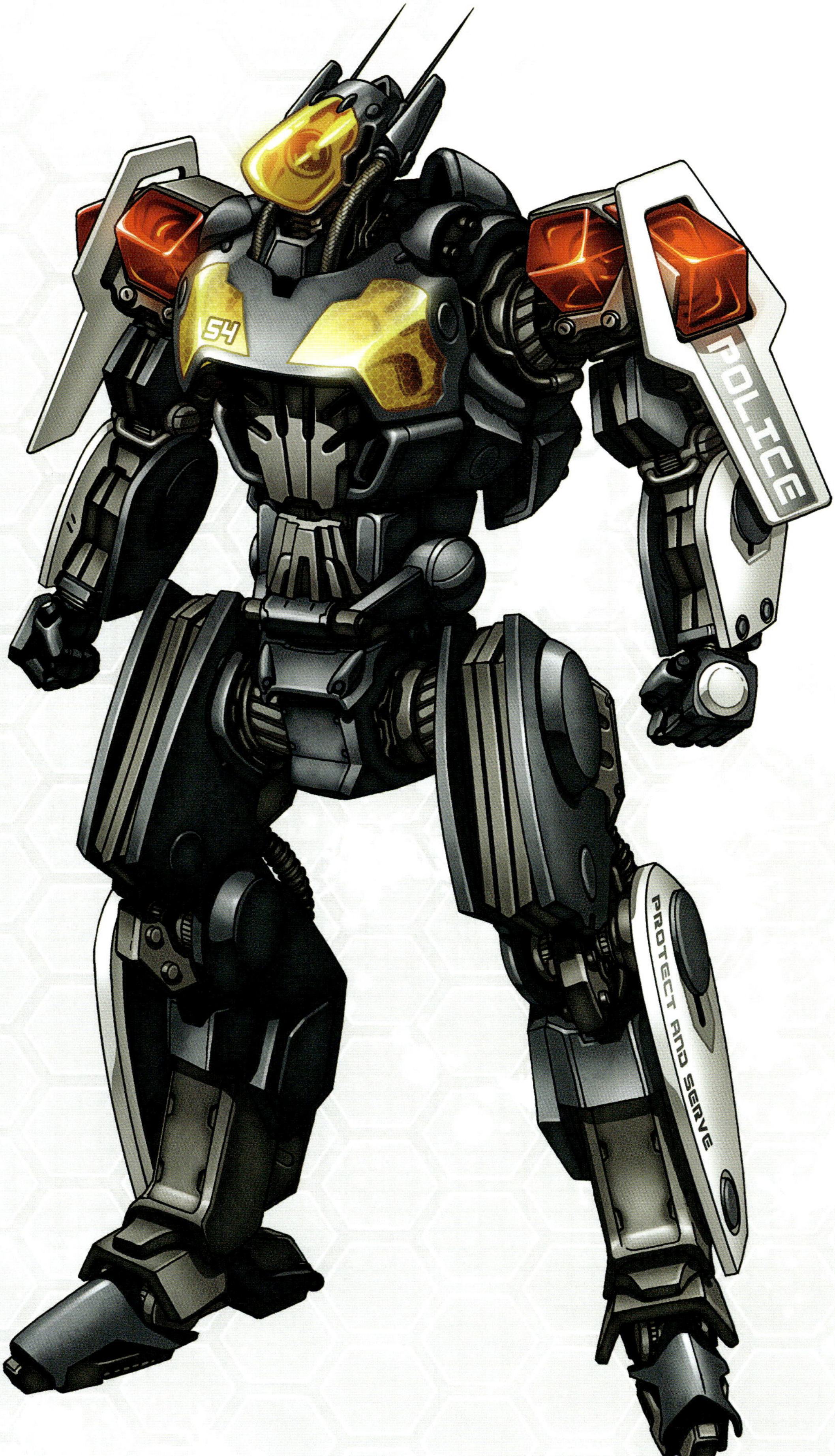

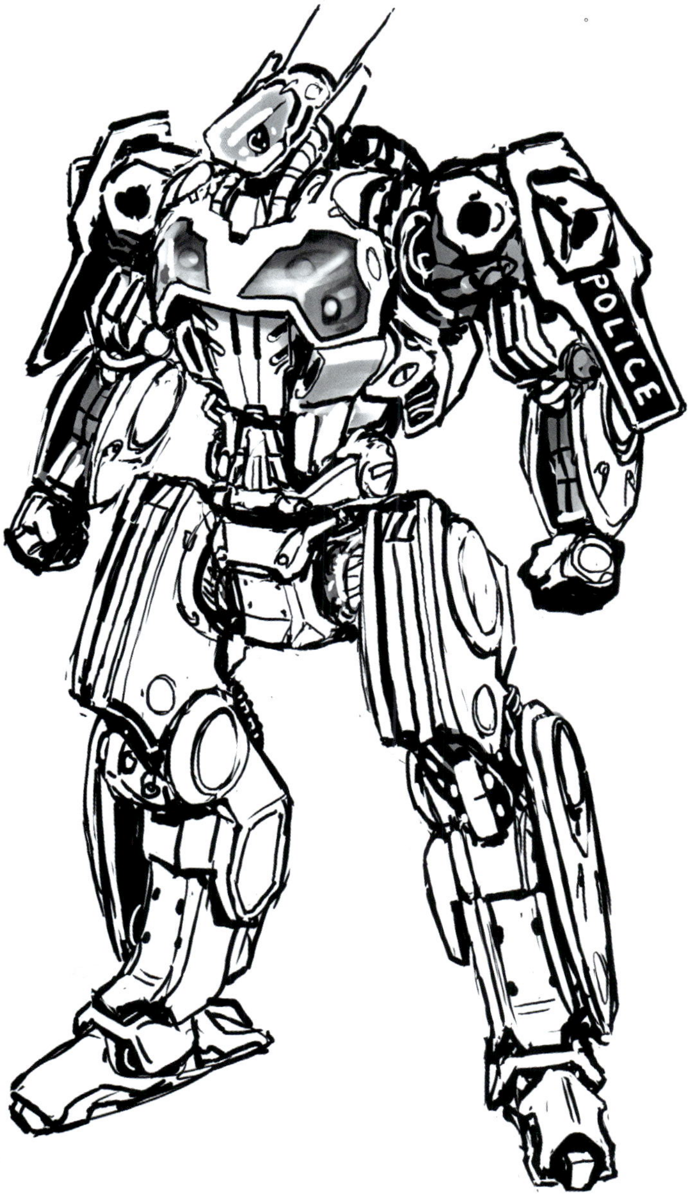

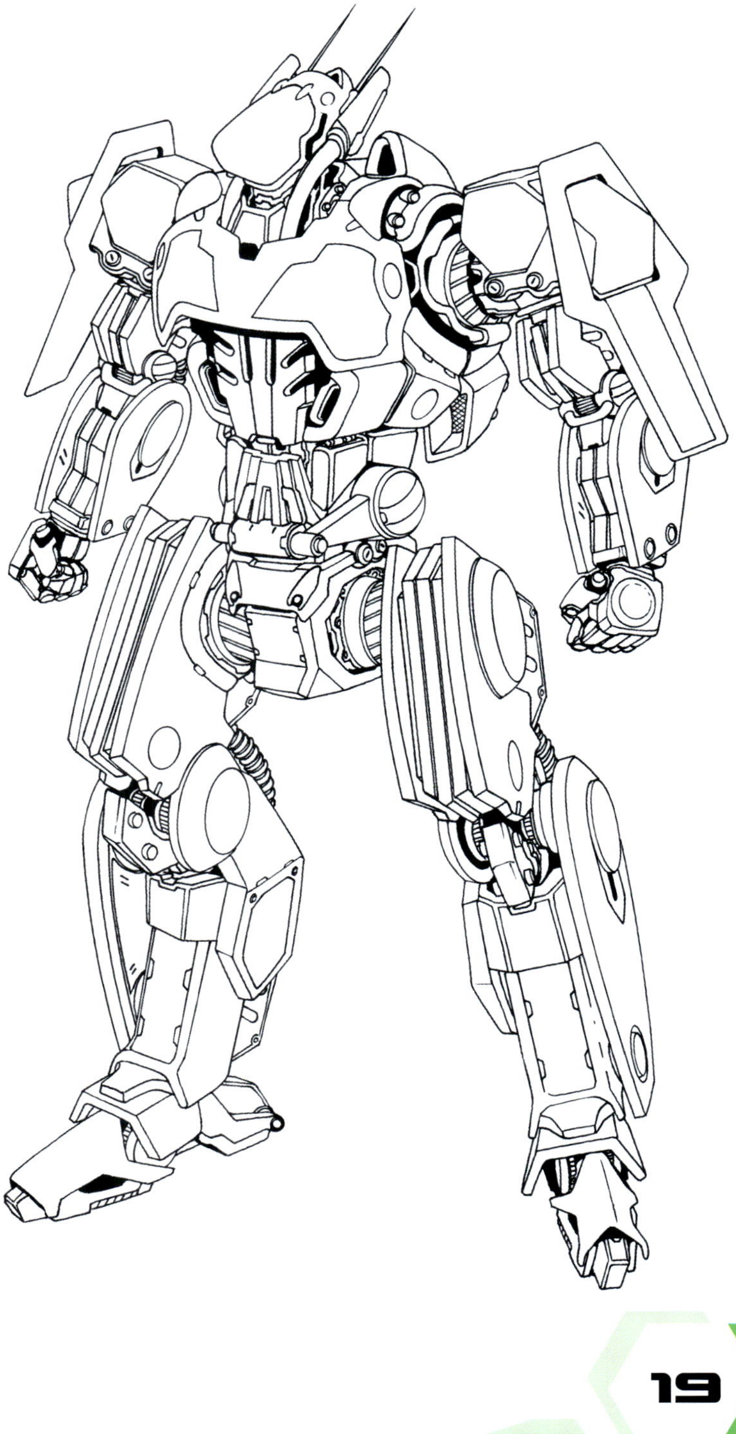

The Police Assault Drone is a re-design of a mecha I sketched while I was in college. The old drawing can be seen on page 20.

A human pilot remotely operates this unit. The pilot resides inside a nearby armored vehicle.

This mecha relies on hand-held tools and weapons. Its only built-in weapon is a non-lethal sonic cannon used to stun and subdue criminals. It can also be equipped with a riot shield.

Police Assault Drone II

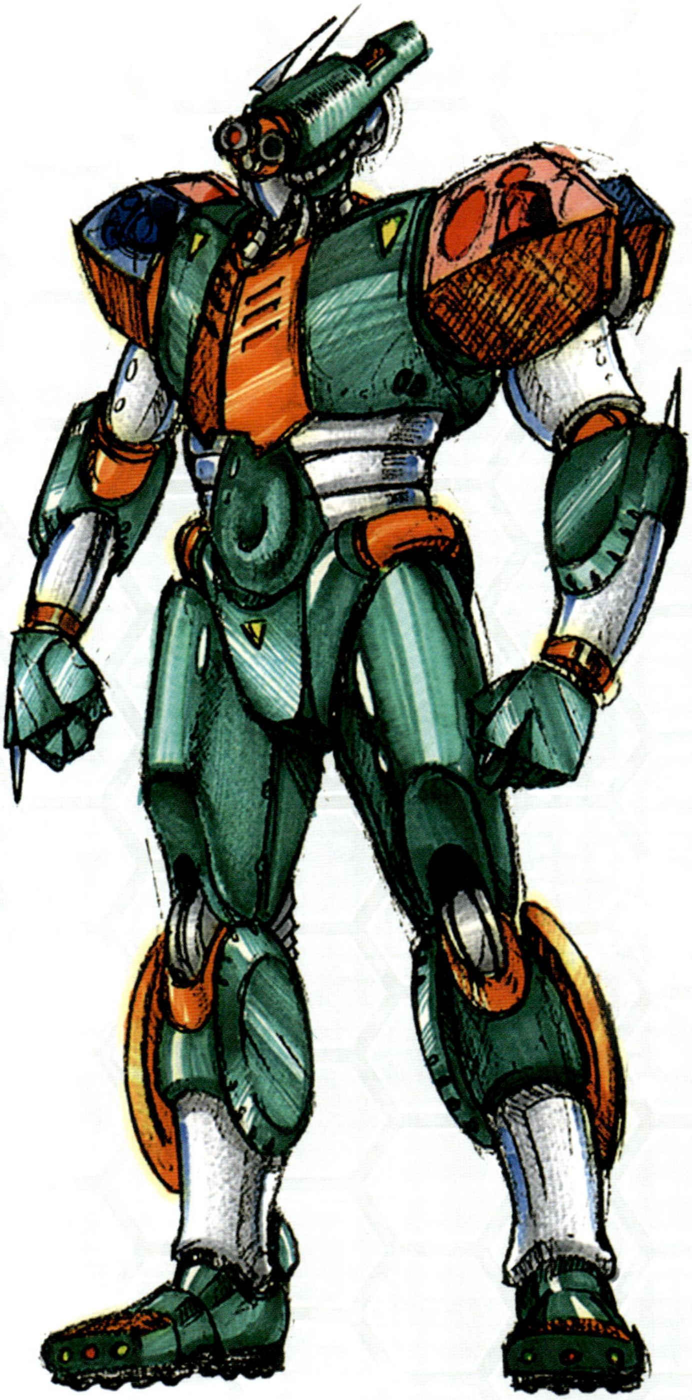

The image to the left is the original marker sketch I made many years ago. I tried to keep the same feel and personality when I was making the new design. The shoulders and legs were the easiest parts to update.

The three images below show slightly different chest details. I used the design from the middle image.

Opposite page: A series of color studies showing possible color combinations. I liked the original teal color, but it didn't feel like the best representation of "police".

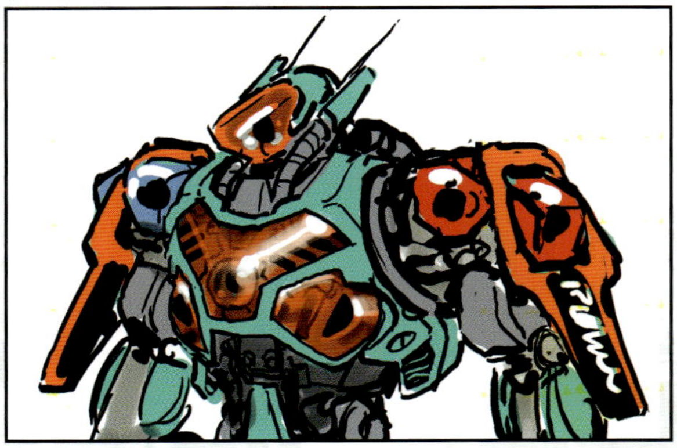

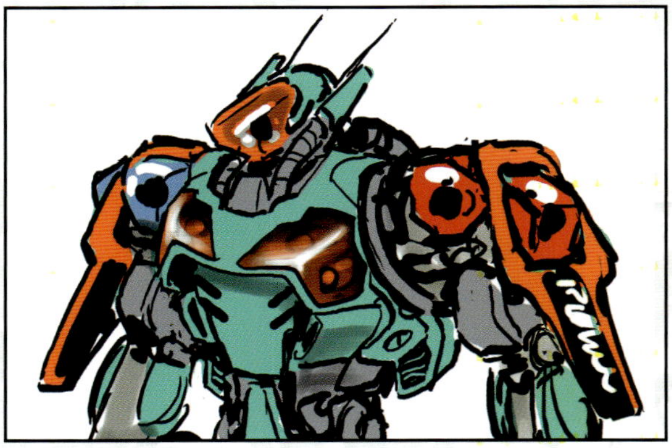

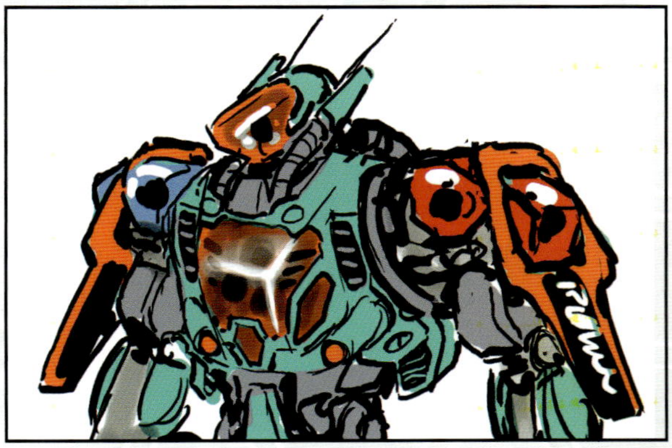

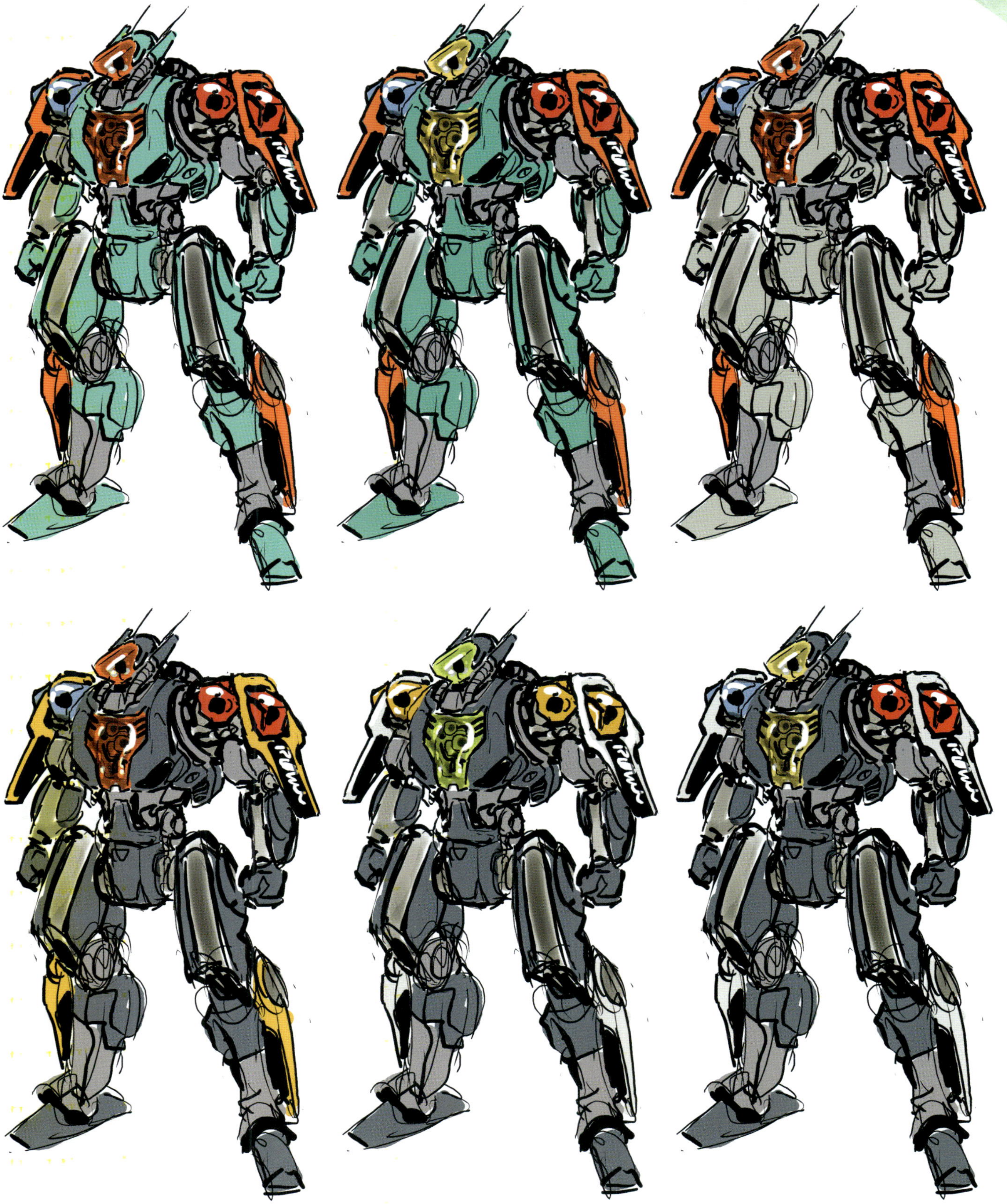

CHAPTER 2

Chapter 2 showcases 6 designs that were created between 2004 and 2009. Some of the designs were created specifically for the original edition of *Mecha Zone 1*.

I was working as a video game artist at the time and I was in the process of making the *MechWarrior 4* games. This inspired me to experiment by adding more aggressive weapons to my designs.

This was also when I started experimenting with making 3D models of my mecha.

CLASSIC MECHA

JAGUAR

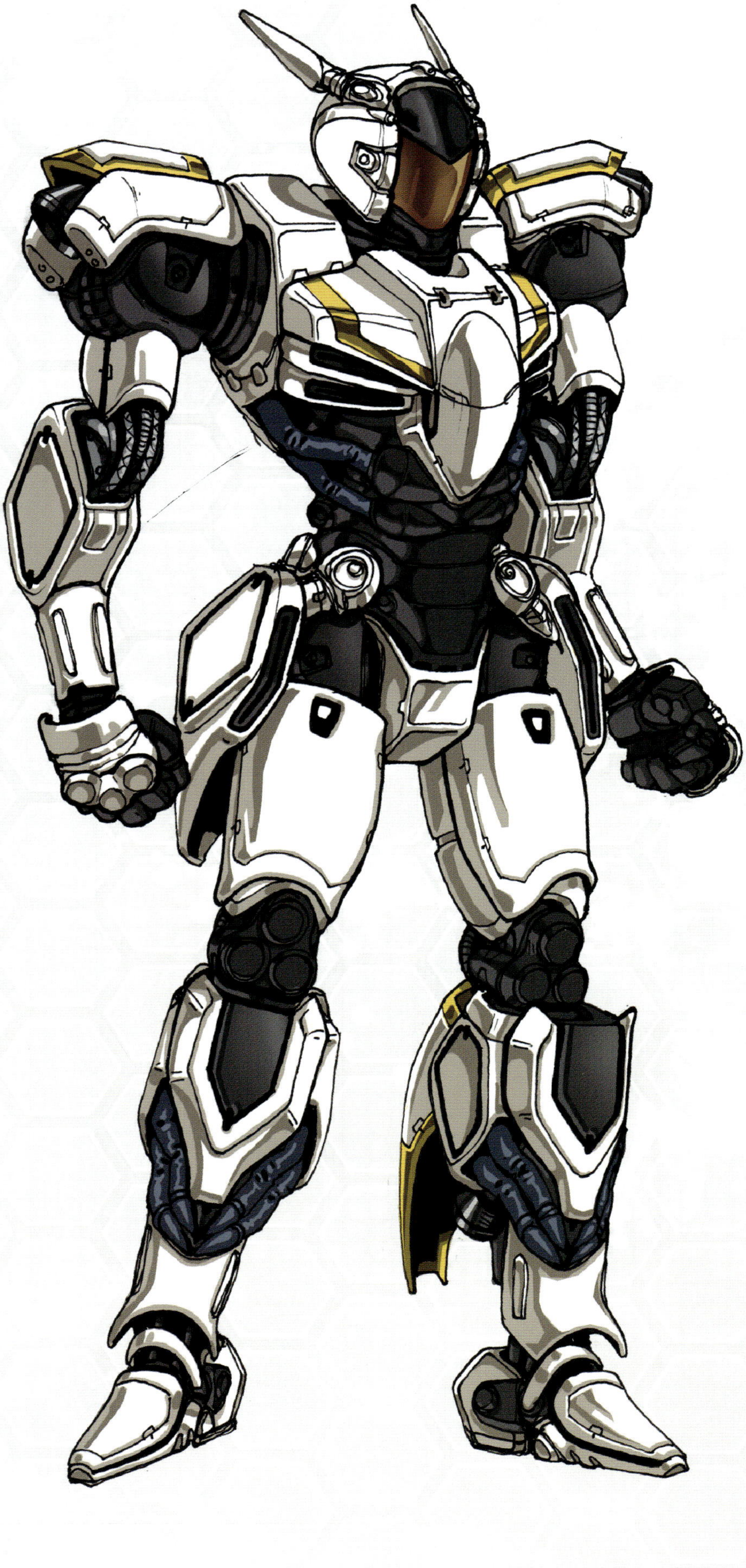

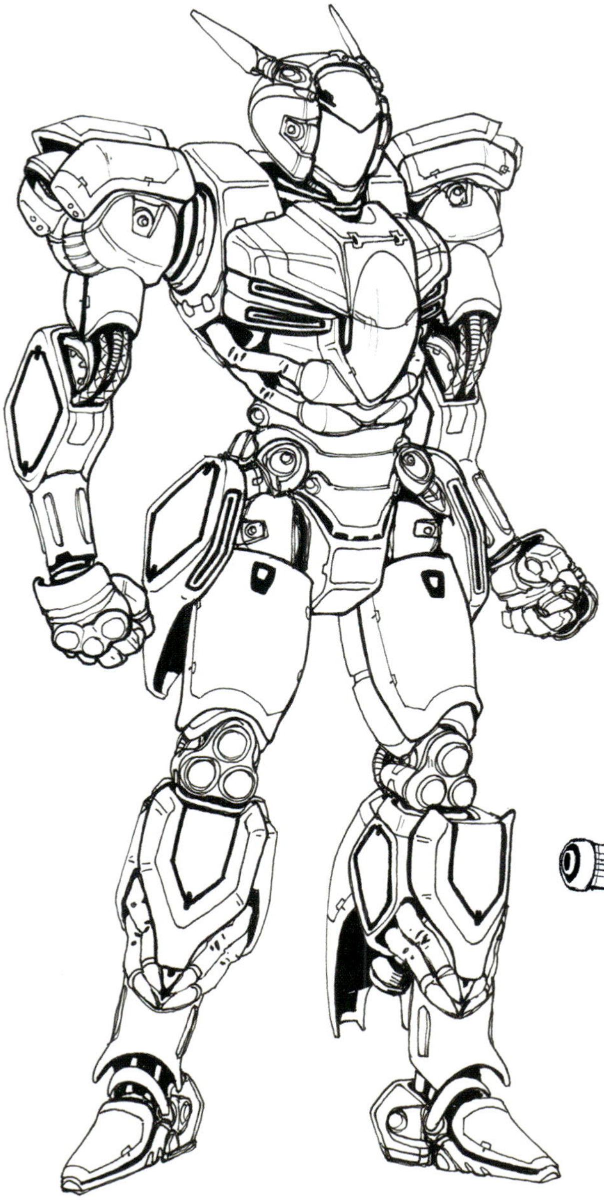

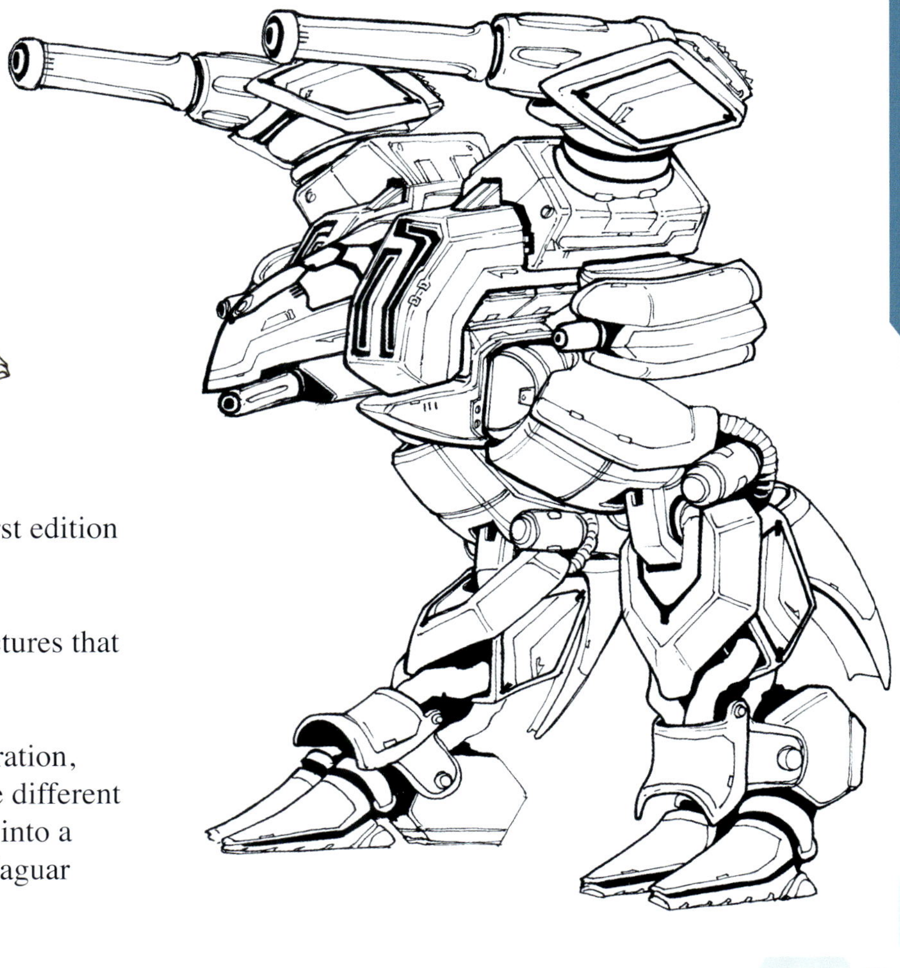

The Jaguar was created specifically for the first edition of *Mecha Zone 1*.

It is agile and quick with advanced joint structures that allow a great degree of flexibility.

The image to the right is an alternate configuration, which uses many of the same parts to achieve different results. The regular Jaguar unit could be sent into a combat situation for recon while the variant Jaguar could provide cover fire from afar.

STRIKER 15

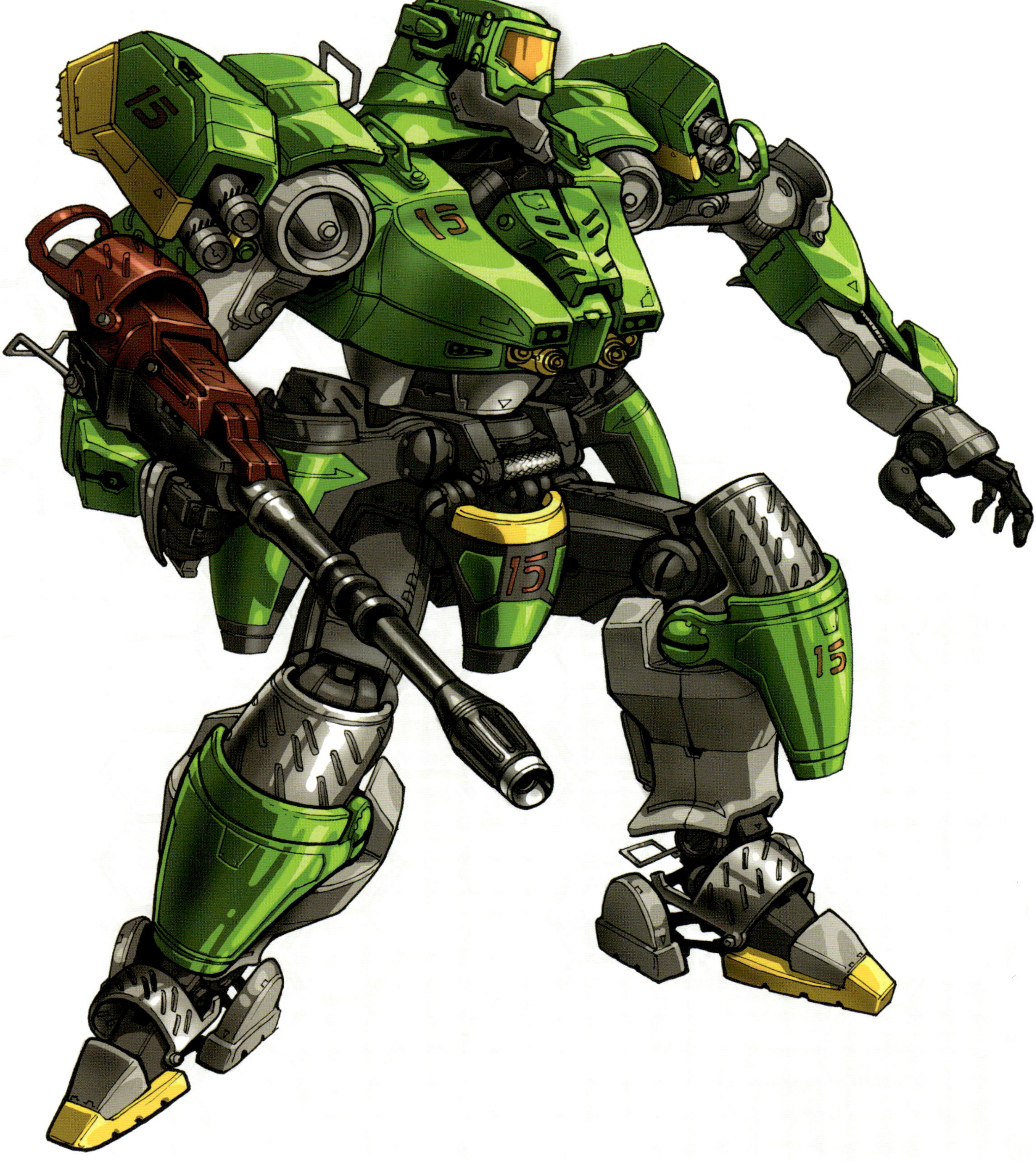

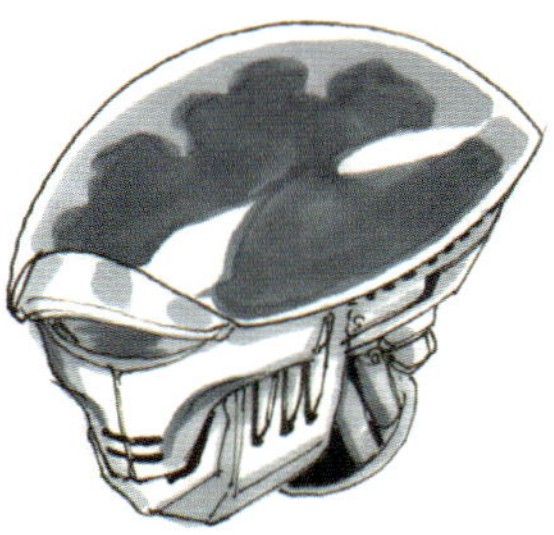
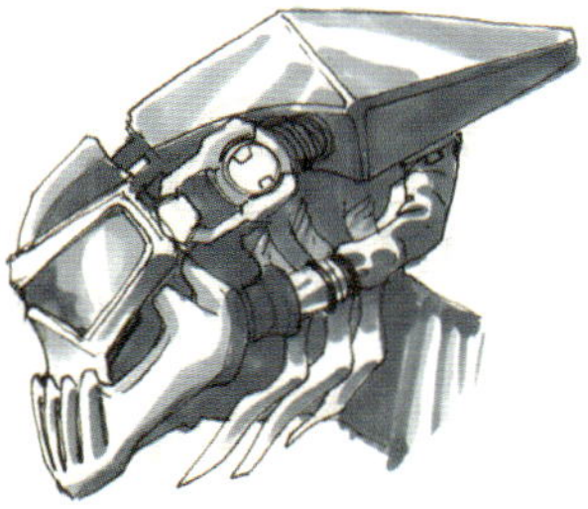
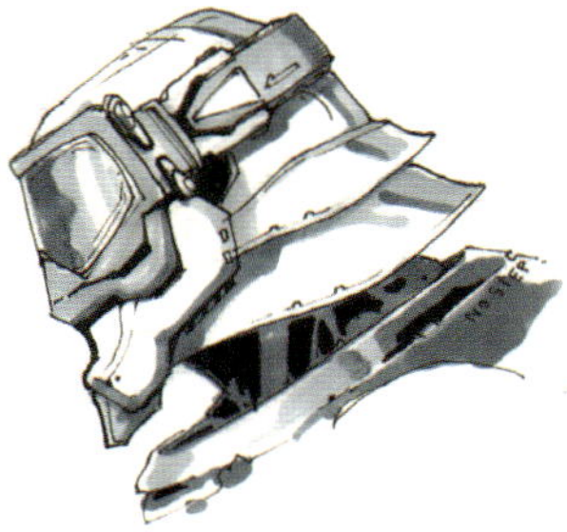
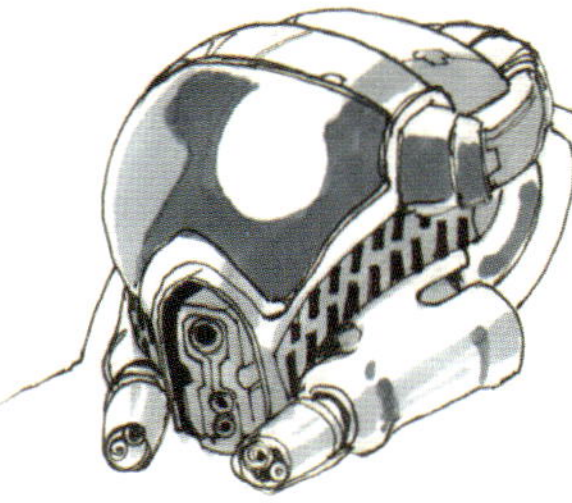
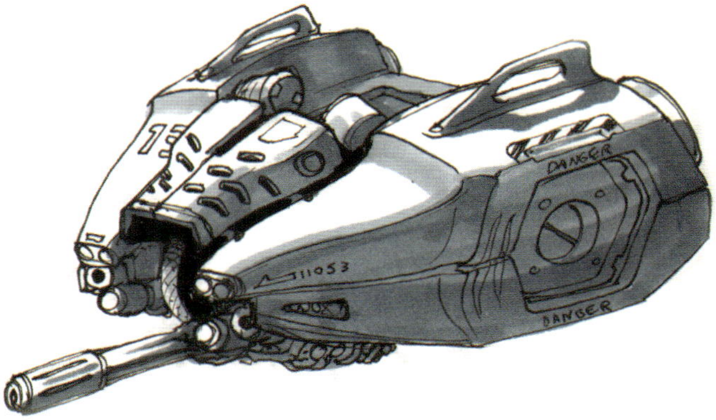

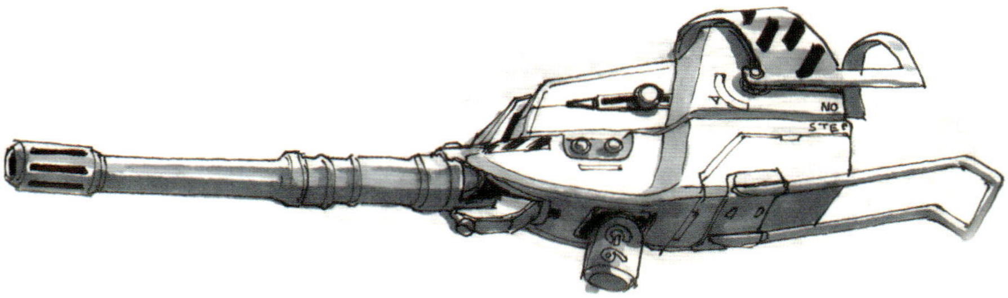

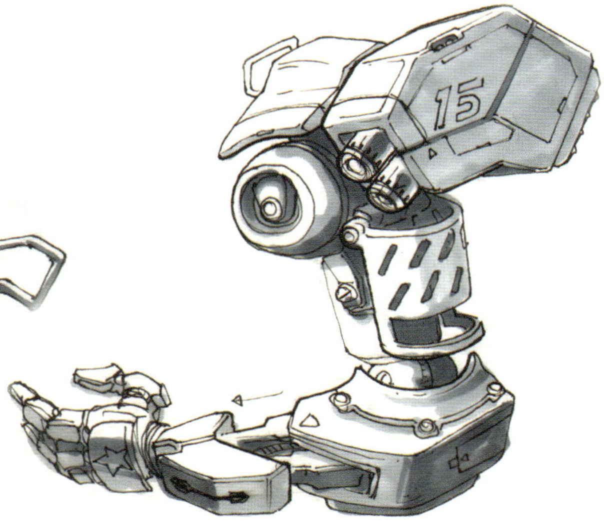

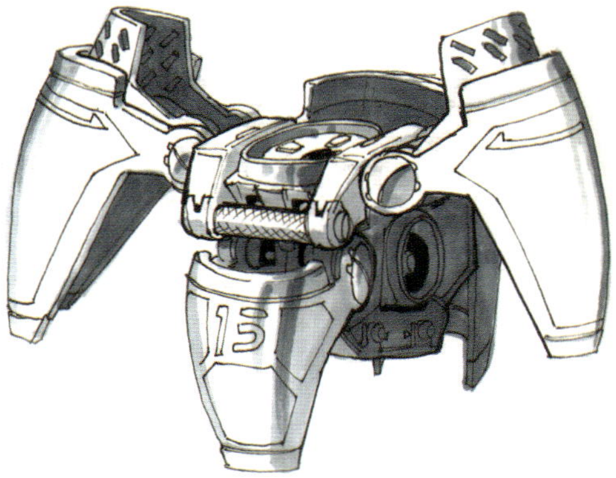

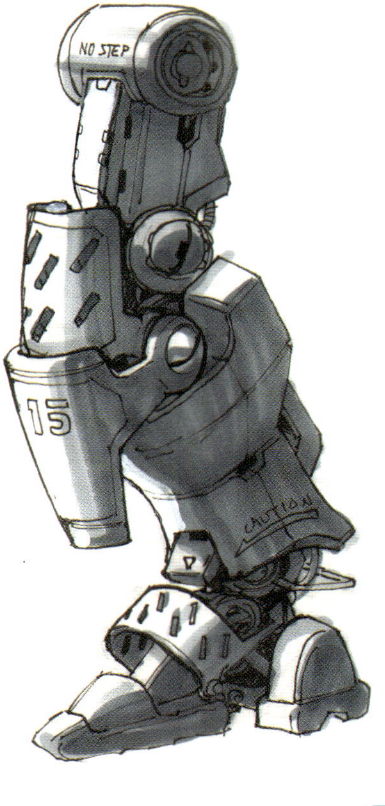

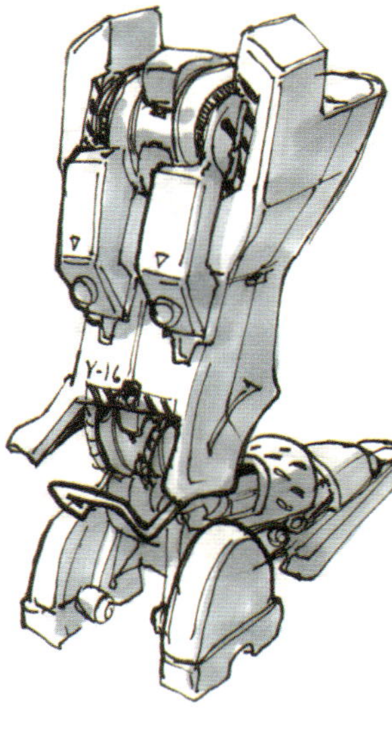

Striker 15 was created after the release of the original *Mecha Zone* book. Paintball guns and gear that I had seen in a sports magazine inspired the design.

I tried a different approach to creating this mecha. Instead of sketching the mecha as a whole, I drew all of the parts separately. Then I combined my favorite parts into a complete robot.

Concussion

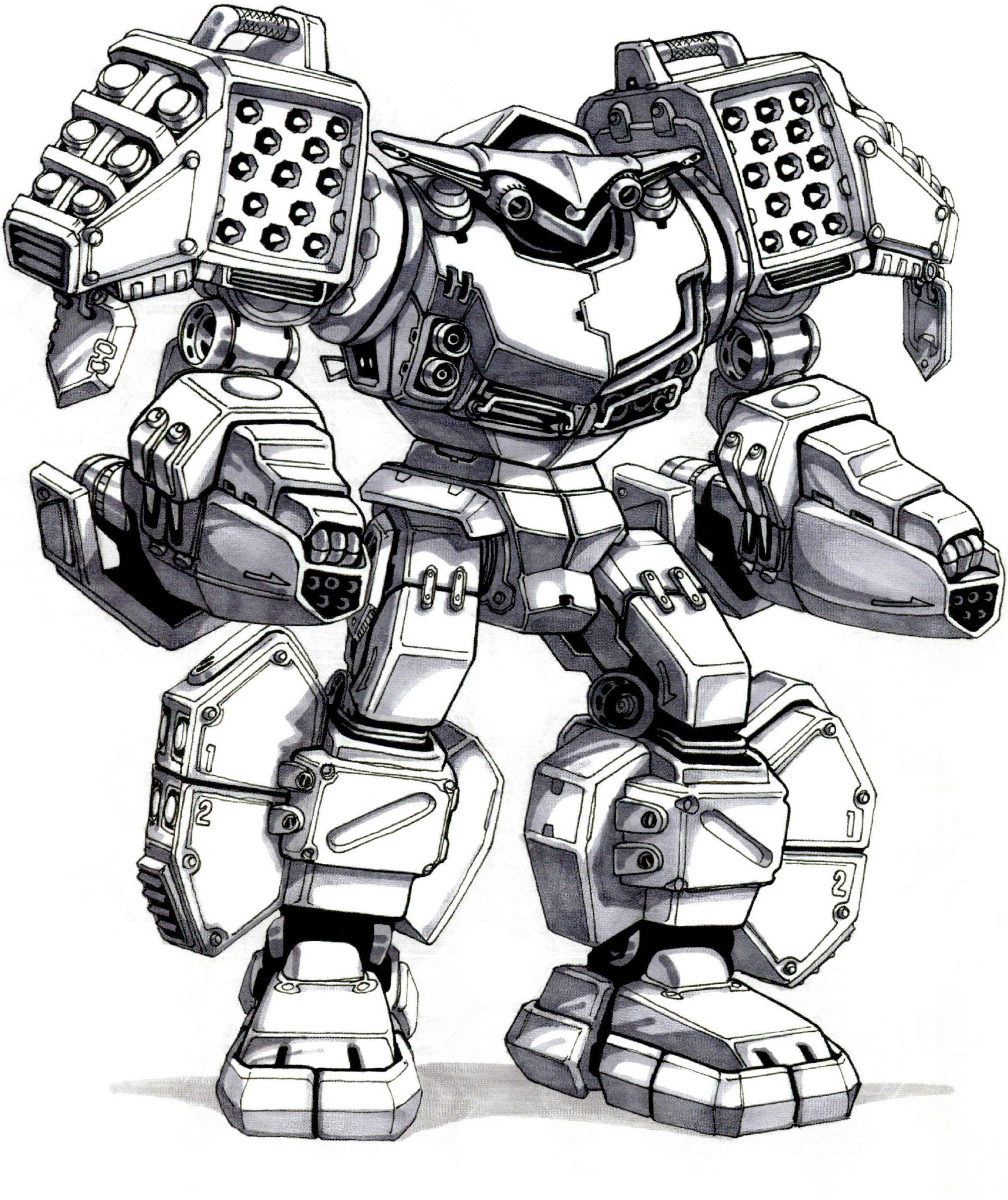

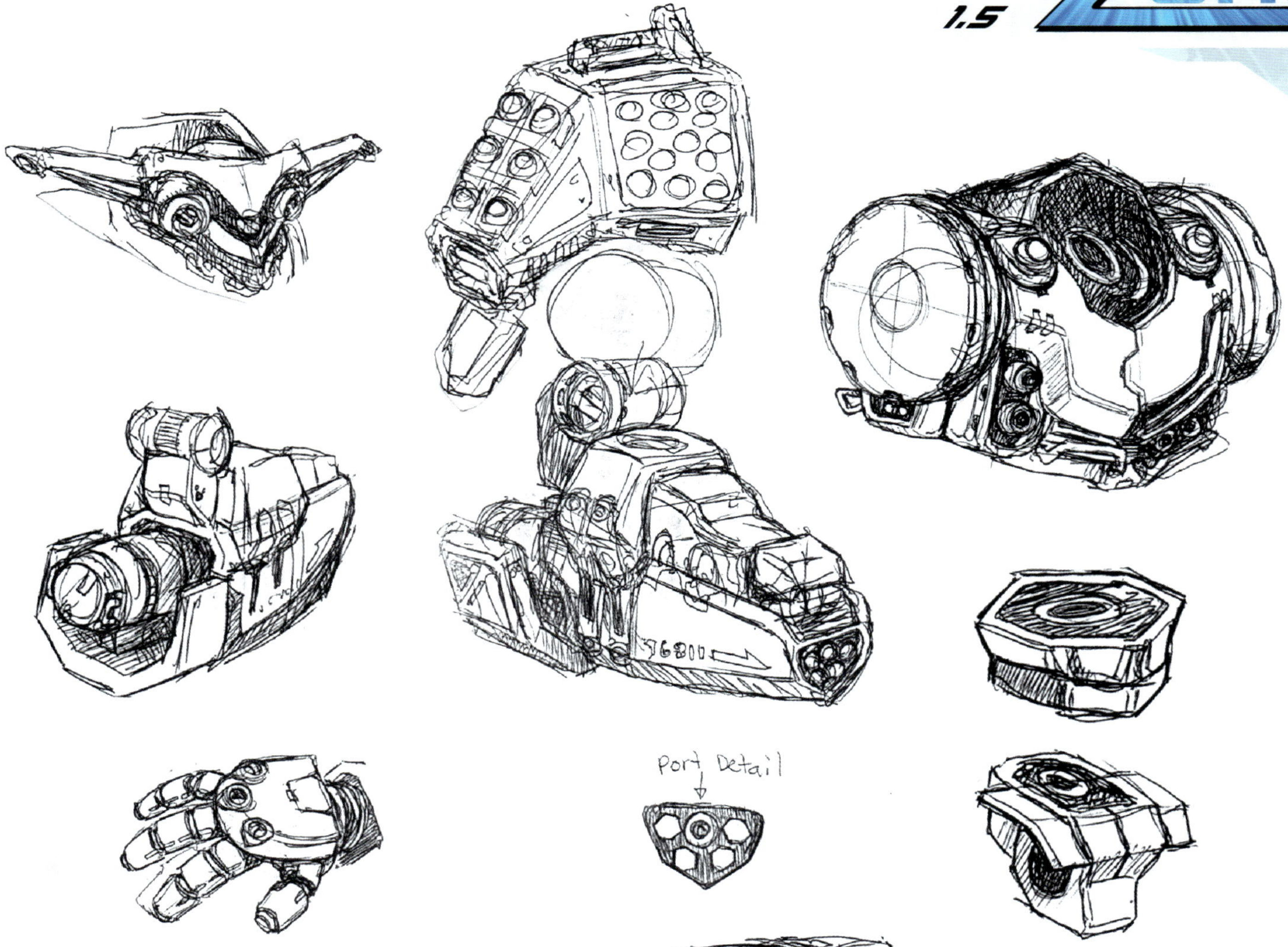

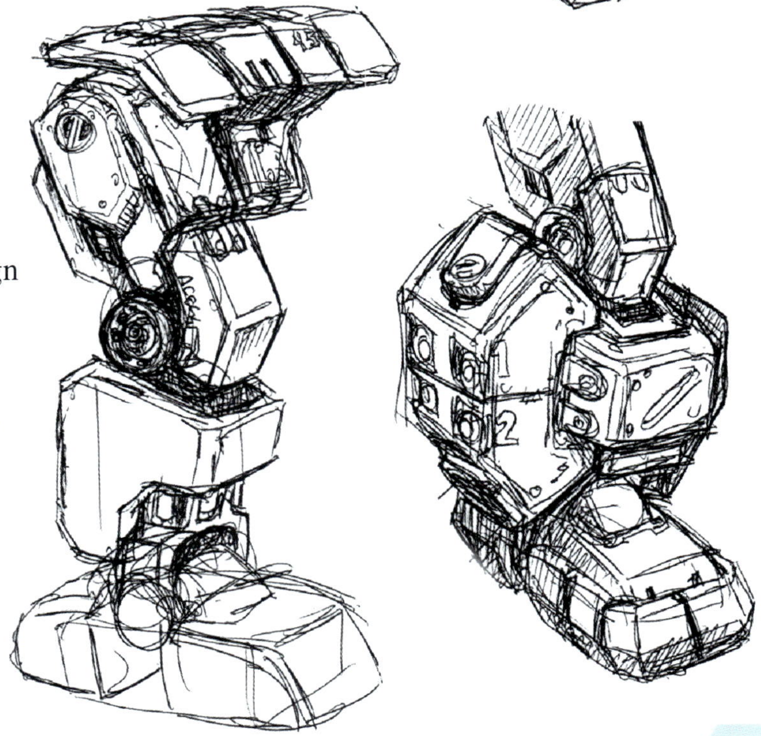

The Concussion is a re-design of an old mecha called the Grenade Bot. You can see the old design on pages 48-49.

The weapons are modular and can be replaced with different pods. The shoulder missiles can be replaced with cannons or machine guns, etc...

The head houses an assortment of sensors that help target enemies and guide the missiles.

Concussion II

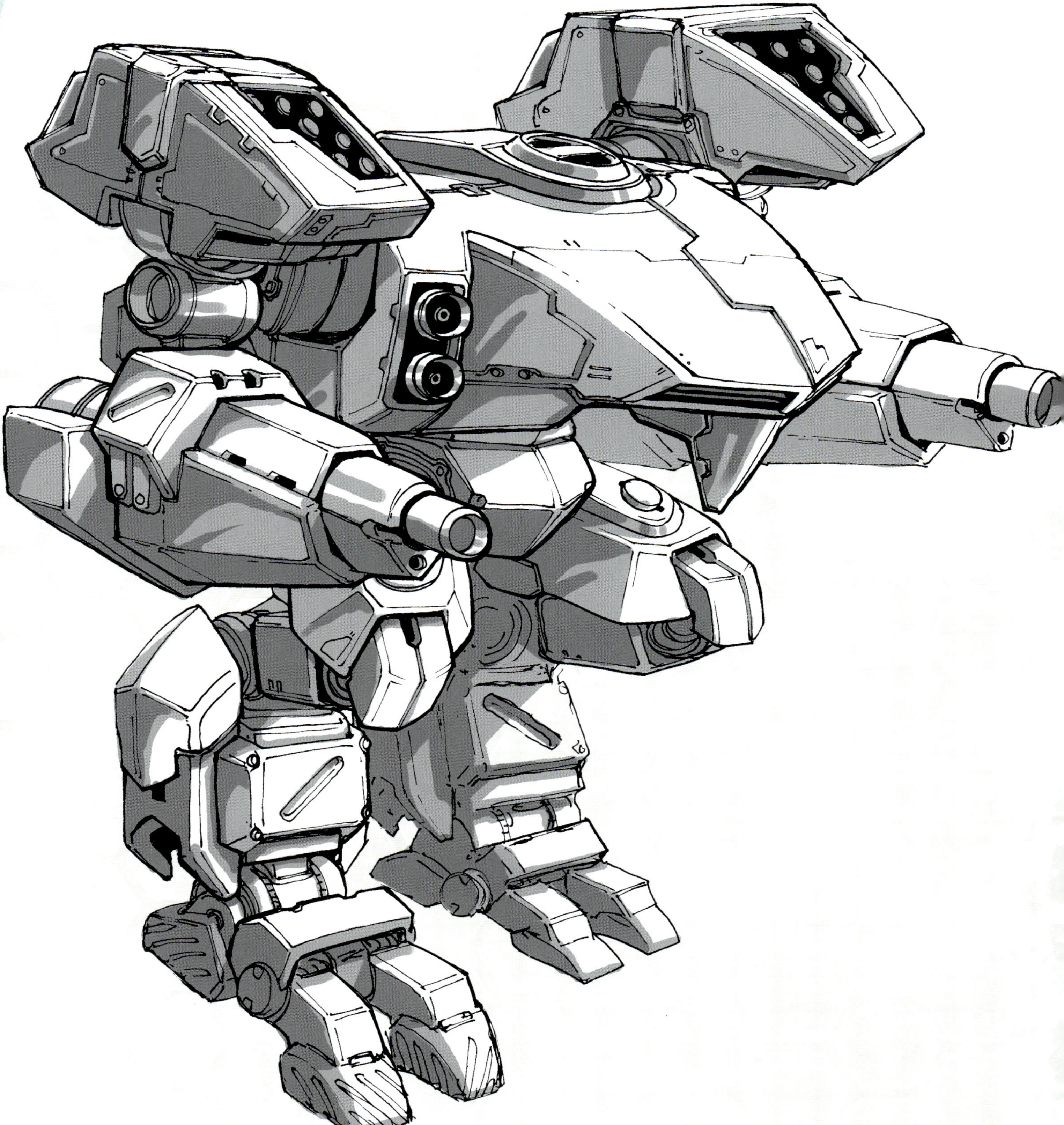

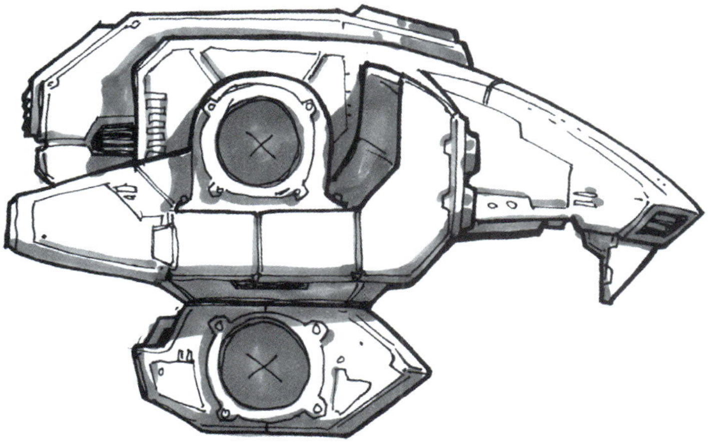

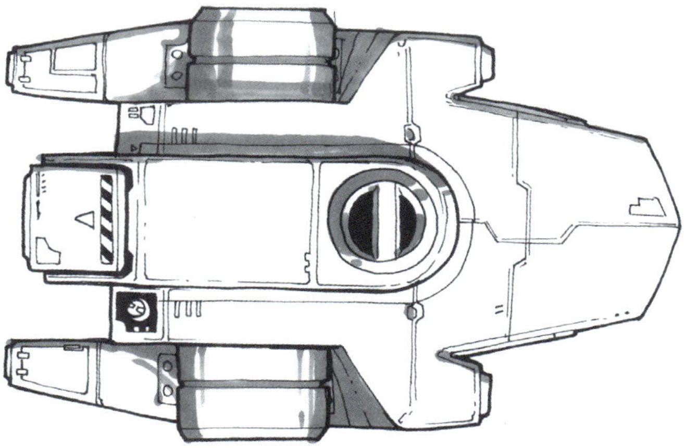

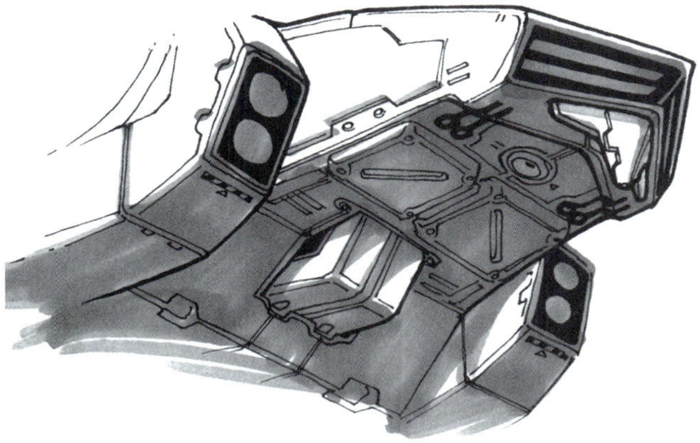

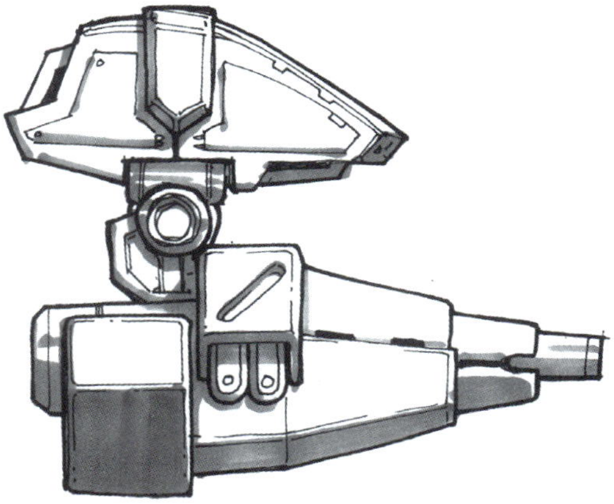

The Concussion II was an attempt to make the Concussion mecha use a more "American" visual style instead of the "Japanese" style of the original.

The head was removed and the body was revised to look more like a tank. The hands were removed and the legs were given new joint structures.

This design was very popular and it was made into a metal miniature for use with tabletop war games.

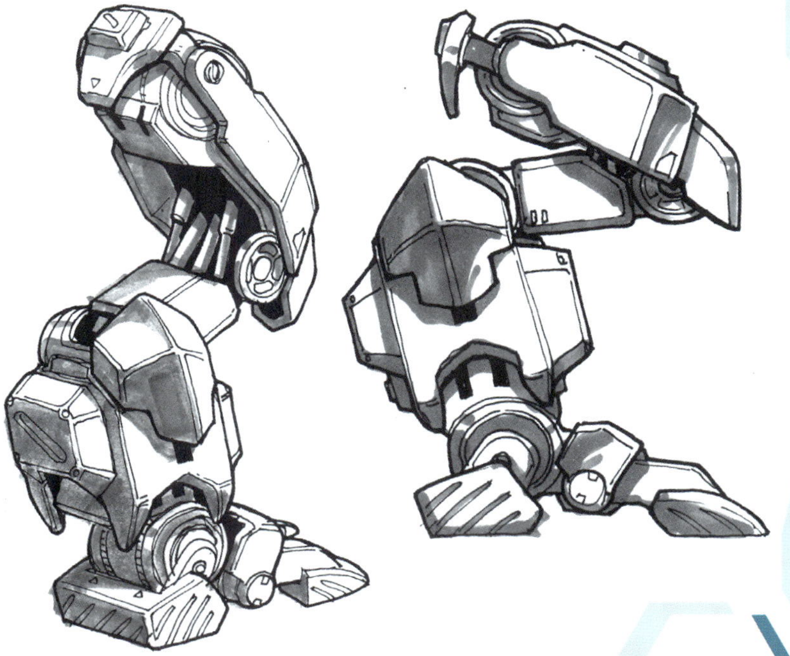

Zero

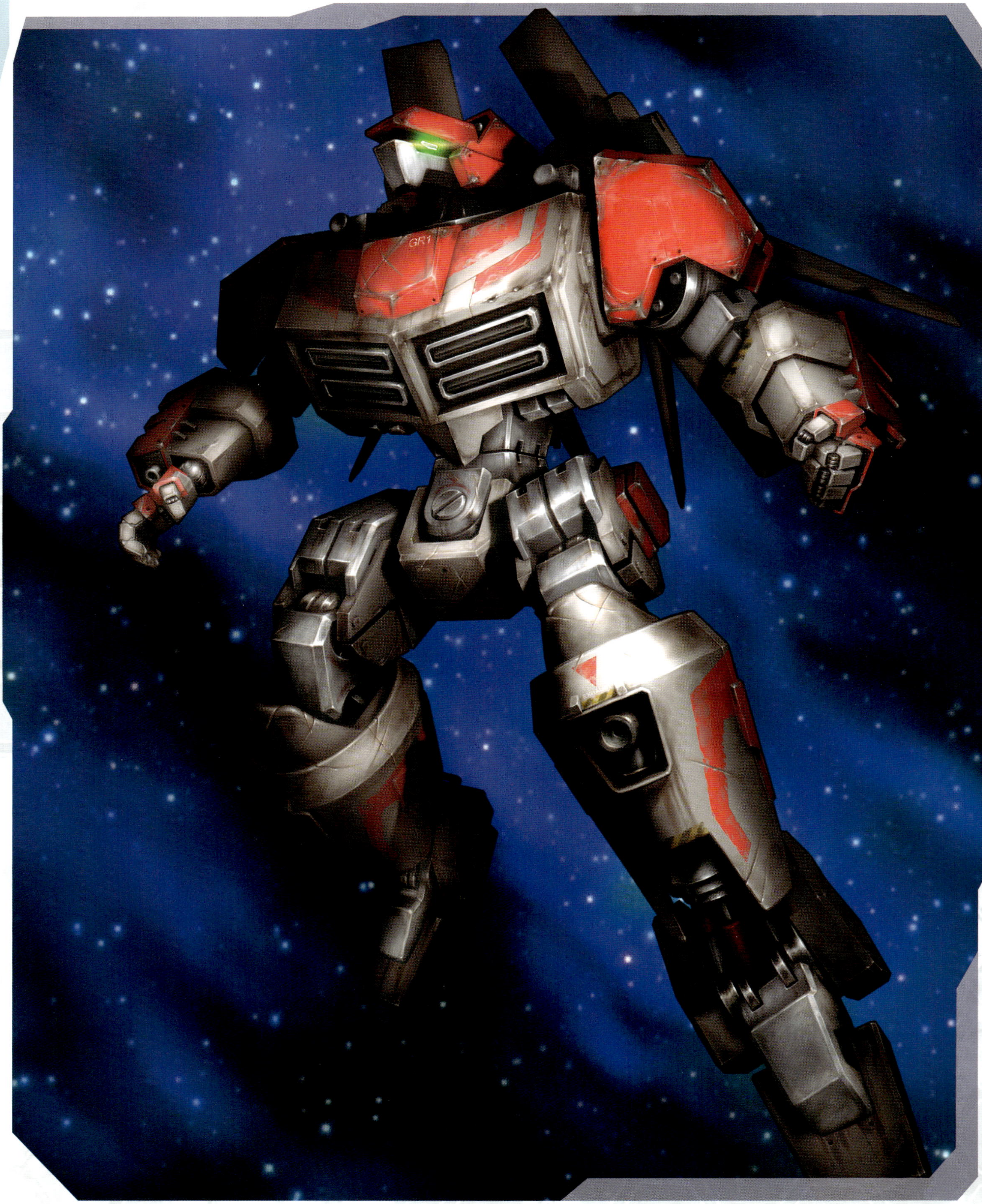

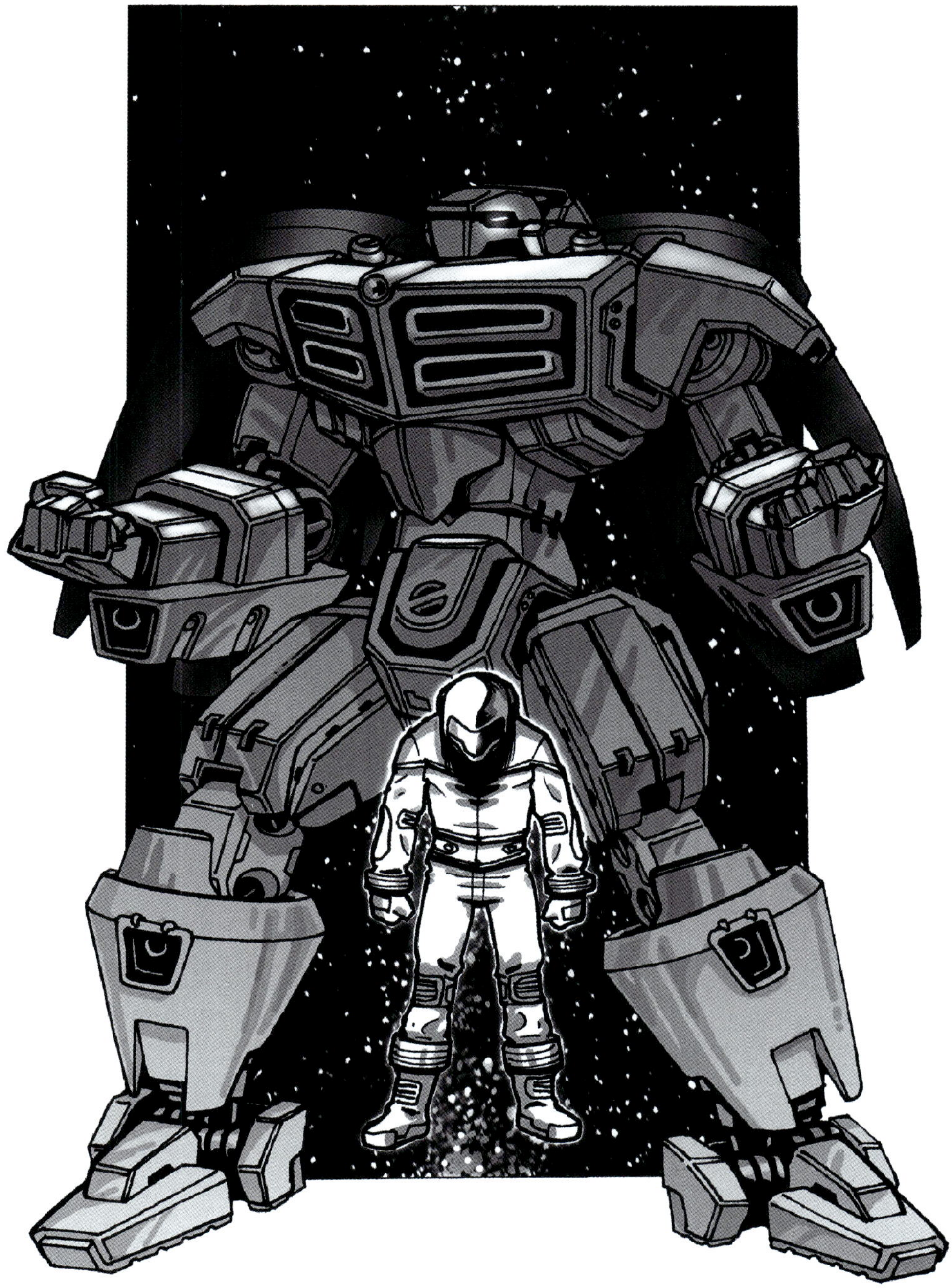

Zero, also called Ace Mecha Zero, was designed for a comic that I never got around to making. The image above shows how I intended to draw the comic.

The image to the left is a poster made by digitally painting over a 3D model I made of the mecha.

This design was very popular and it was made into a metal miniature for use with tabletop war games.

Zero prototypes

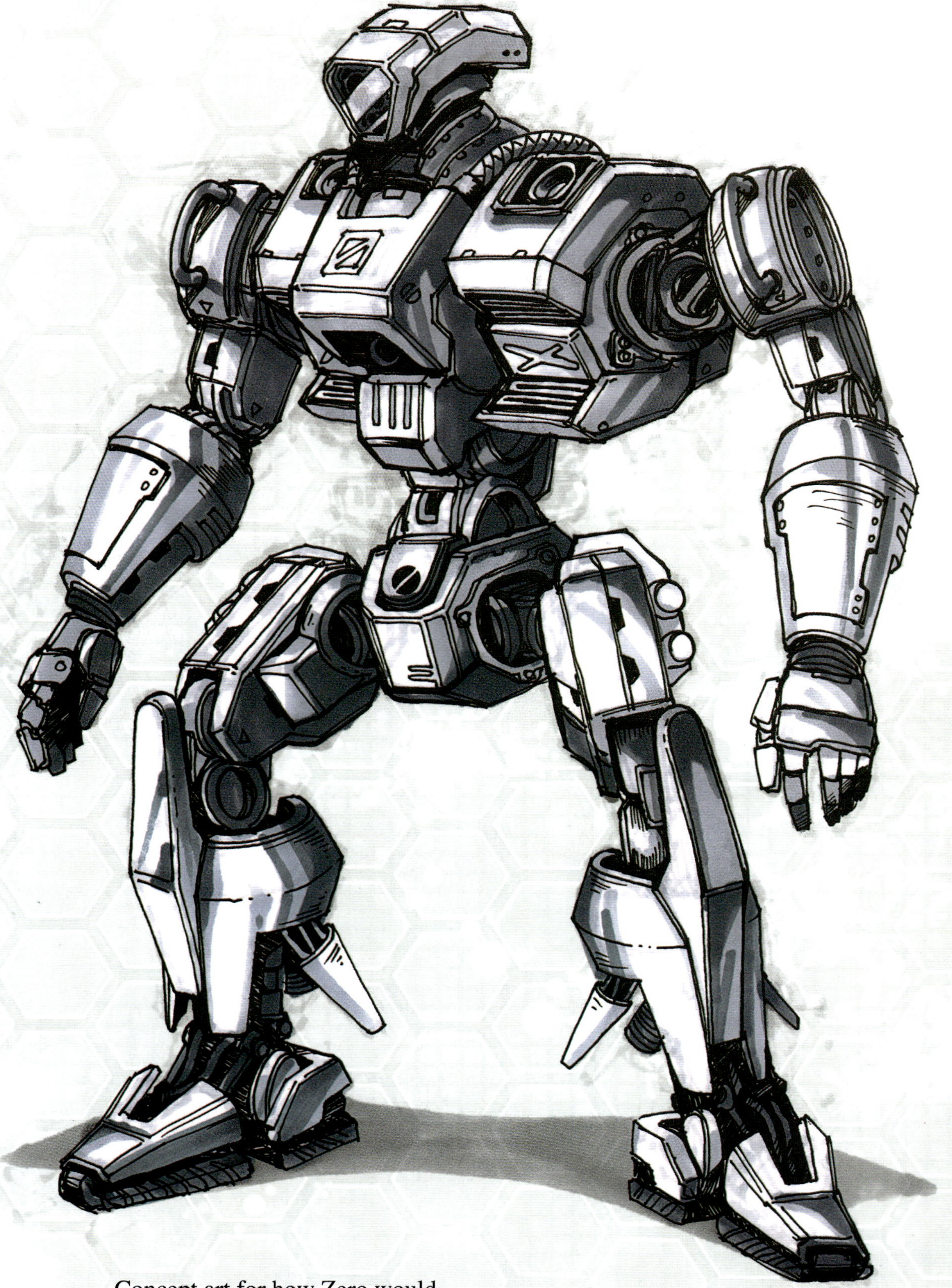

Concept art for how Zero would look as a prototype unit.

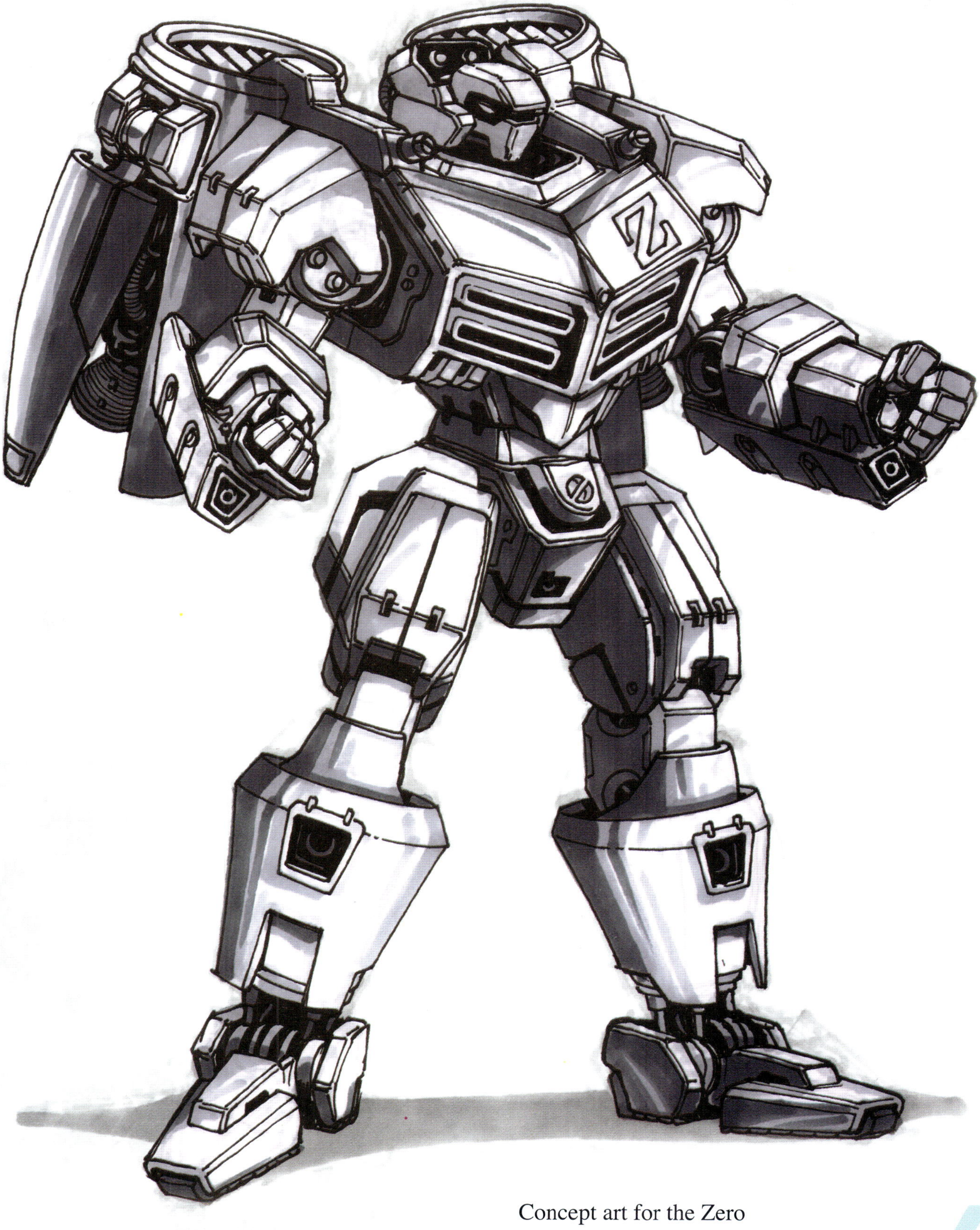

Concept art for the Zero production unit.

ZERO CG MODEL

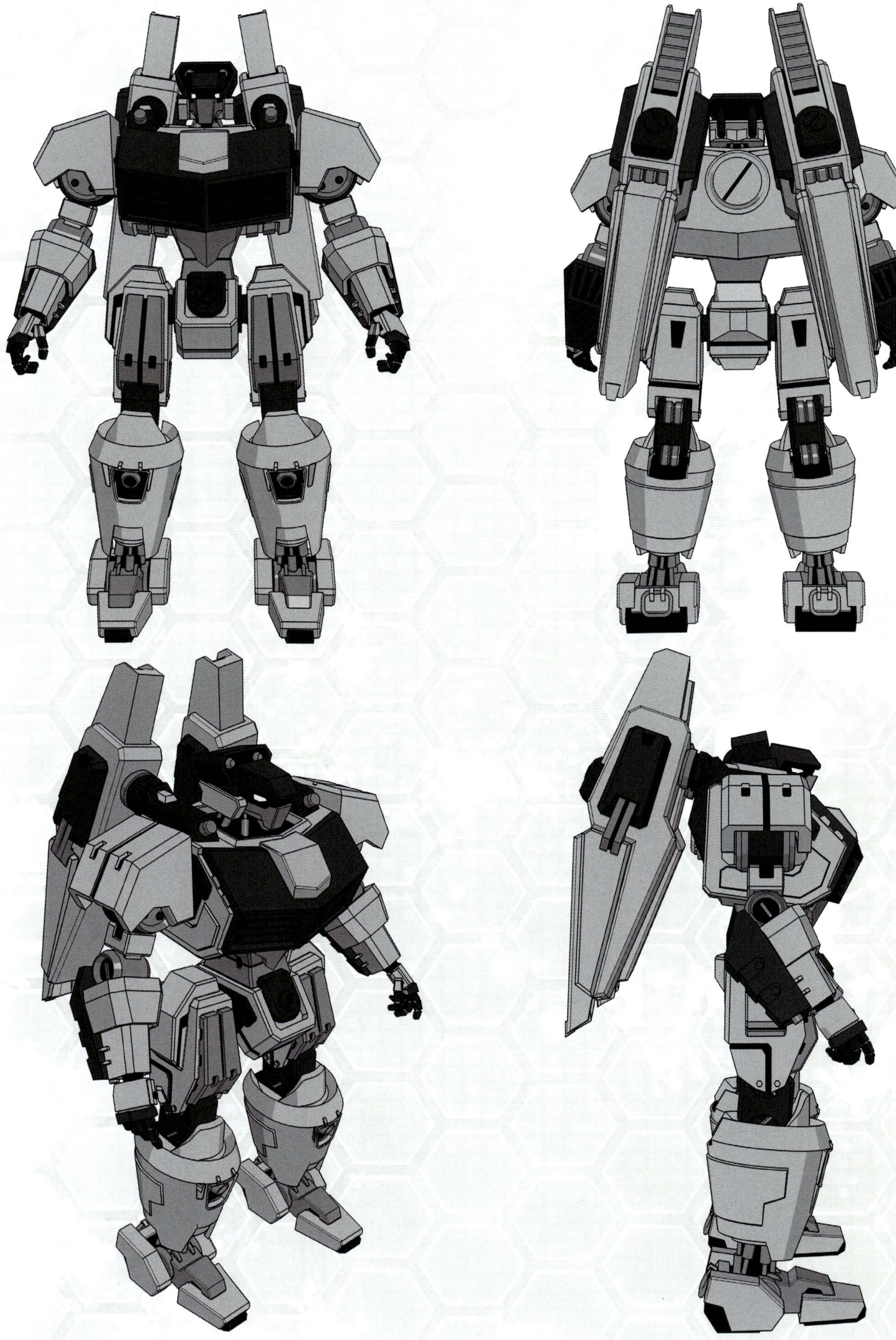

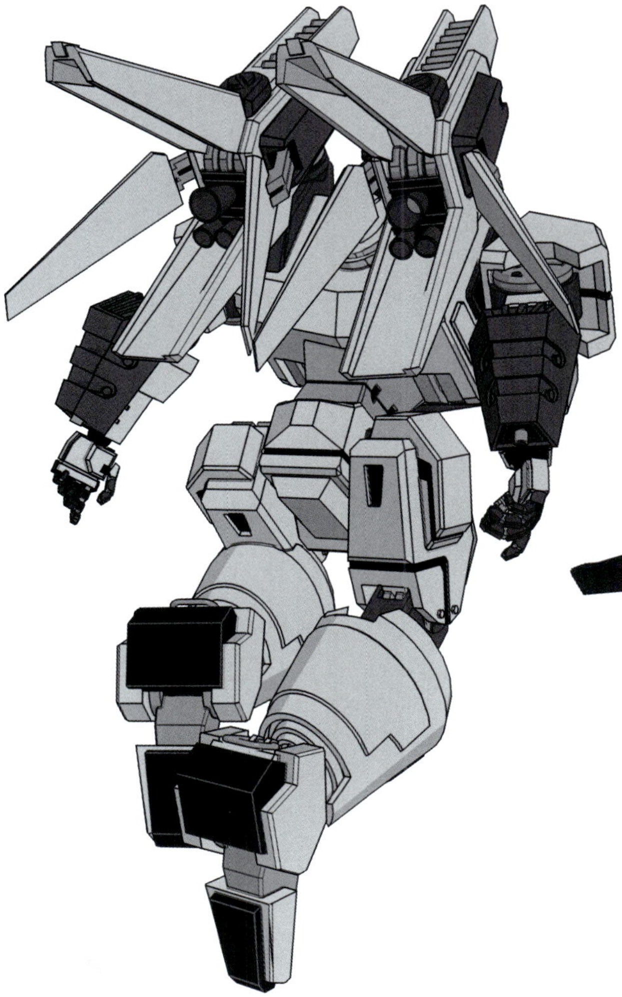

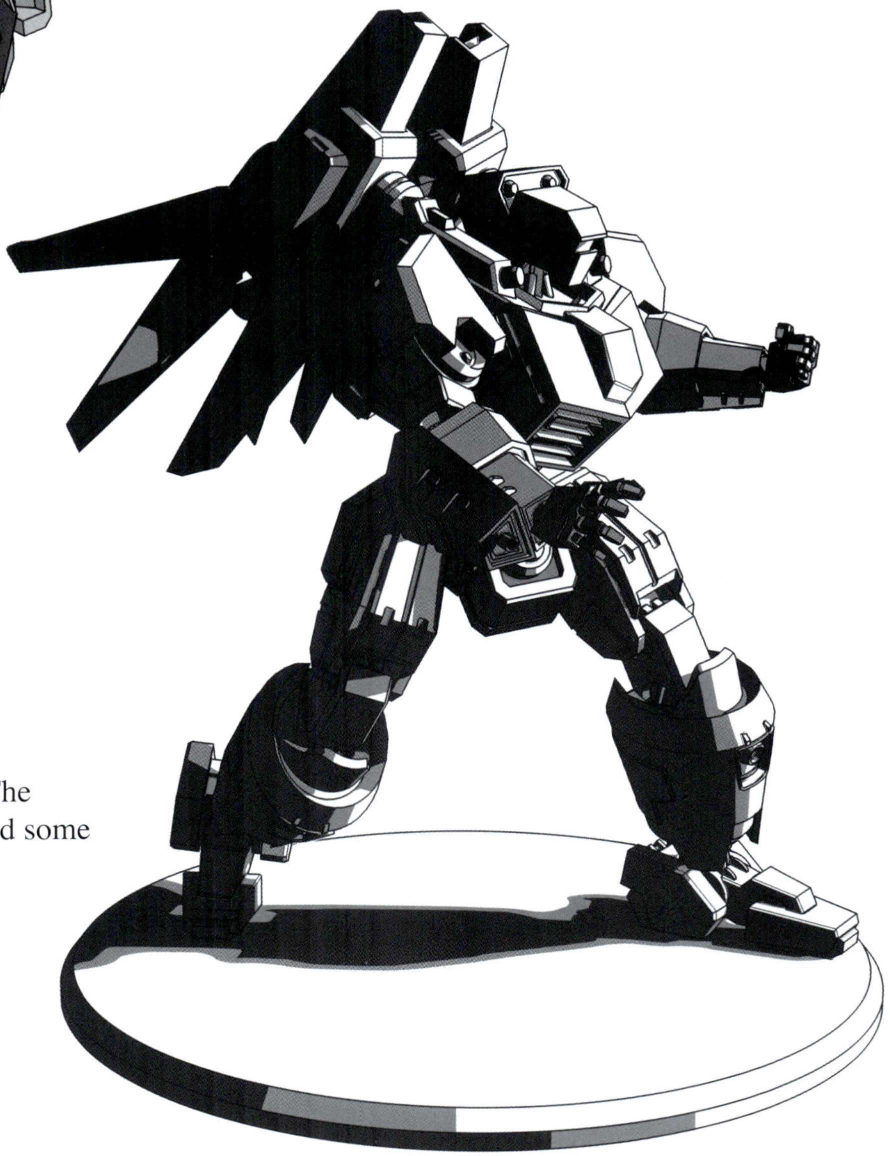

I made a very detailed 3D model of Zero. The model was fully jointed and I even produced some simple animations of it walking and flying.

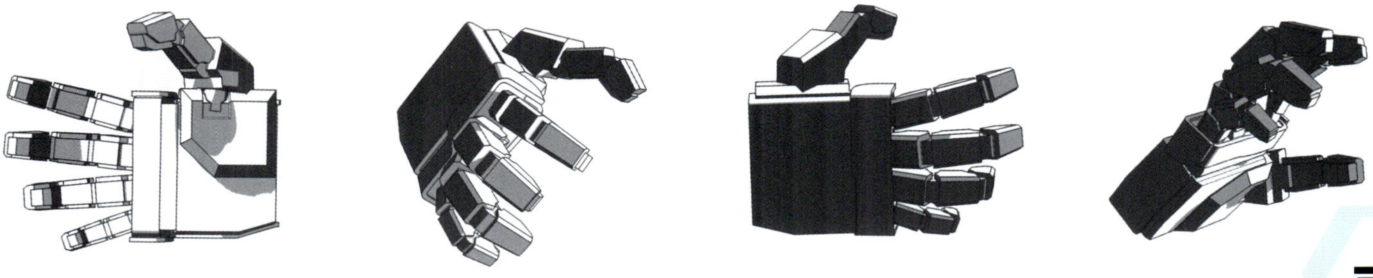

Spider Tank

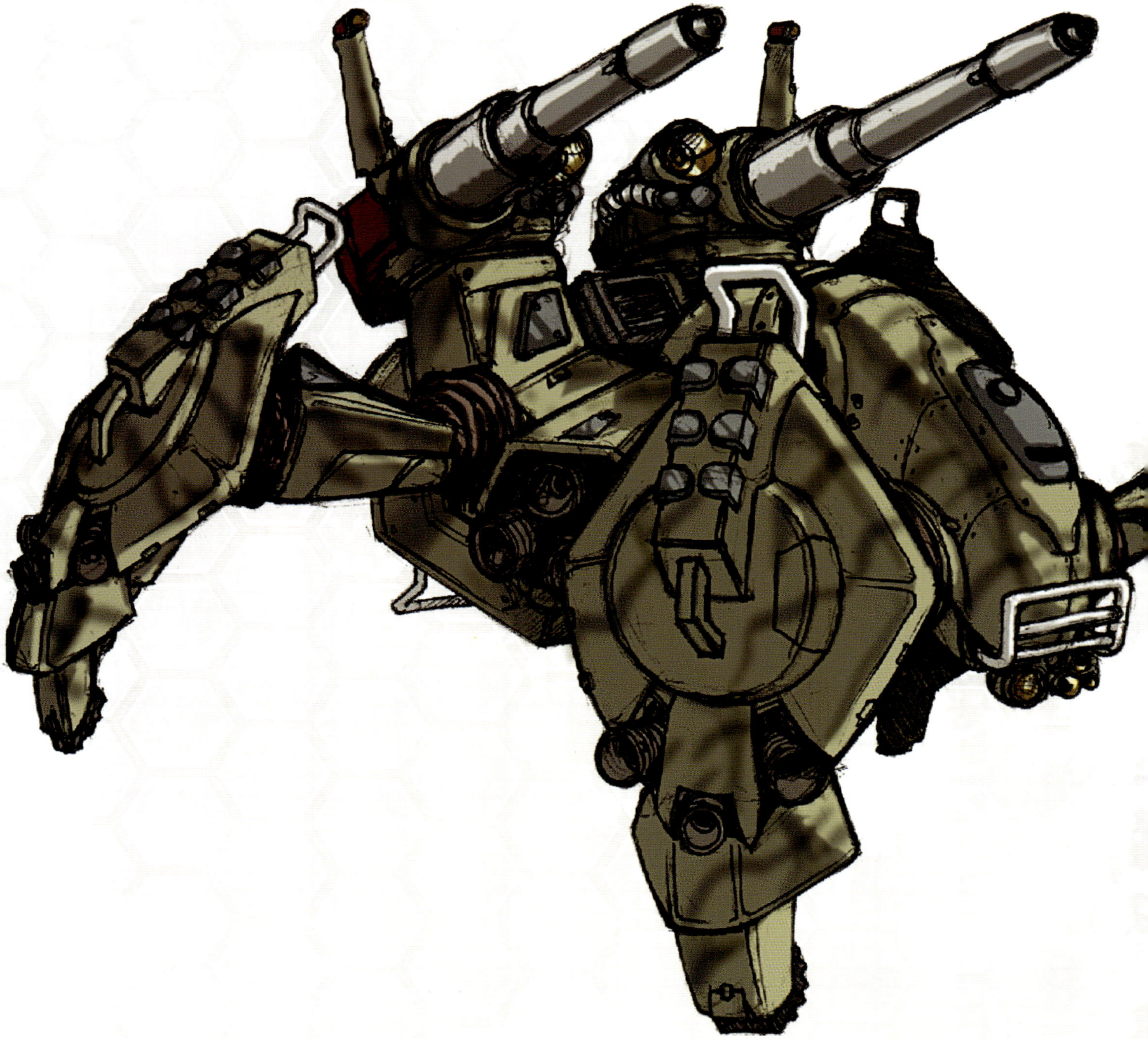

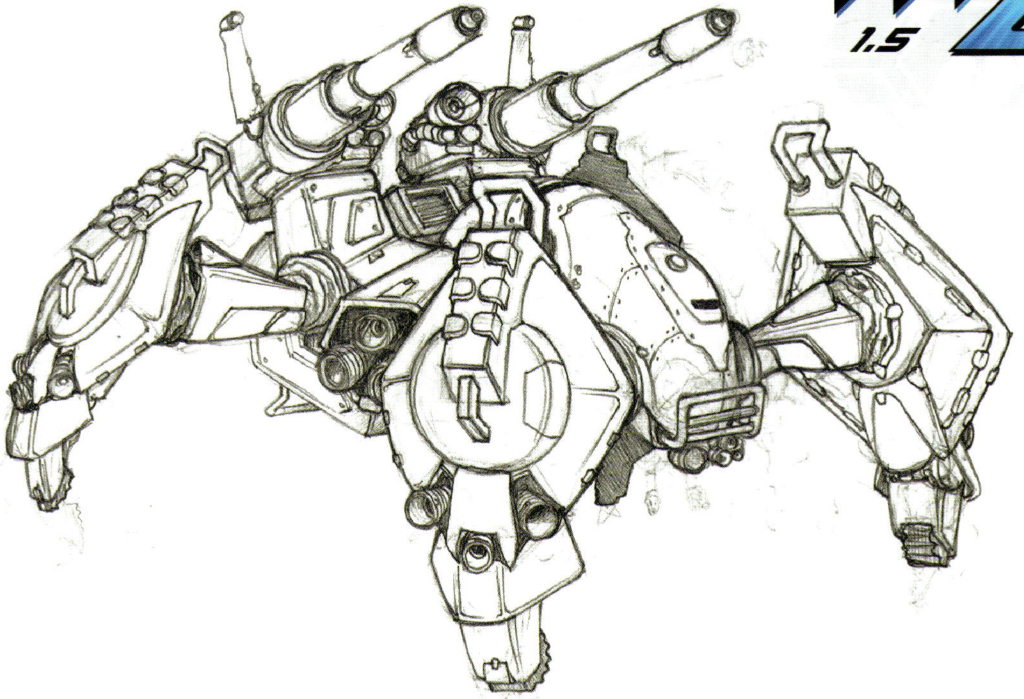

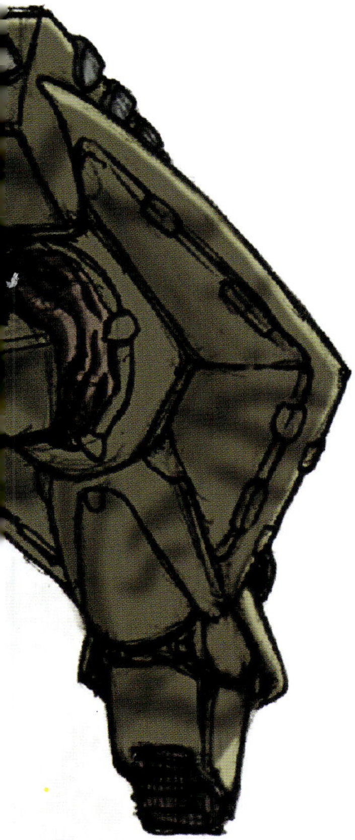

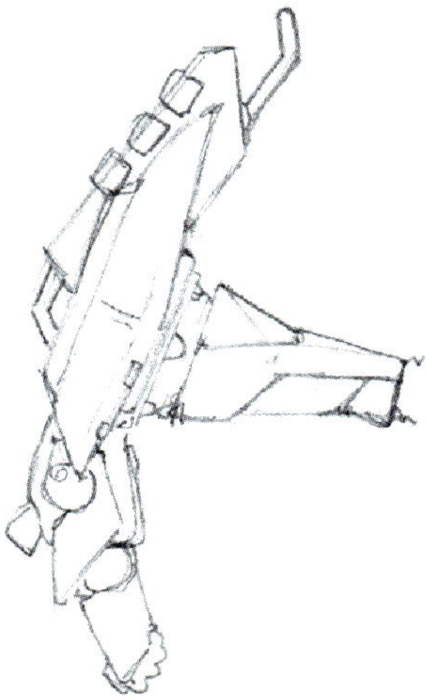

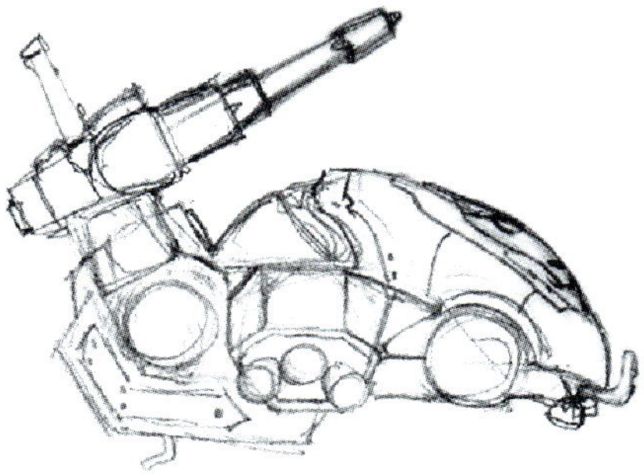

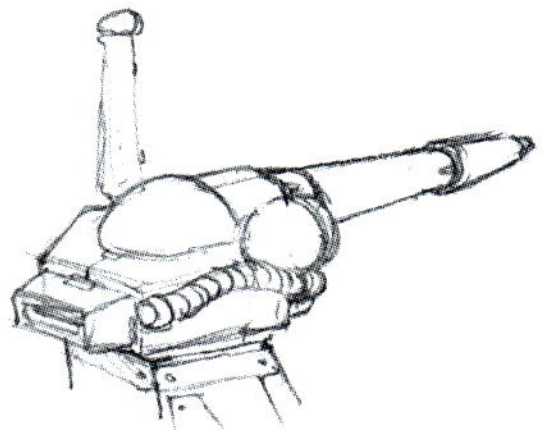

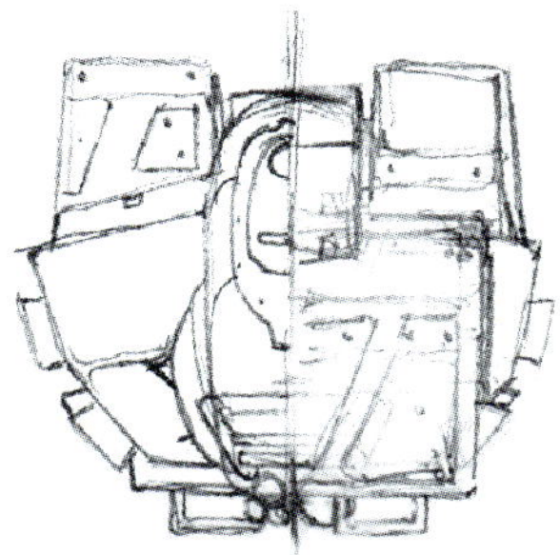

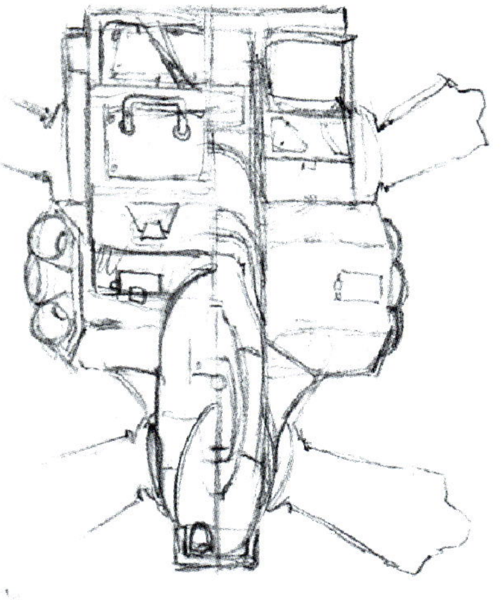

The Spider Tank is very agile and able to traverse rough and uneven terrain that would stop many other mecha.

The legs are equipped with rockets that allow the Spider Tank to jet-jump over large obstacles. This ability is also good for surprising enemy units from behind buildings and hills.

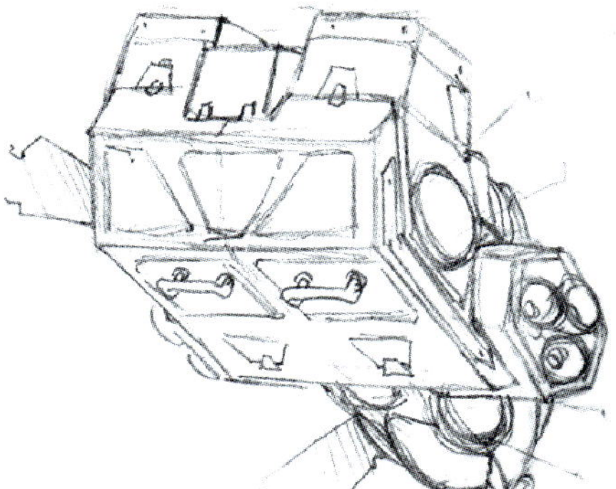

CHAPTER 3

Chapter 3 showcases 10 designs made for my original Mecha Zone web page. My intent was to create one new mecha every month and present it on my web page.

I started creating these images in 1996. I inked all of the images with a brush on vellum paper. The coloring was all done digitally. The idea of coloring art on a computer was still new and the tools were not very powerful, but I found the process fun and flexible.

Unfortunately, I did not know much about printing at the time so I made the images at a very low resolution. Some of the mecha may appear a bit blurry because of this.

MECHA ZONE

Nightingale

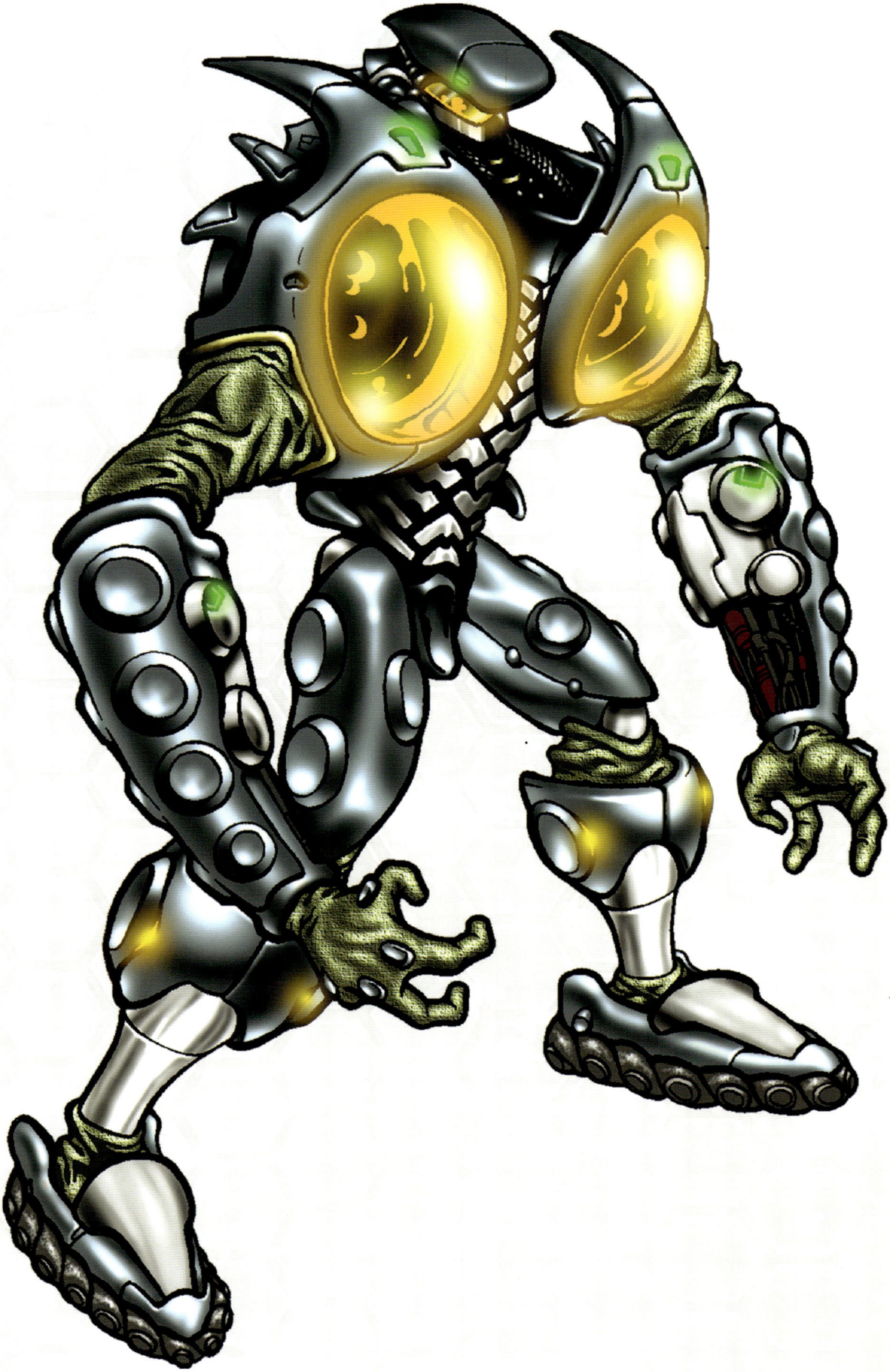

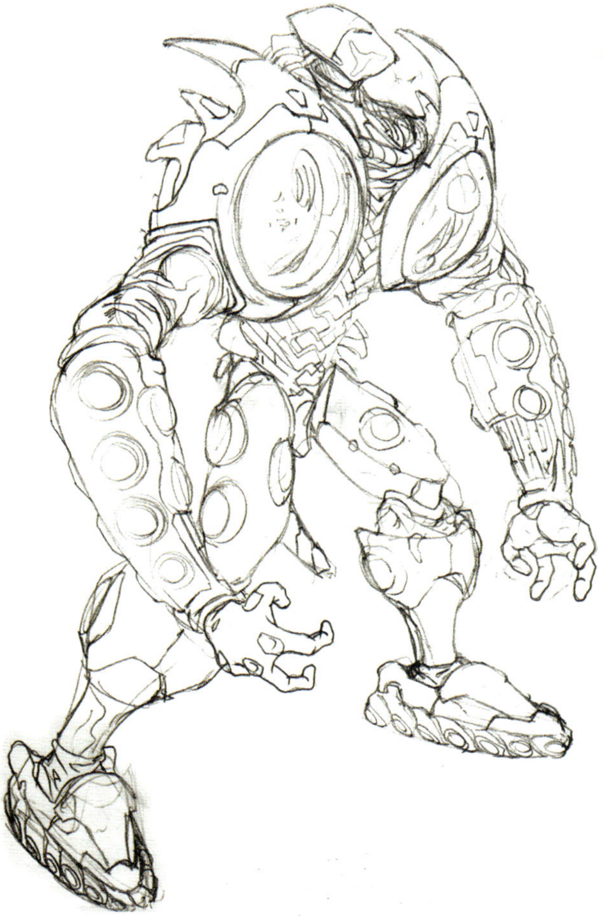

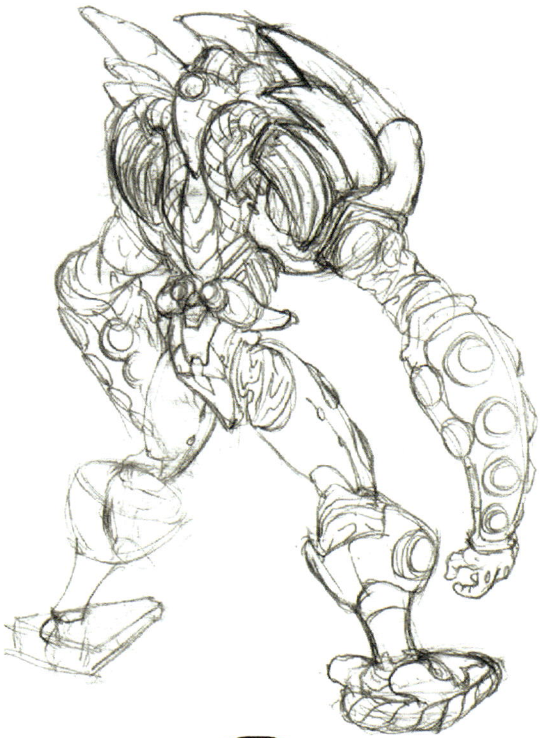

The Nightingale is a research drone developed by an ancient alien civilization. It roams the universe looking for knowledge and enlightenment.

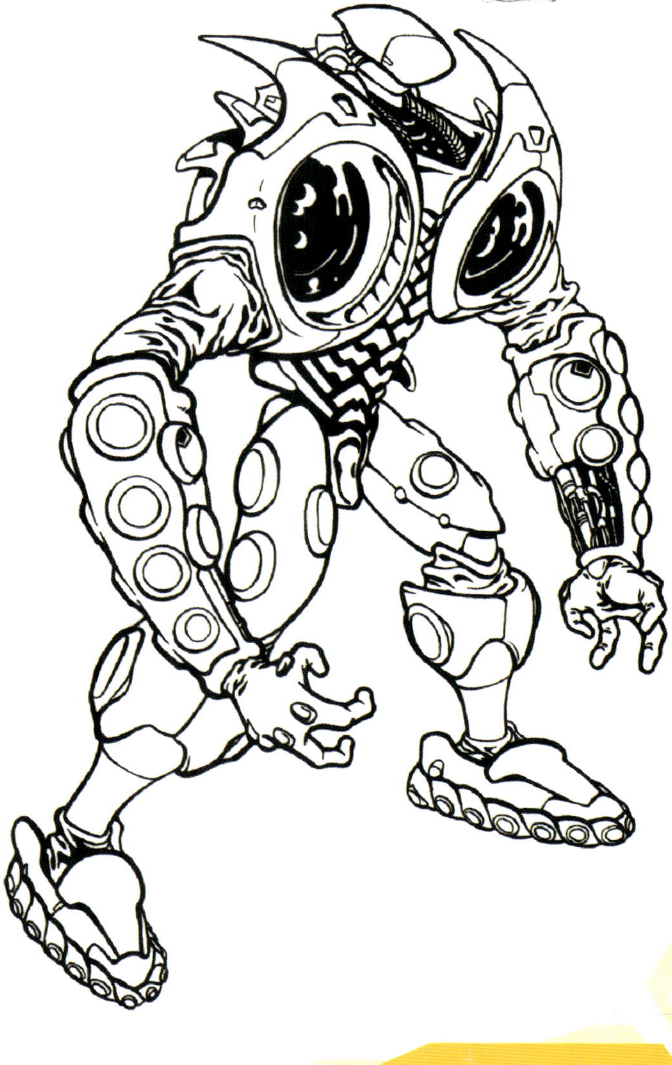

CHAINSAW BOT AKA RIPPER

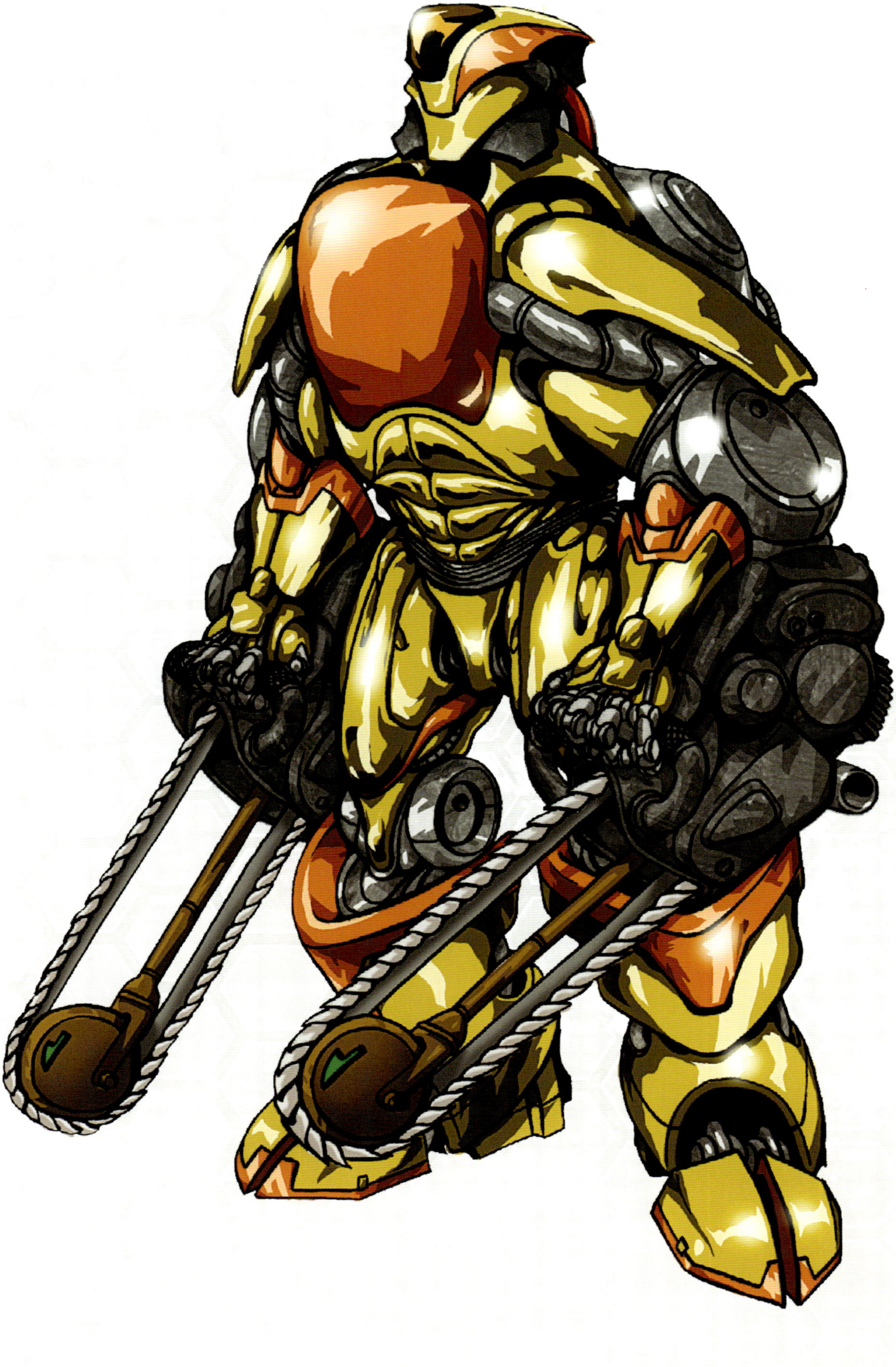

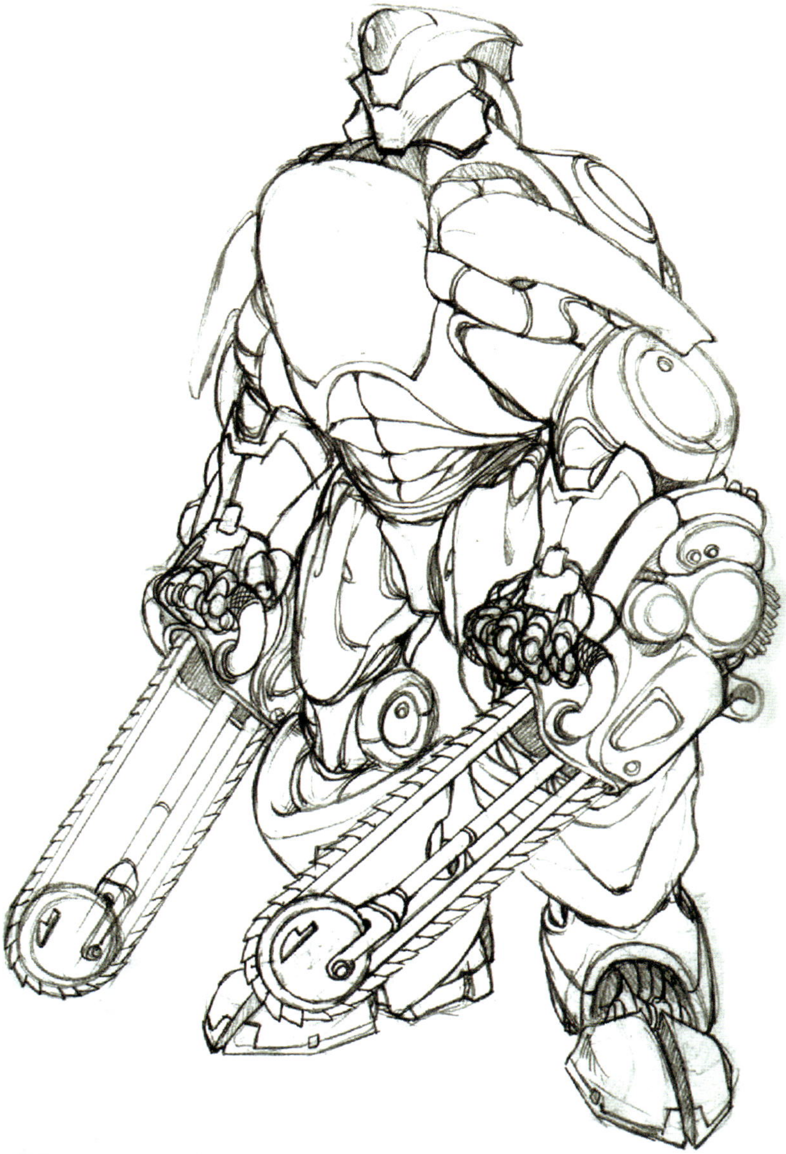

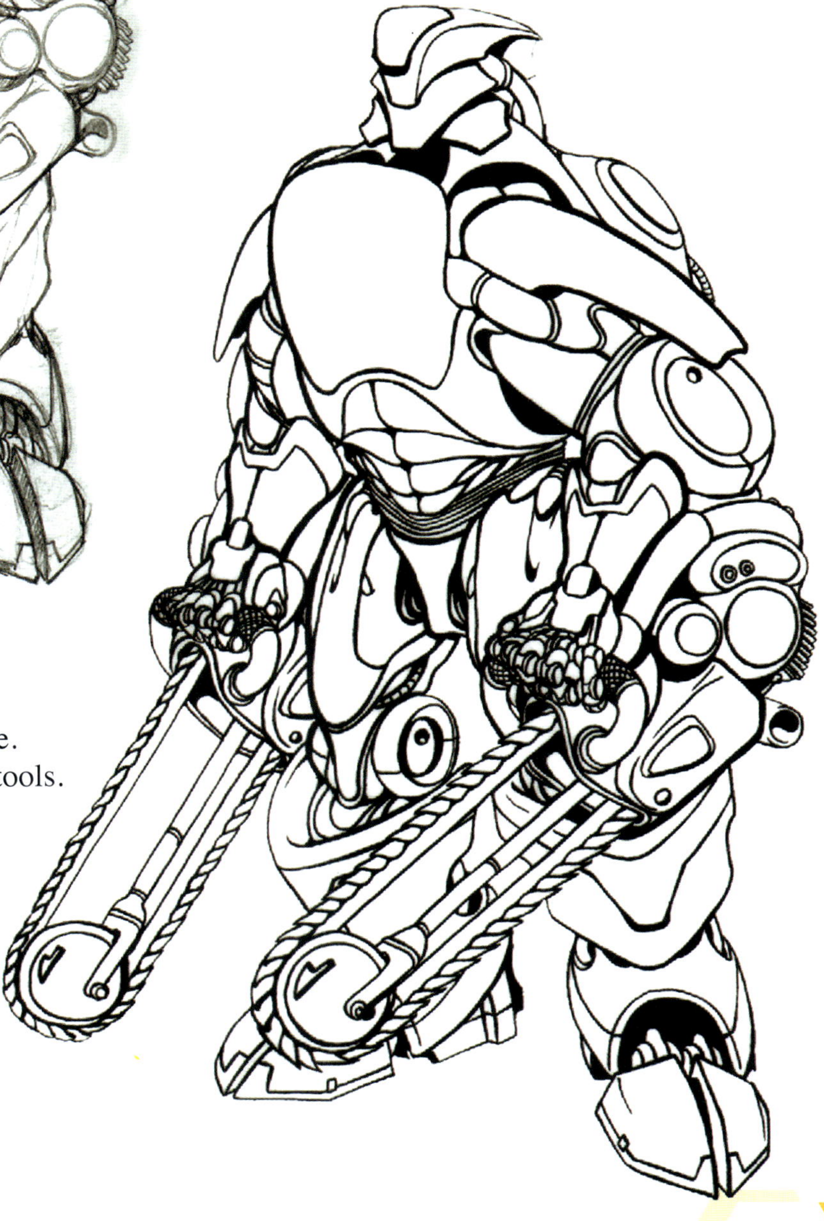

The Chainsaw Bot was designed for industrial use. Variant models replace the chainsaws with other tools. Military models are rumored to exist.

MISSILE BOT

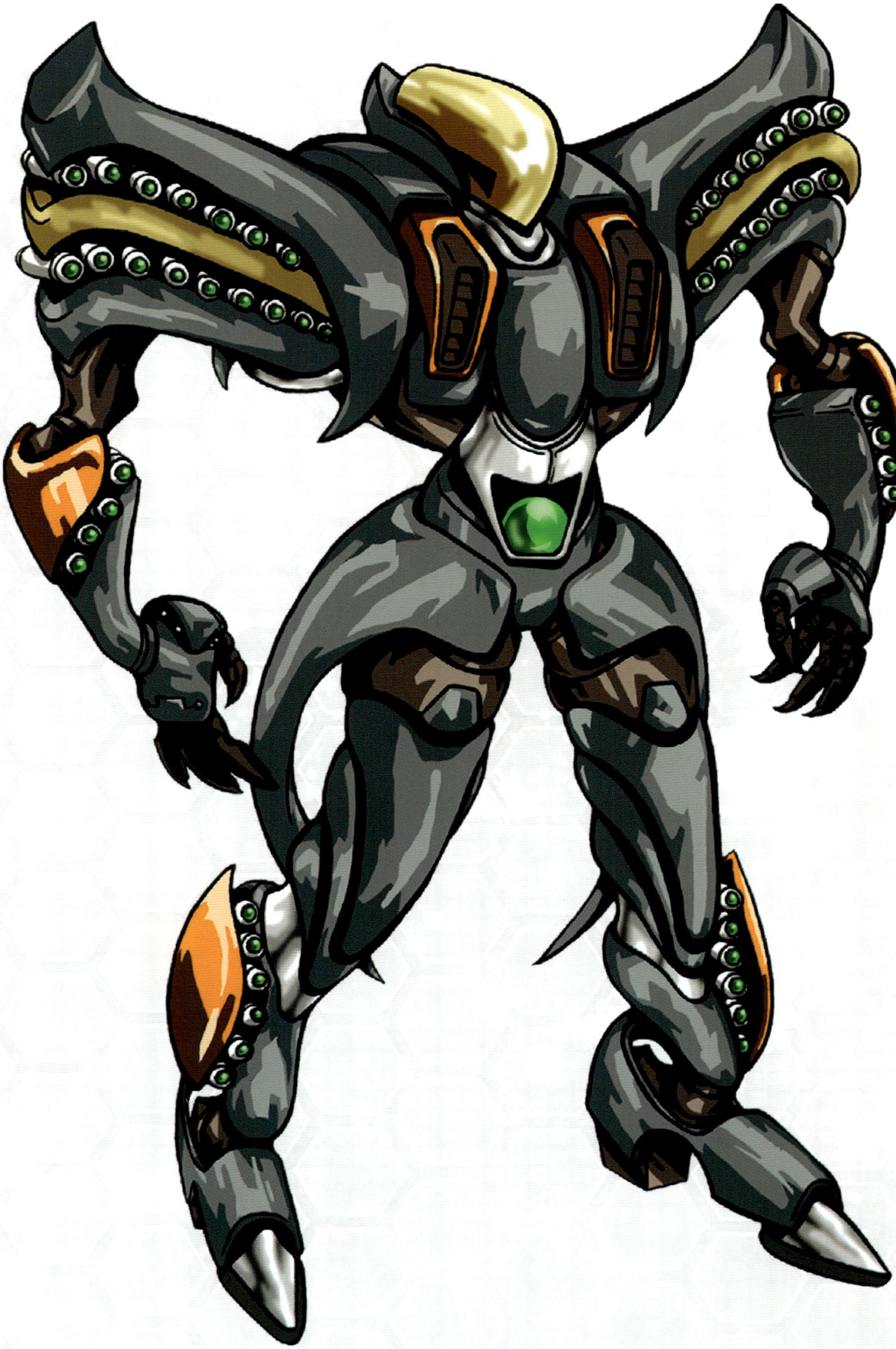

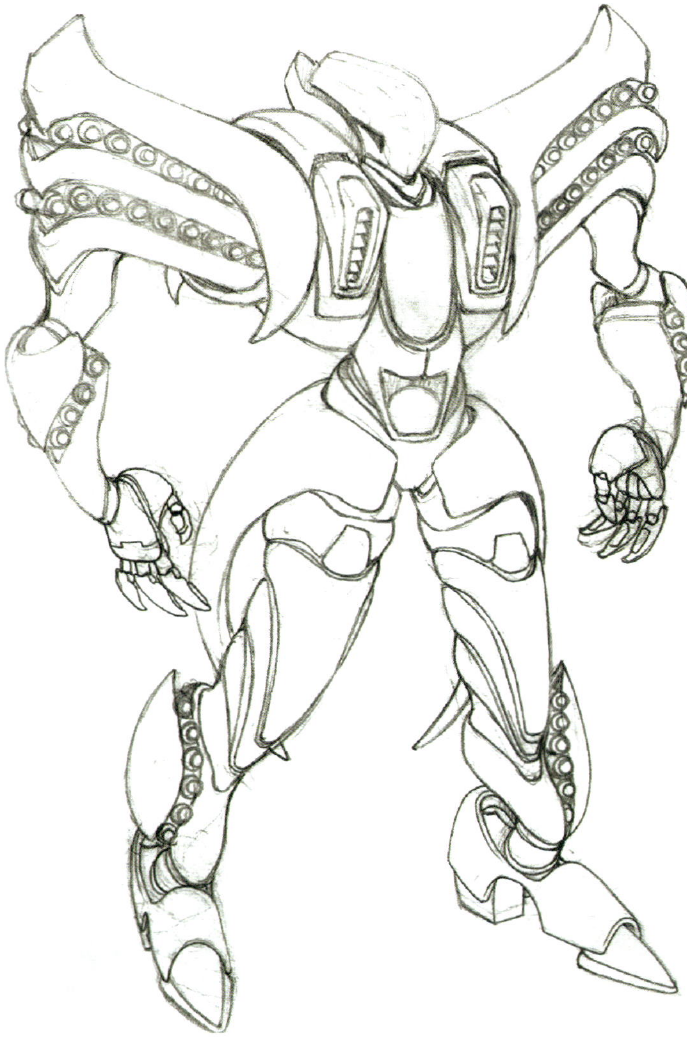

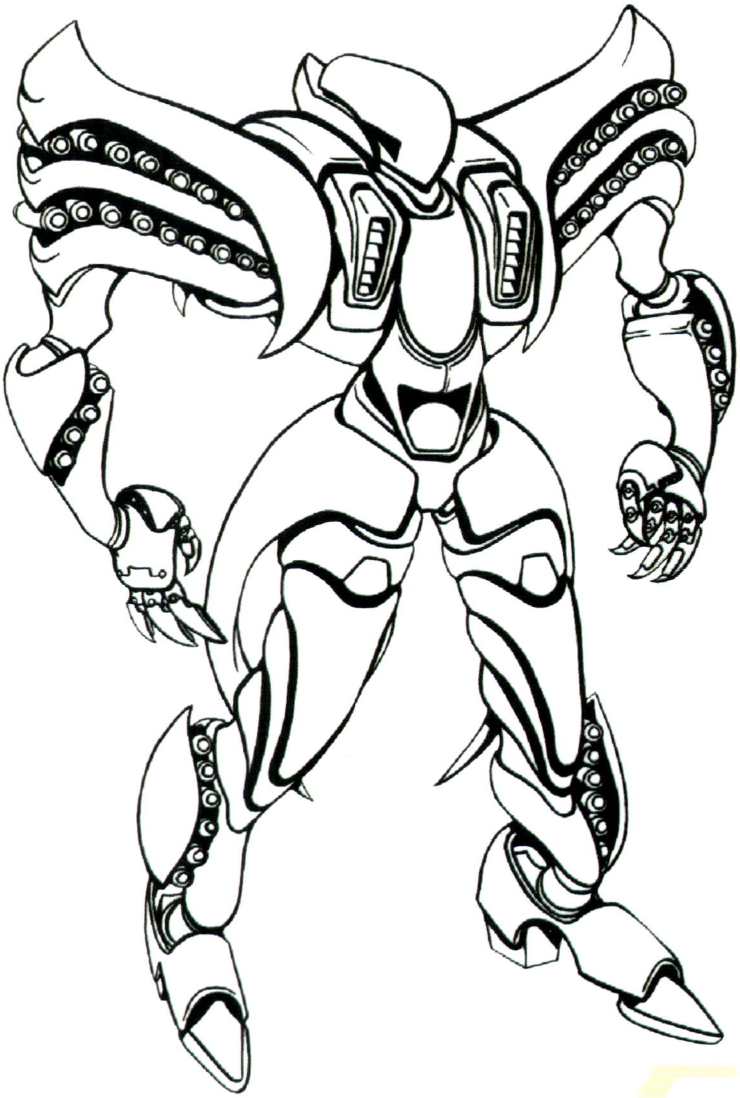

The Missile Bot was designed for high altitude and long-range combat. The missile compartments can be closed for transport and increased aerodynamics.

GRENADE BOT

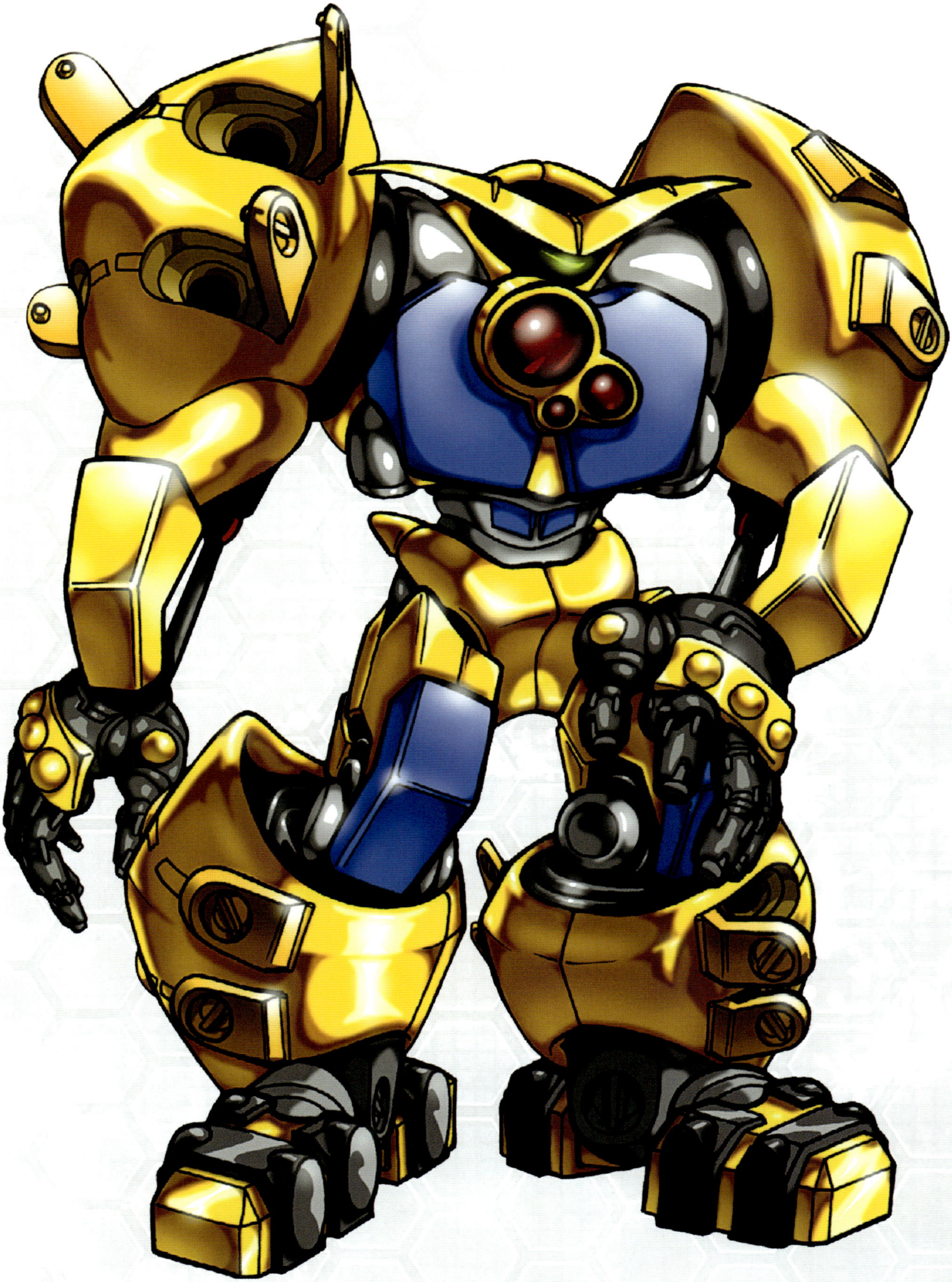

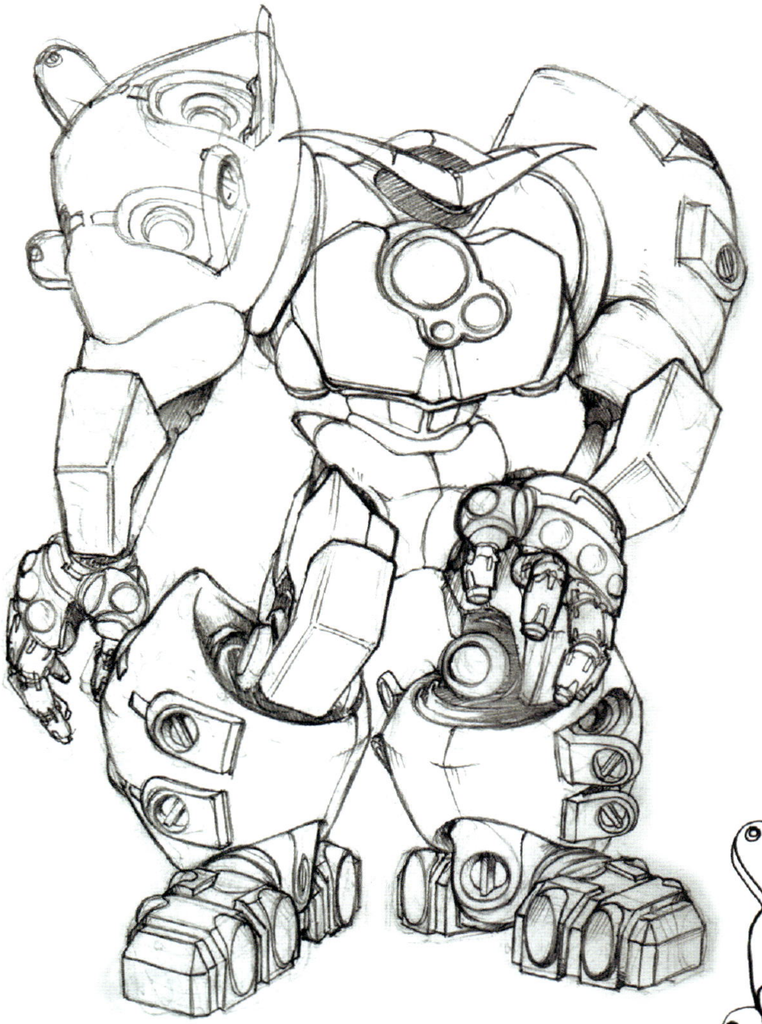

The Grenade Bot is a re-design of an old sketch called the Construction Mecha, which can be seen on pages 92-93.

The Grenade Bot keeps the same basic feel as its predecessor, but adds a more militaristic flare with the addition of missile tubes.

This version has also been re-designed again! You can see that re-design, called the Concussion, on pages 28-29.

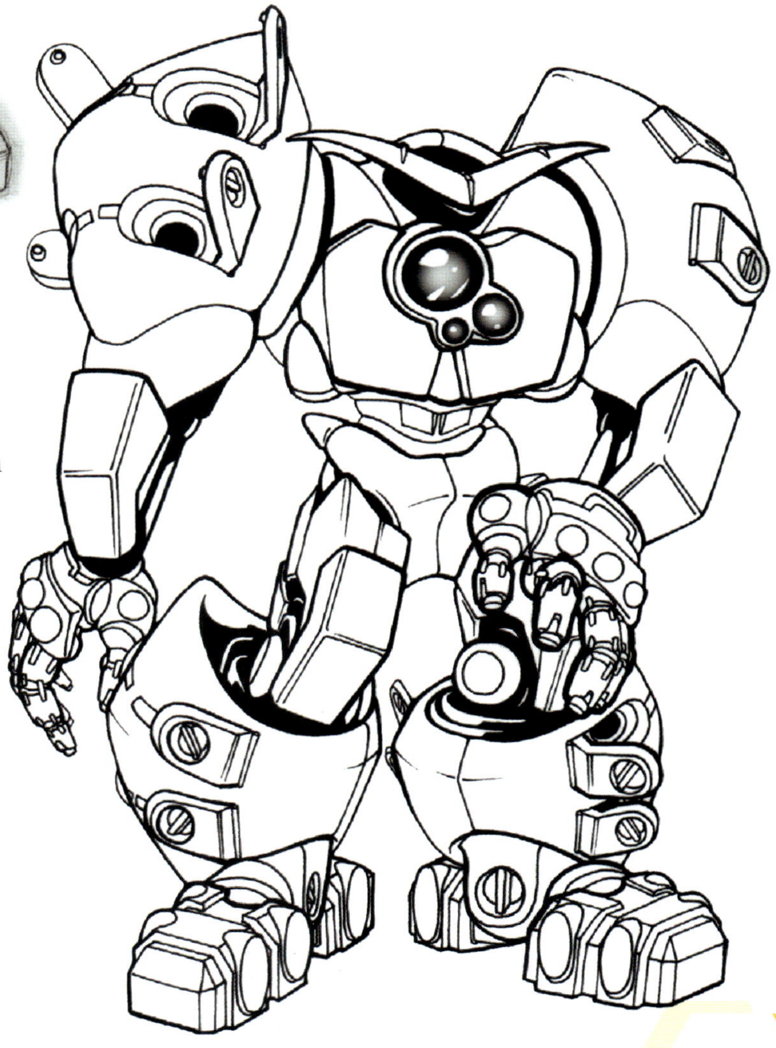

Command Bot

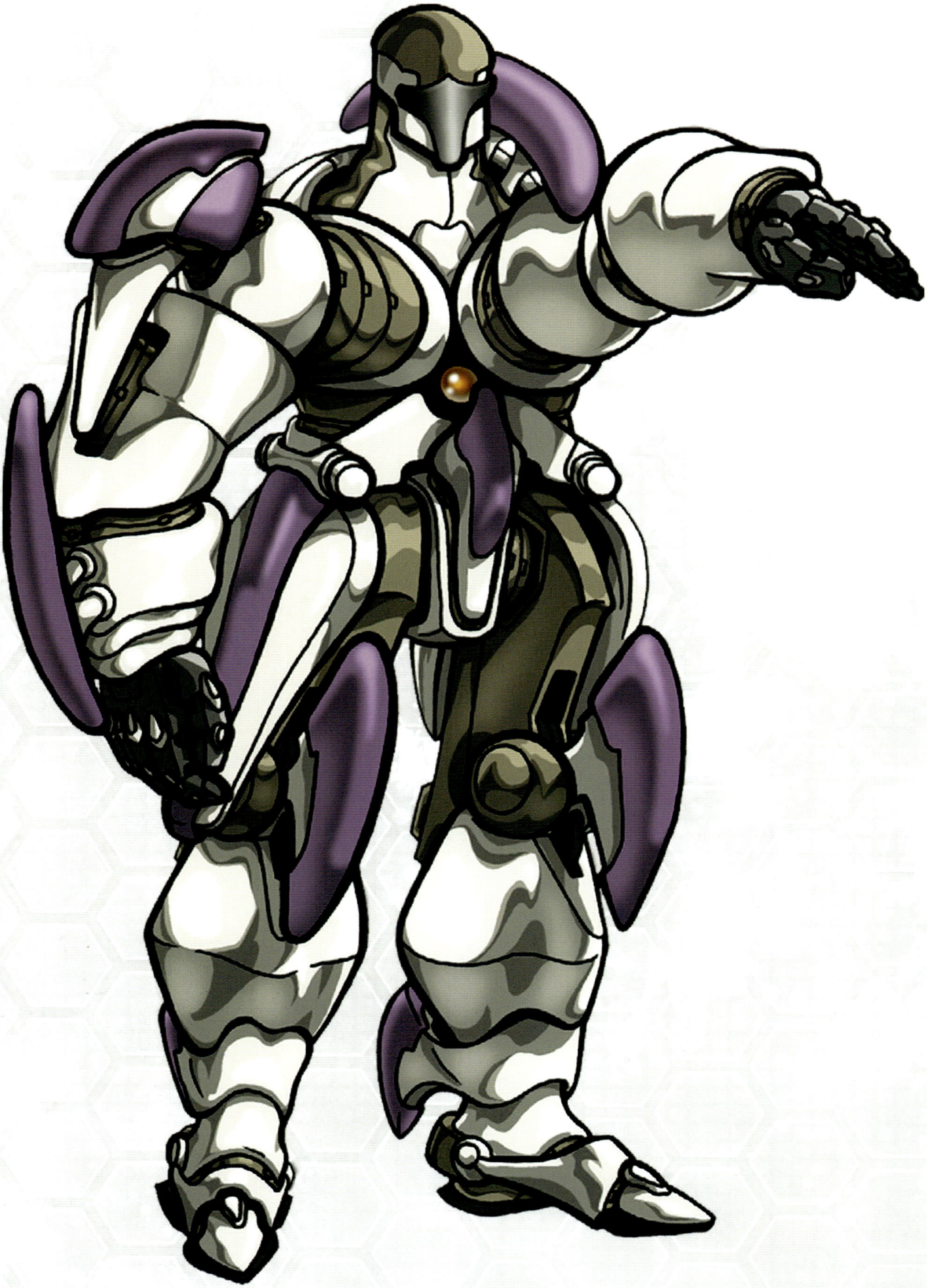

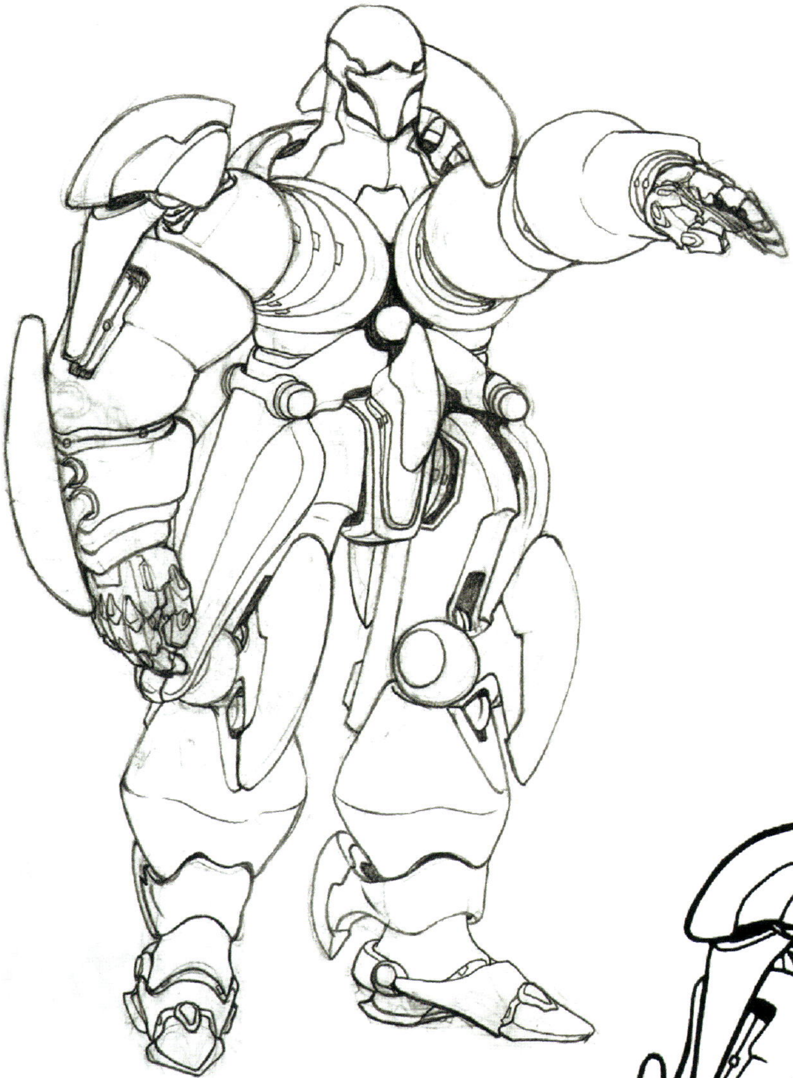

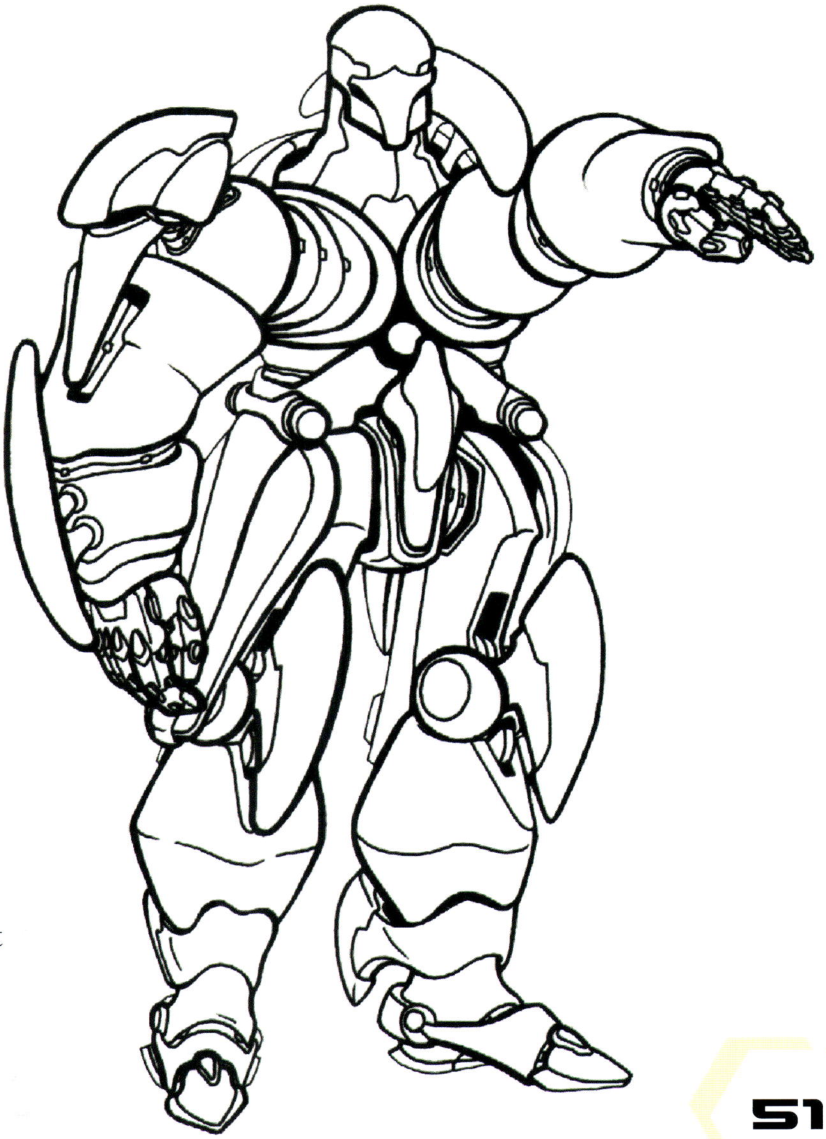

The Command Bot has no weapons. Its purpose is to evaluate the battlefield and direct the other combat mecha.

The thick, layered armor is intended to provide maximum protection against damage so the Command Bot can remain functional throughout the battle.

Command Bot X-Ray

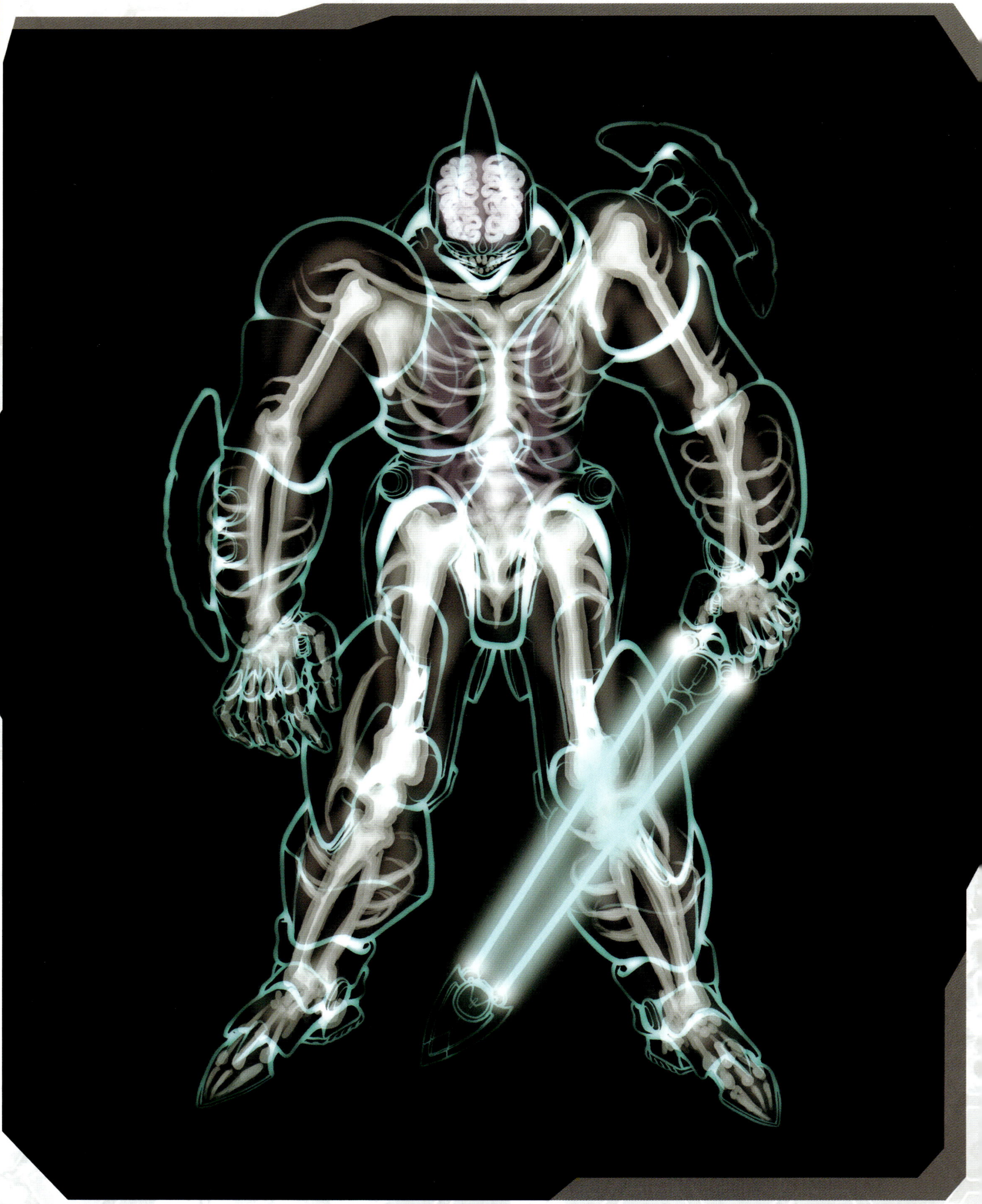

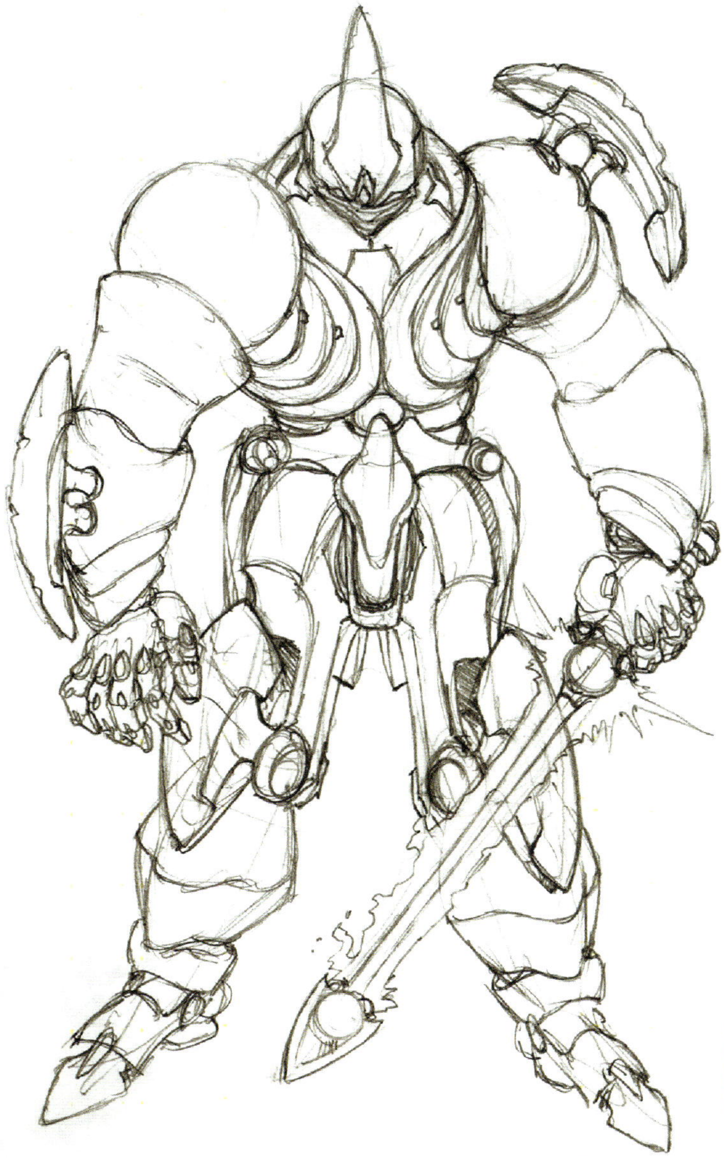

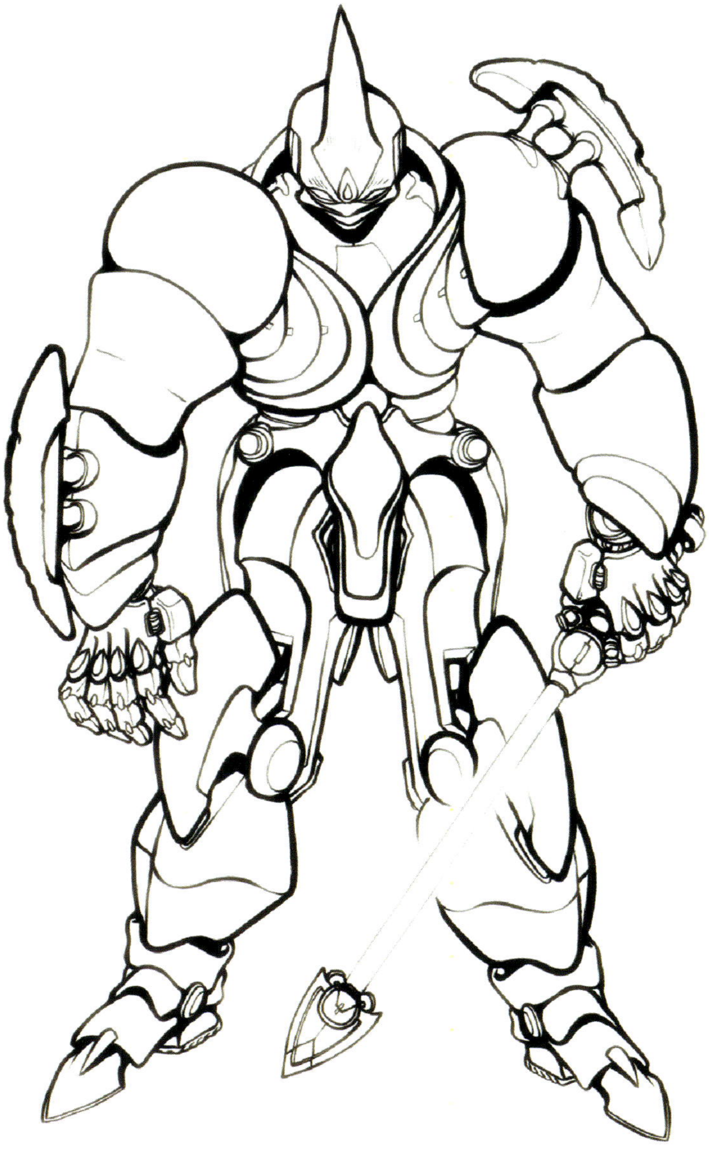

TOP SECRET:
The Command bot is actually a cyborg unit. The organic neurological systems give it superior battlefield judgment and quick decision-making skills.

Later models were equipped with an energy sword for self-defense.

SWORD BOT

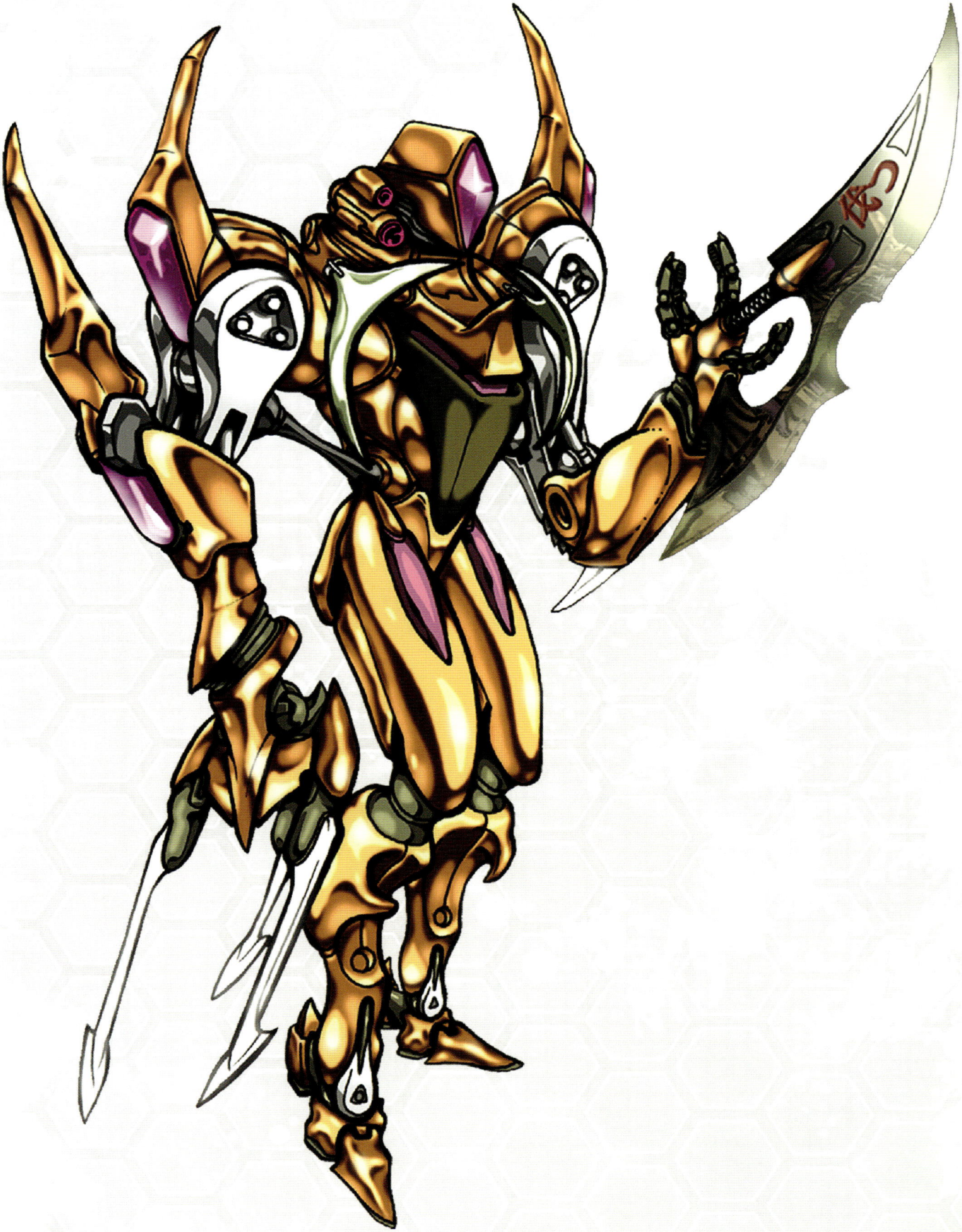

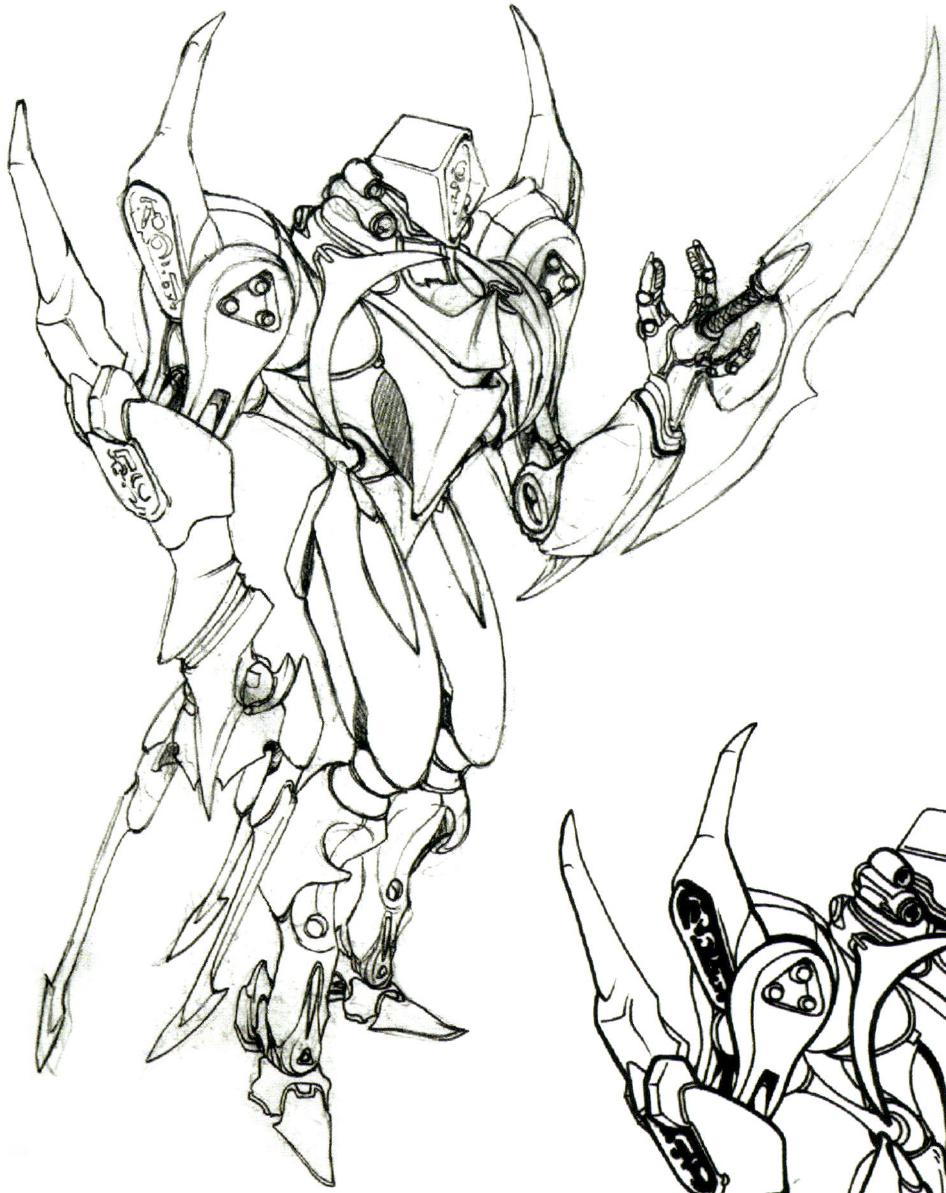

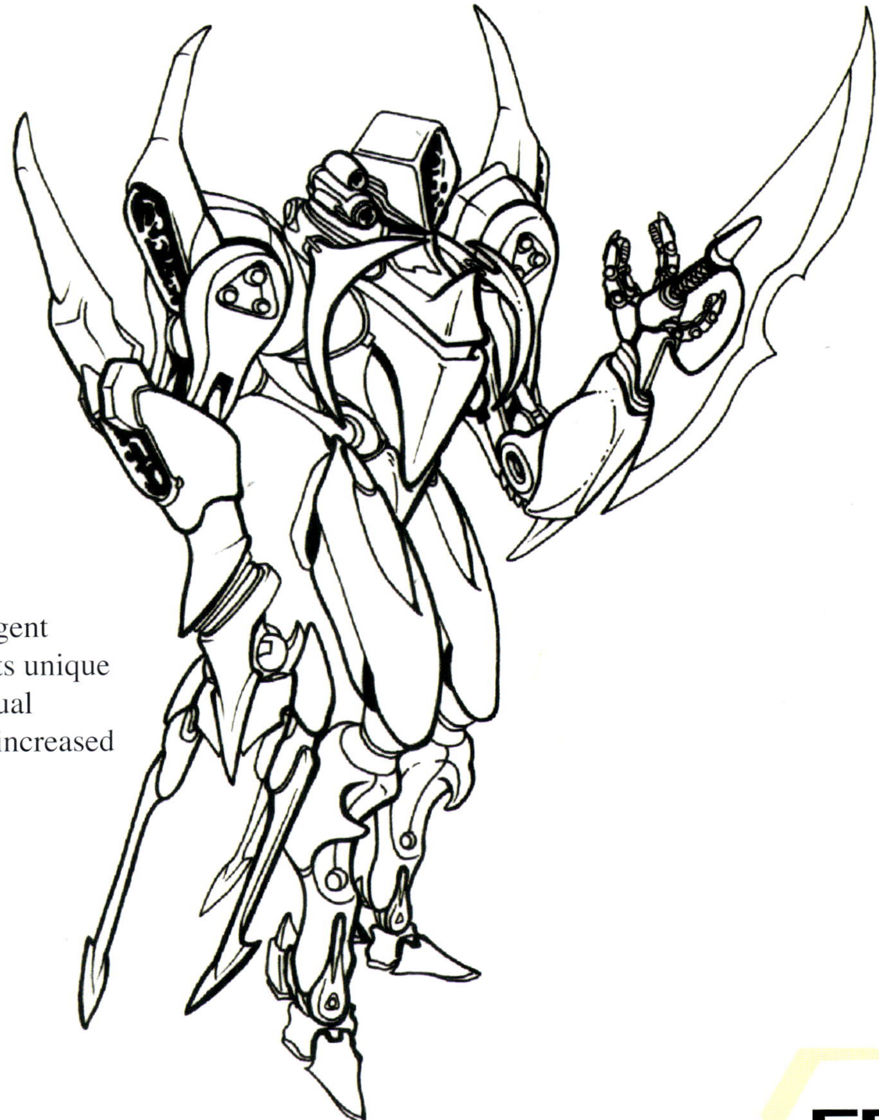

The Sword Bot is a stealth unit used for urgent combat missions on hostile alien planets. Its unique and flexible skeleton can adapt to the unusual physiology of almost any alien soldier for increased combat effectiveness.

Laser Bot

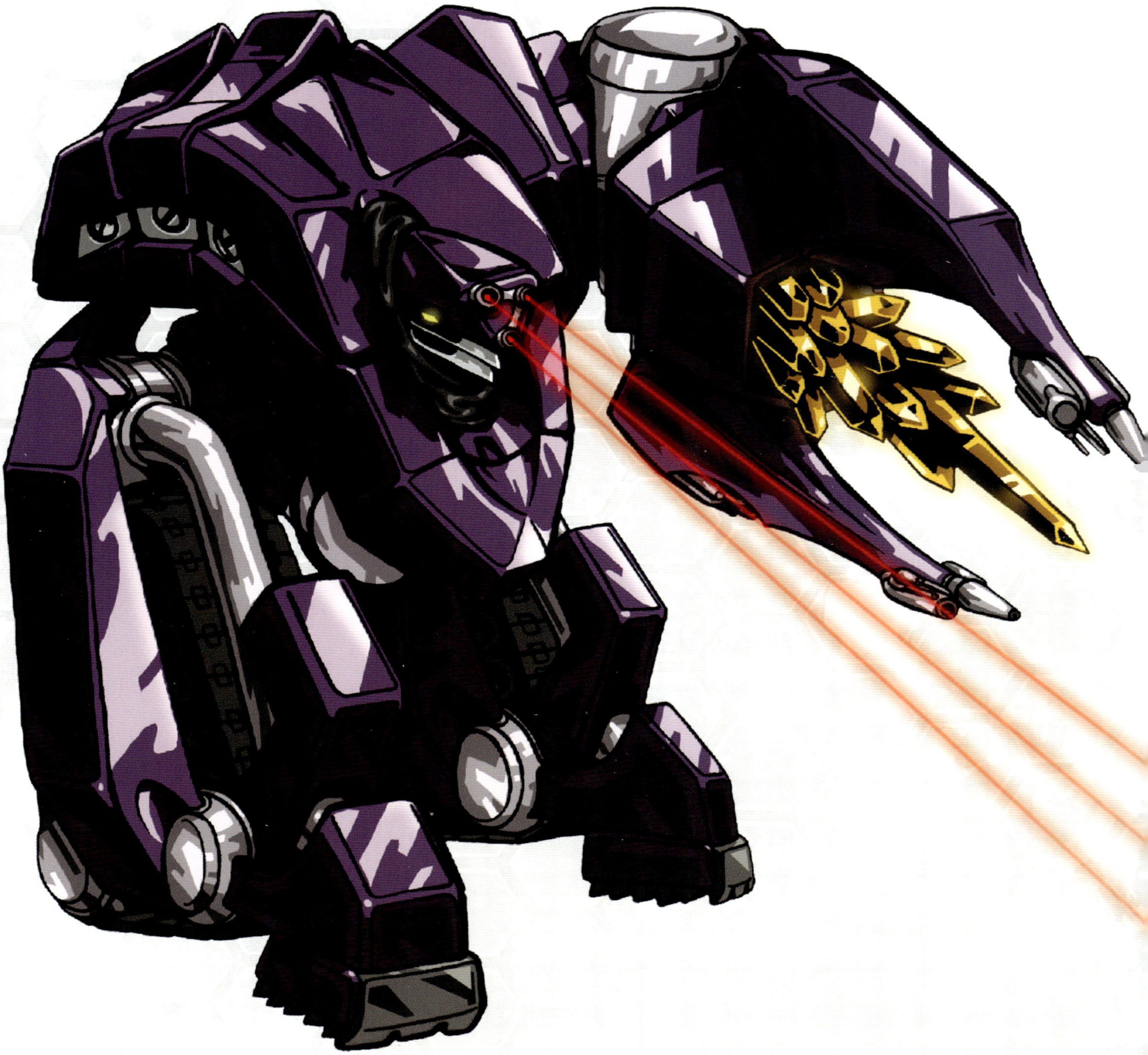

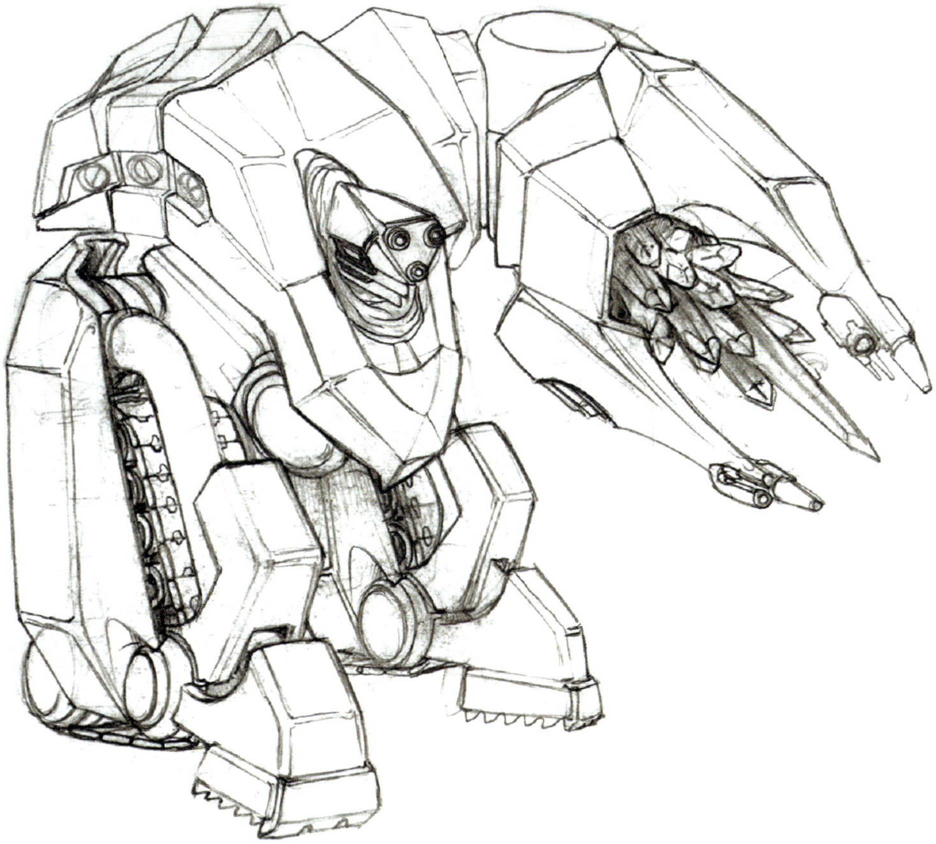

The Laser Bot is a slow and lumbering mecha designed to stay hidden and bombard the enemy with powerful lasers.

There are treads hidden in the legs and the Laser Bot can fold itself into a tank for increased mobility or long-range travel.

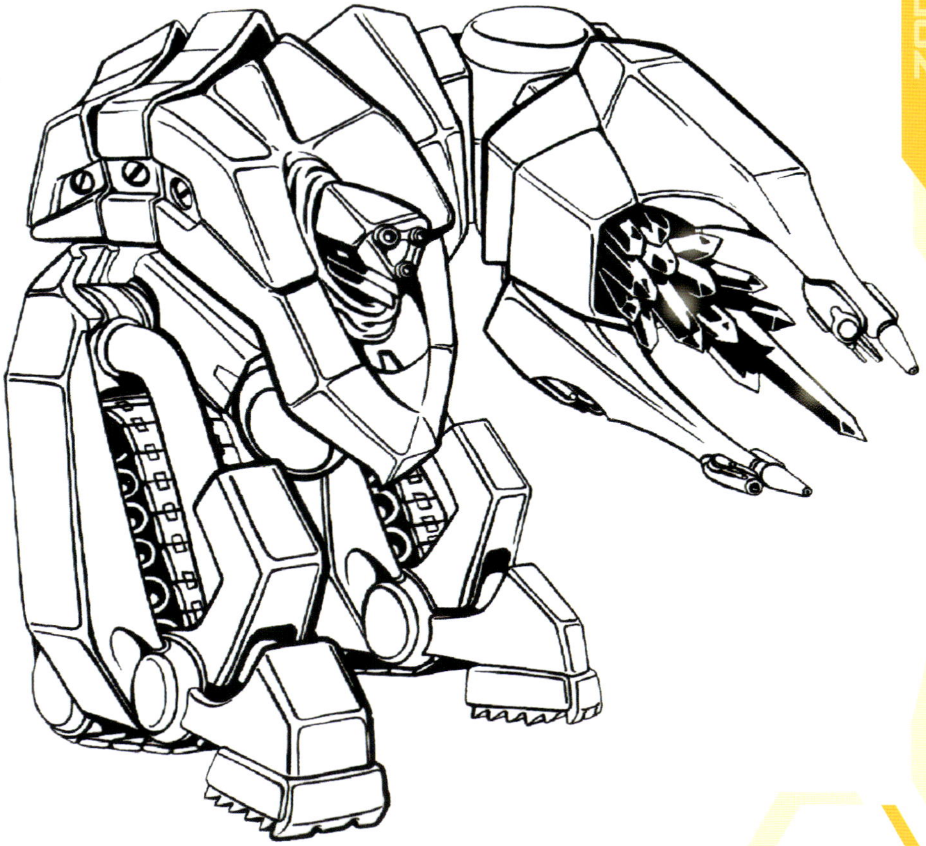

Winner

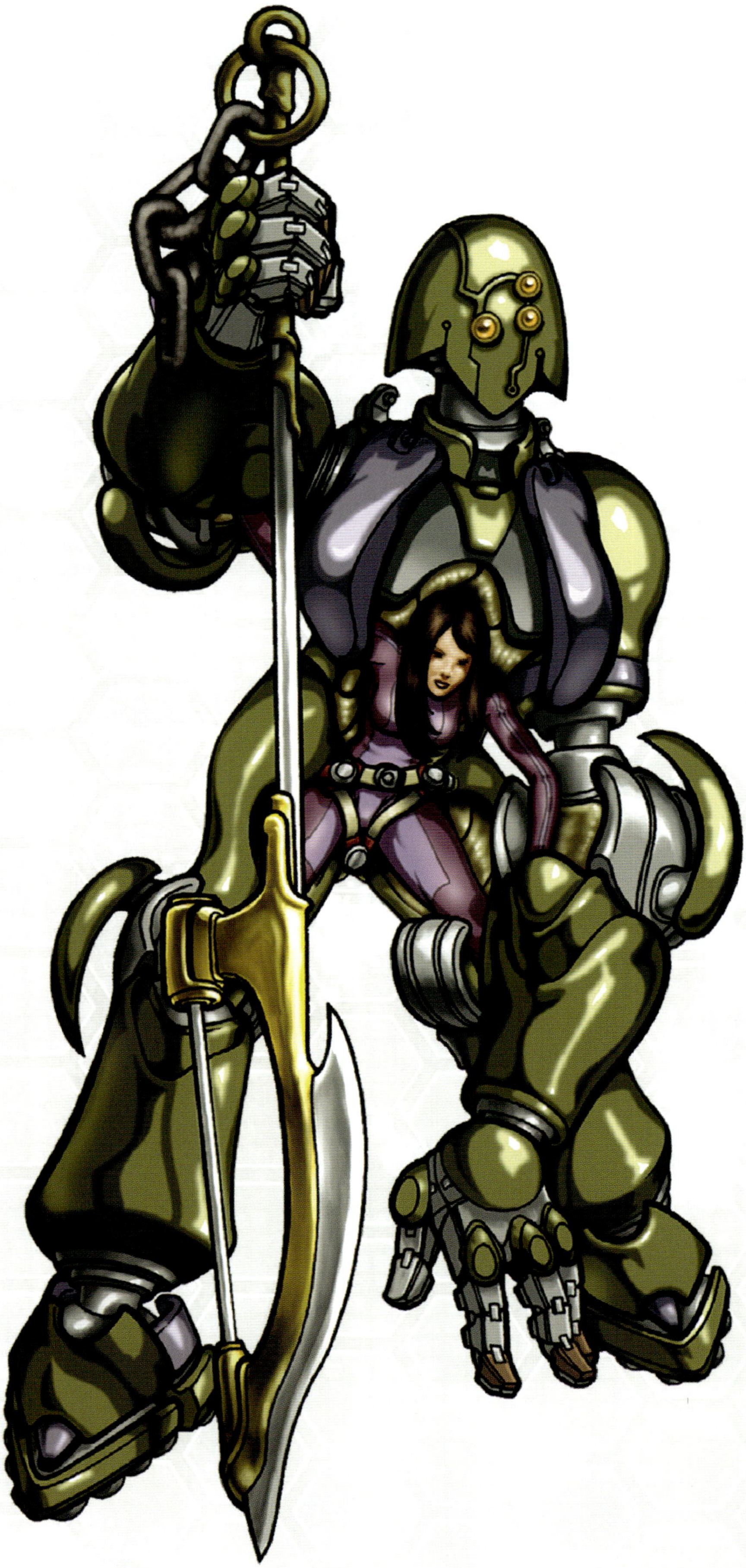

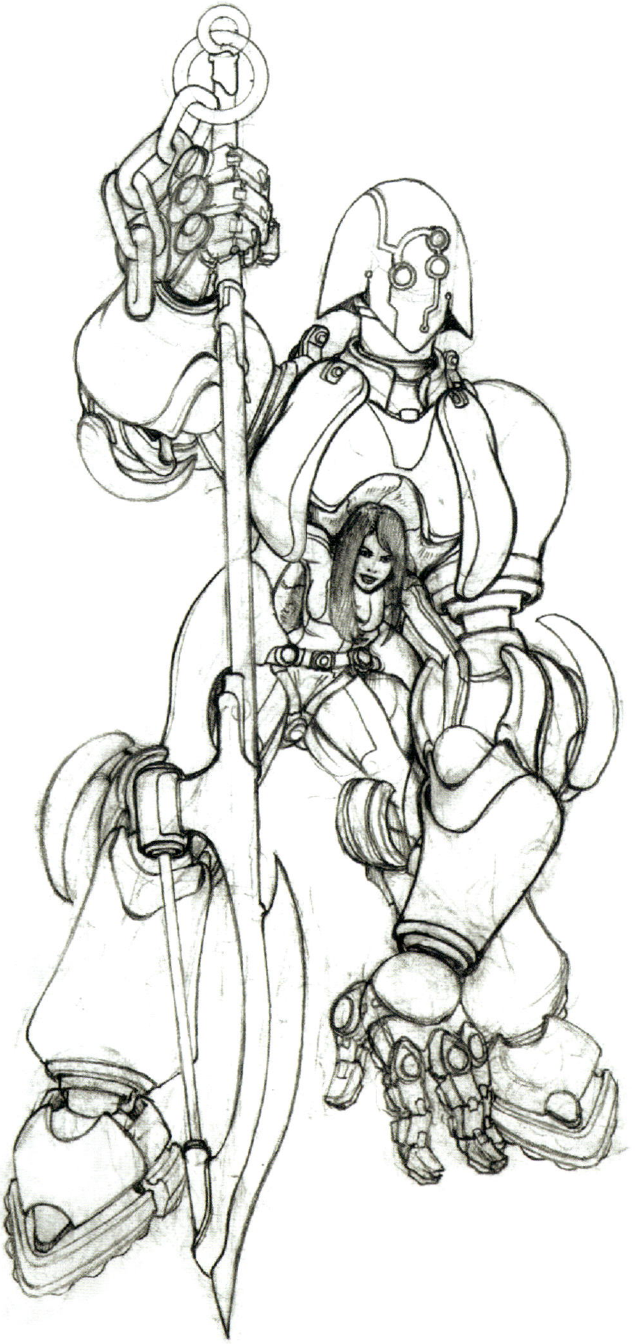

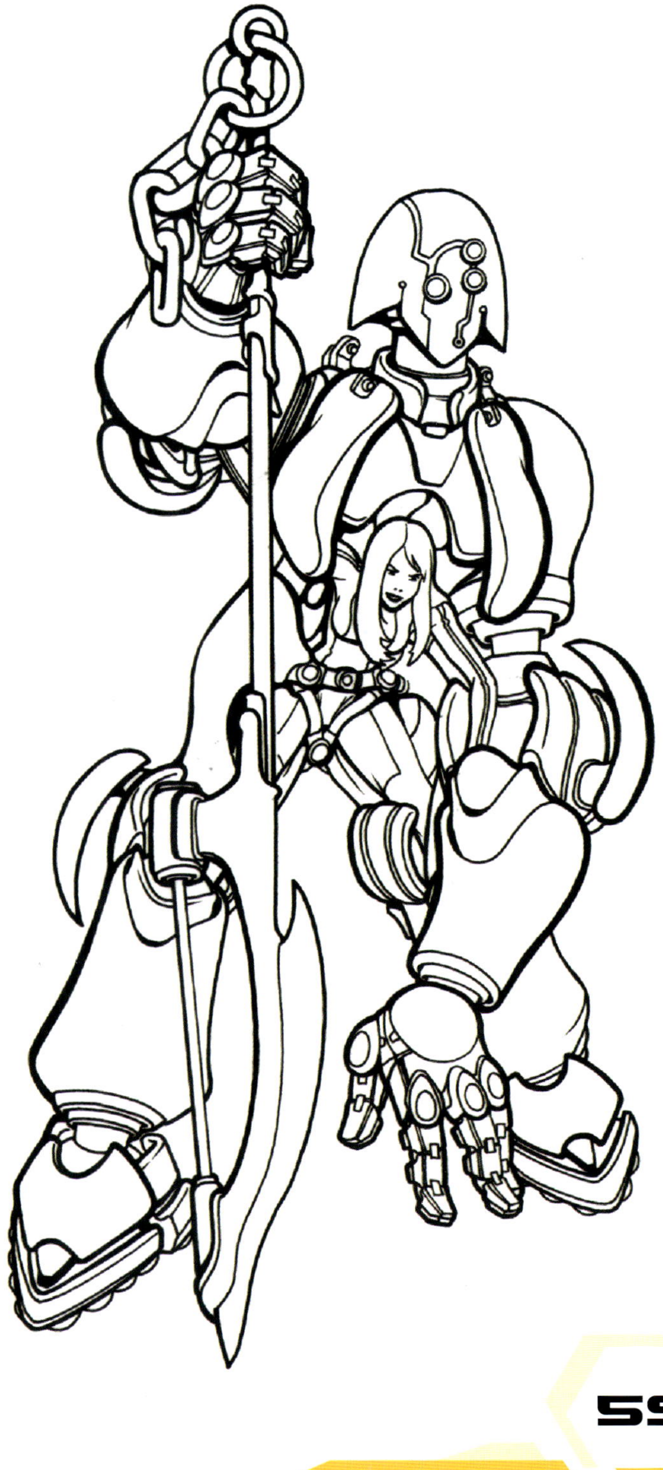

The mysterious Winner is a veteran of the underground fighting championships. Her lithe armor and quick reflexes always give her an advantage.

Her weapon of choice is a crystal edged pike, able to slice though any alloy or compound.

Claw Bot

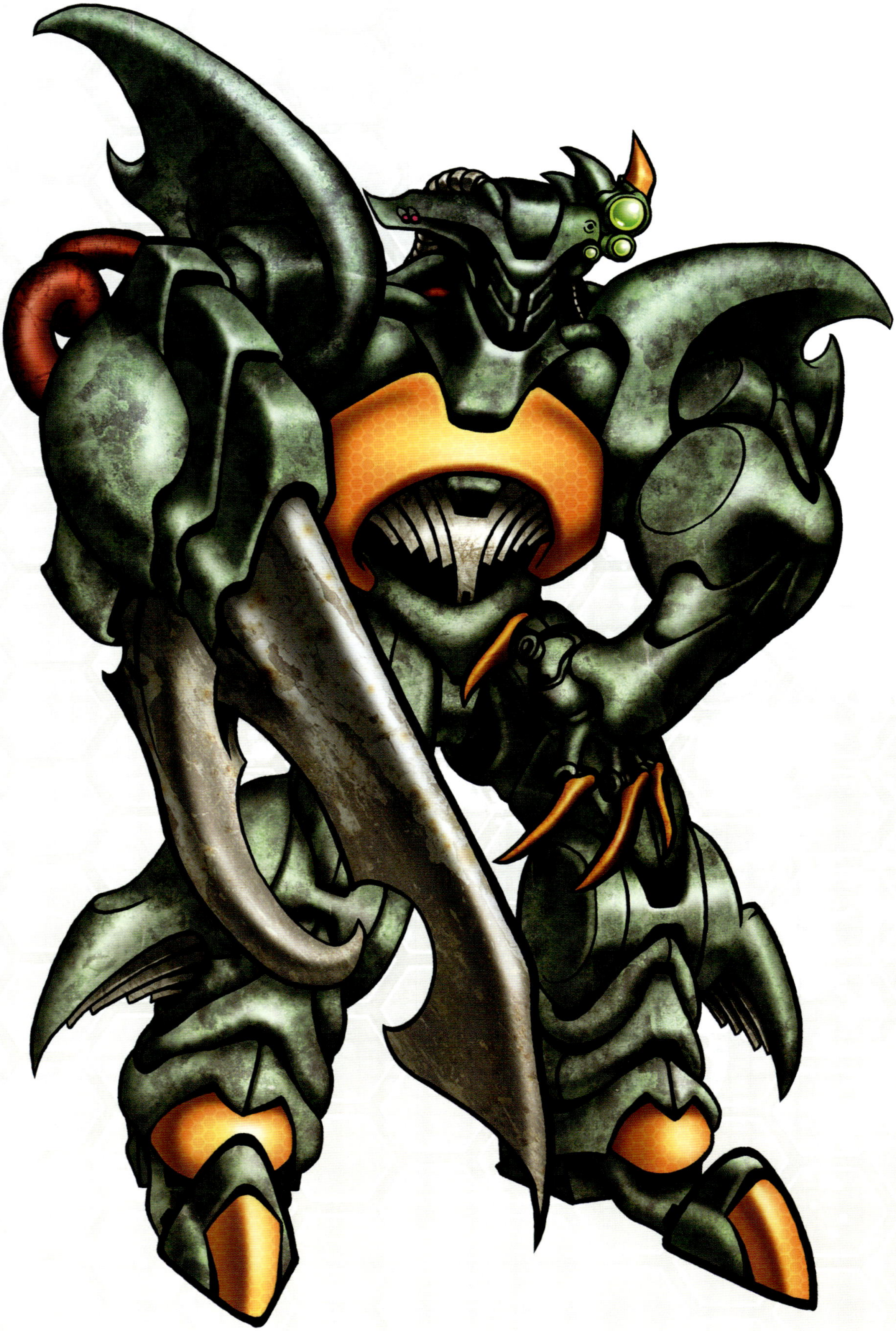

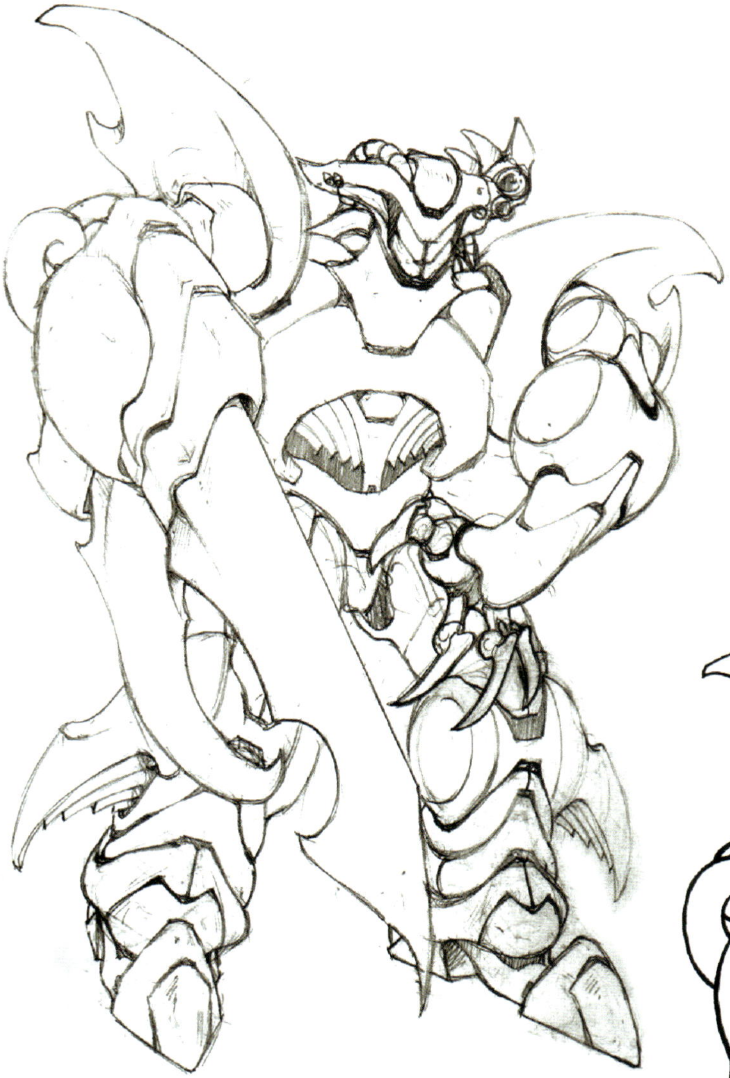

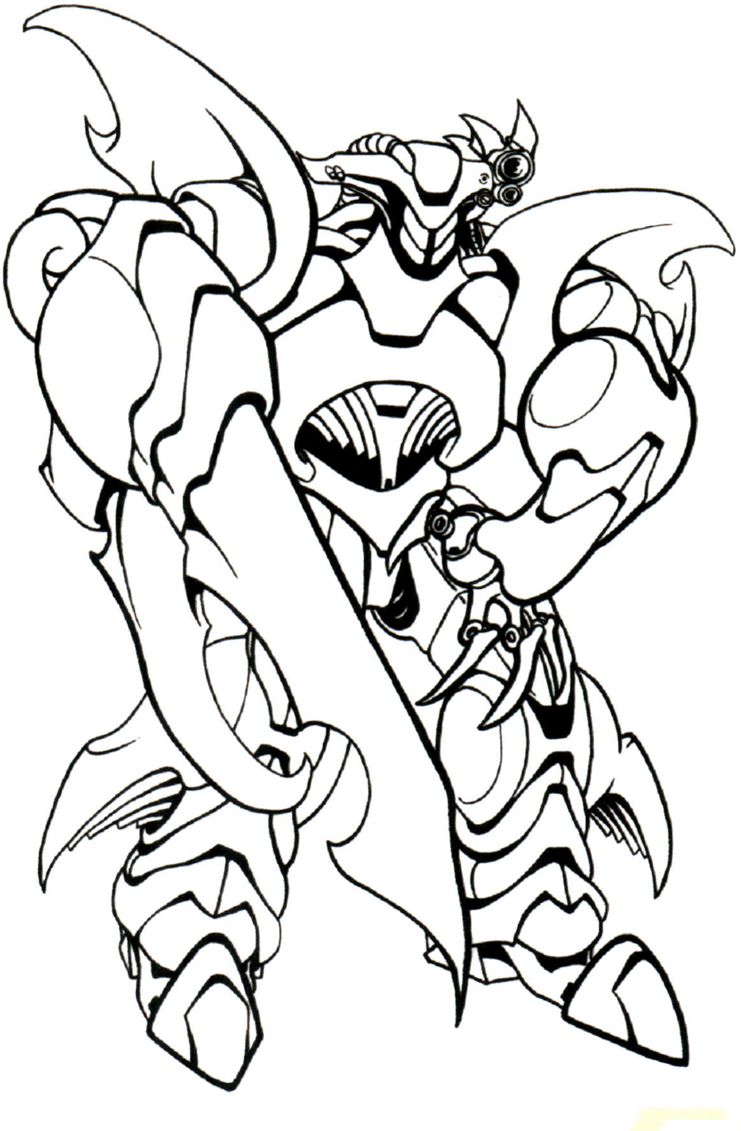

The Claw Bot is a fierce warrior that uses its massive pincers to chop and cleave inferior opponents.

Advanced optical camouflage allows the Claw Bot to remain unseen until it is within striking distance of a target.

CHAPTER 4

Chapter 4 showcases 6 mecha that were commissioned by clients for various projects. Some of the mecha were for books while others were intended for games.

Creating a mecha that meets your client's demands and satisfies your own artistic aesthetics can be very challenging. I think all of the mecha presented in this chapter were successful on both fronts.

Of all the design in this chapter, only the U.N. Mecha was ever actually used in a final product.

FREELANCE MECHA

P.A.S.S. SUIT

POWER ARMOR FOR SERIOUS SPORTS

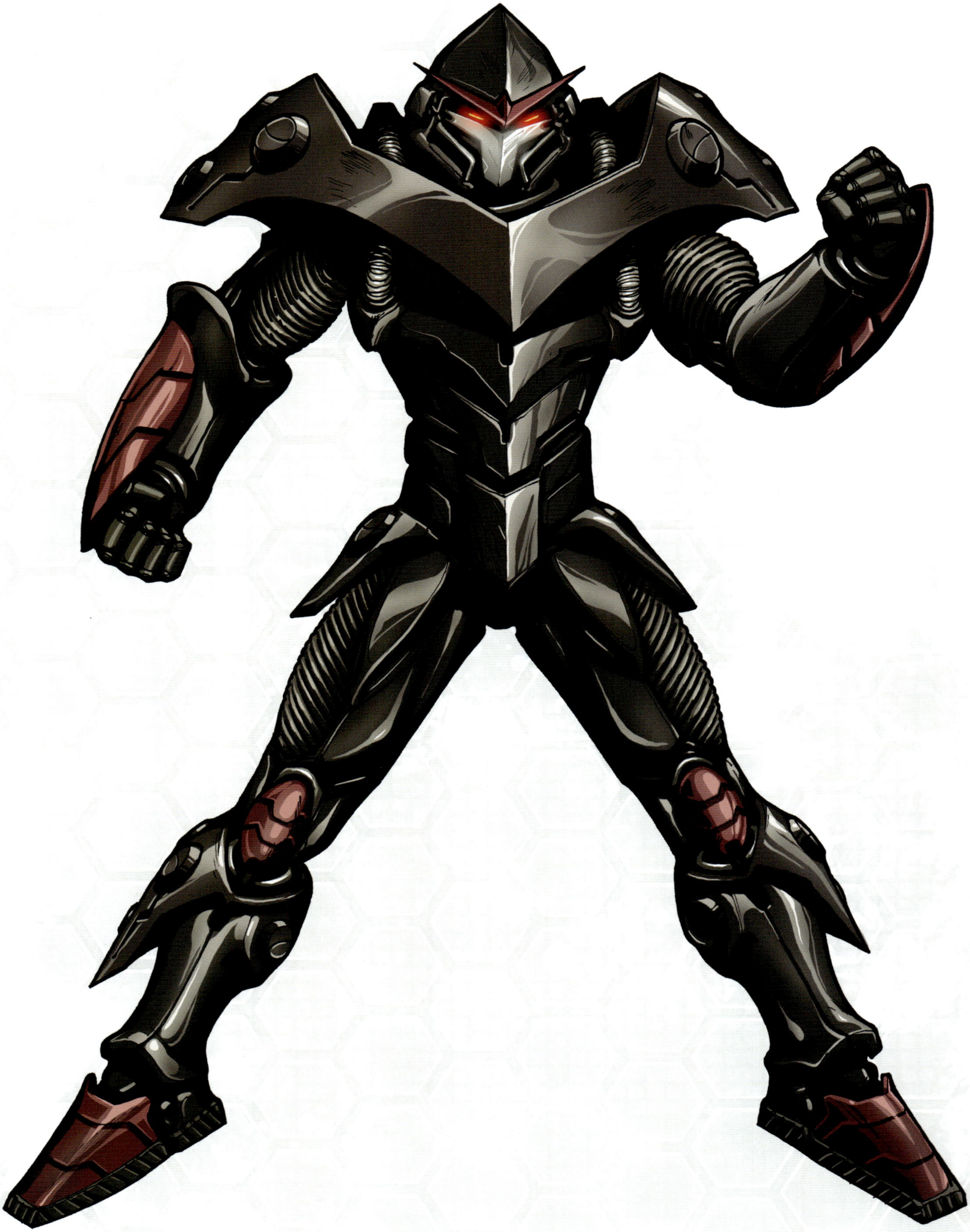

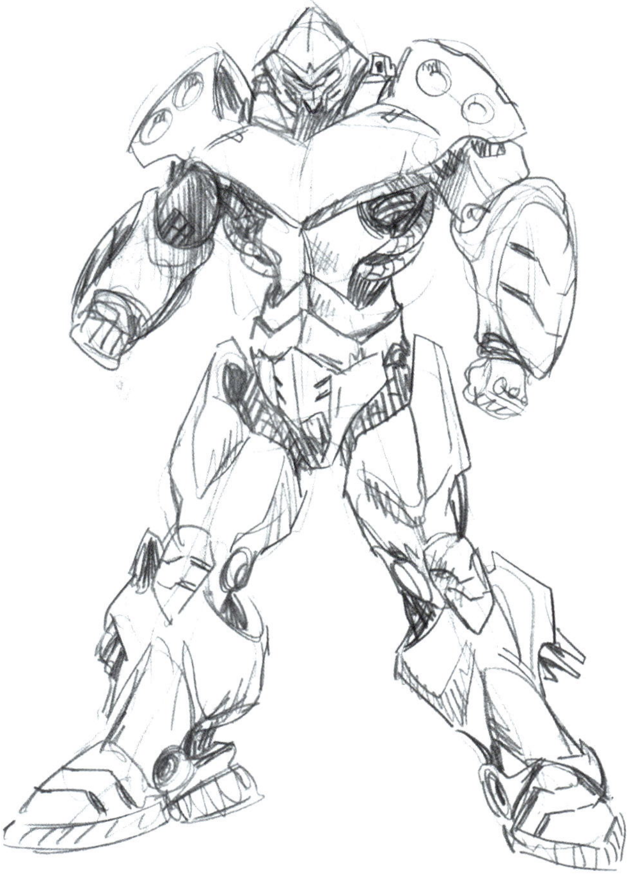

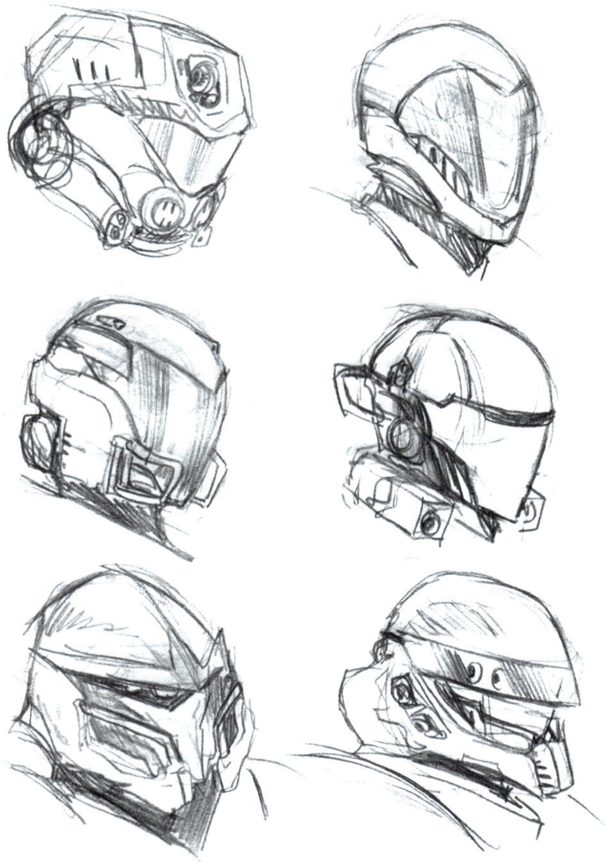

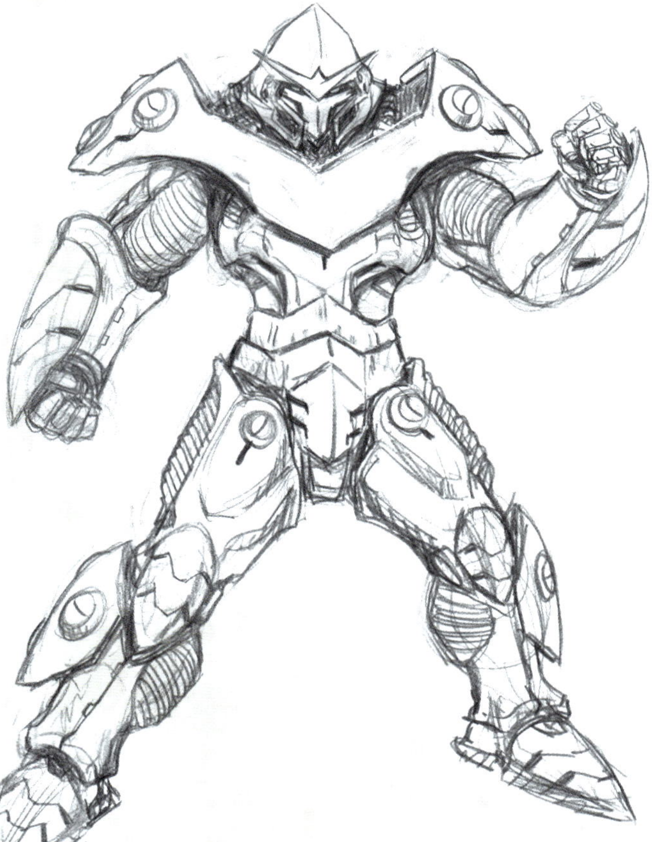

The P.a.s.s. suit is used in all modern aggressive sports to augment the athlete's natural abilities and provide protection. Strength, speed, and visual acuity are all enhanced.

Thanks to Yohan Sohn, the producer for this project, for allowing me to use these images.

U.N. MECHA

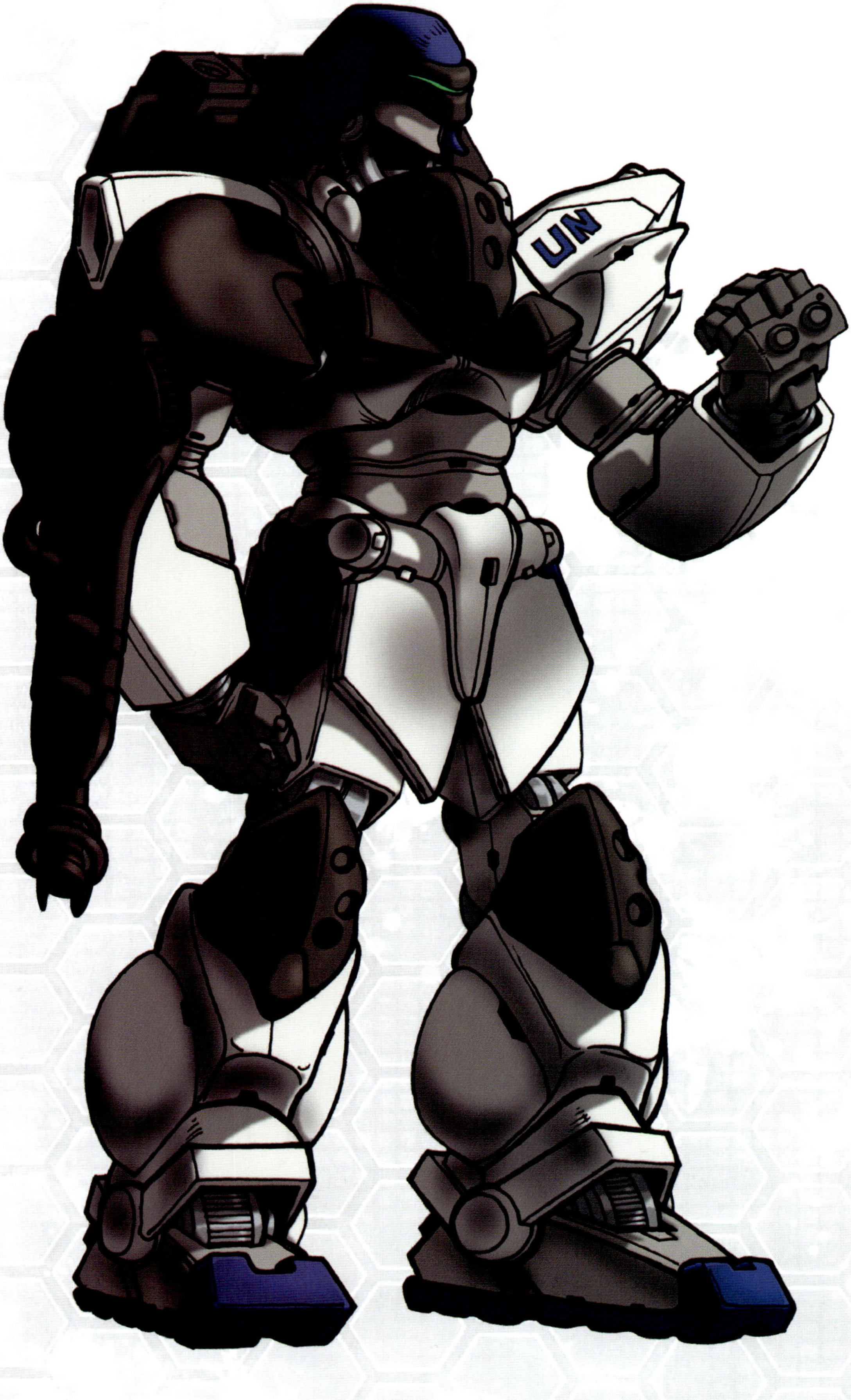

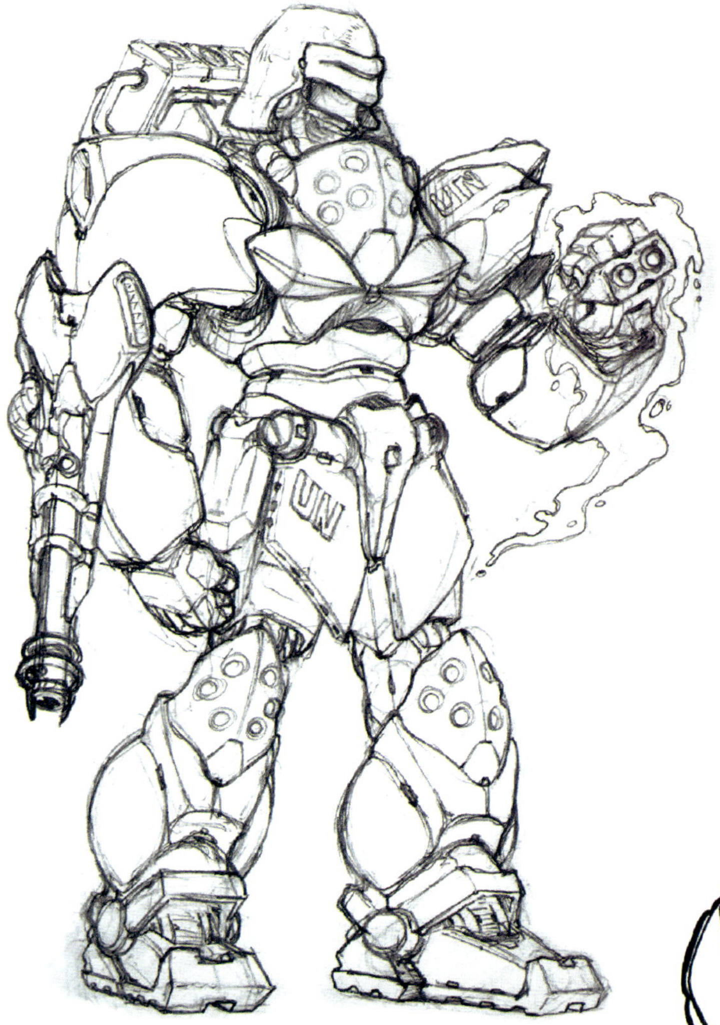

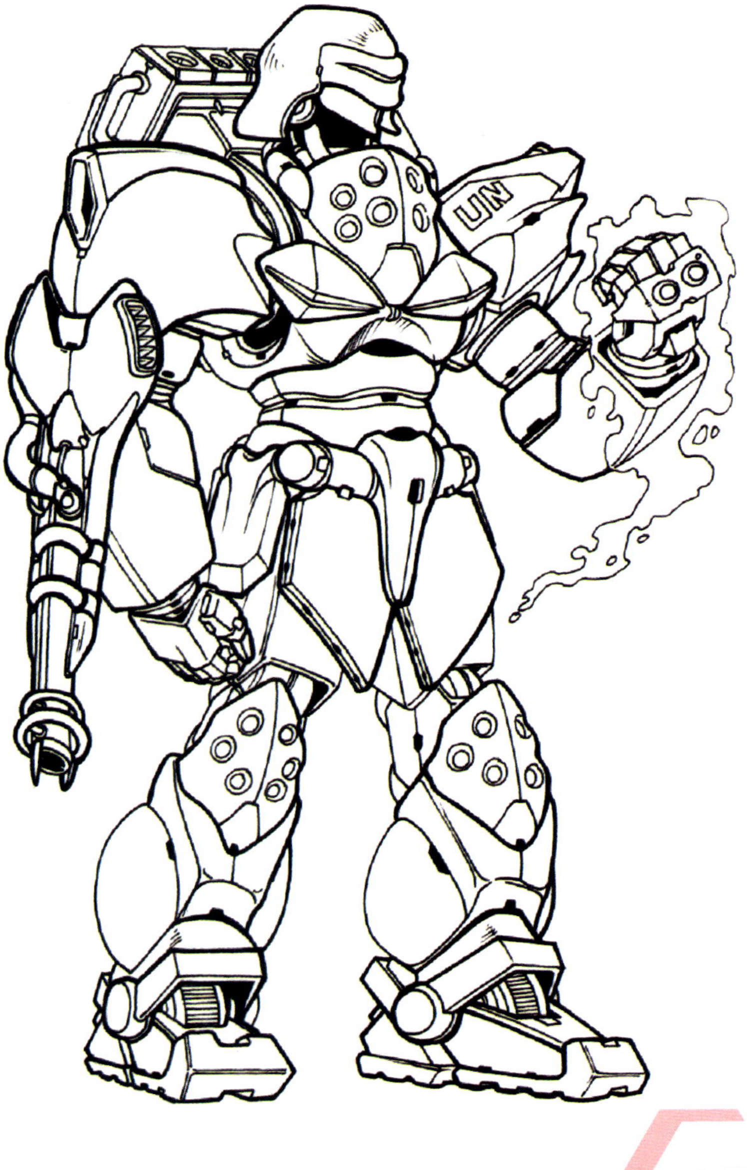

The U.N. Mecha carries a varied arsenal including missiles, an arm mounted rail gun, and shock knuckles. It is equipped to keep the peace, no matter what.

This mecha was originally printed in the game book, *Big Robots, Cool Starships*.

FED-01

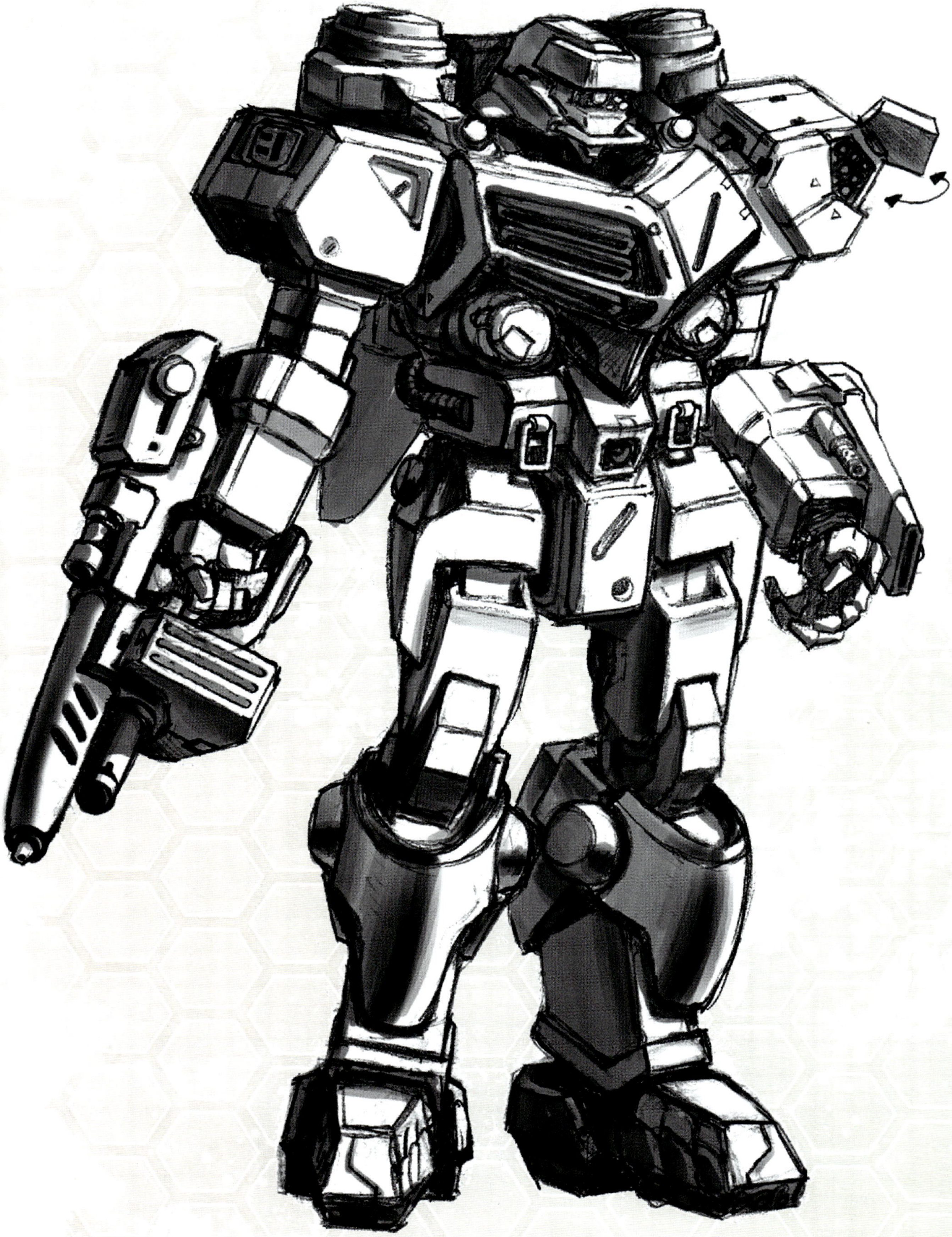

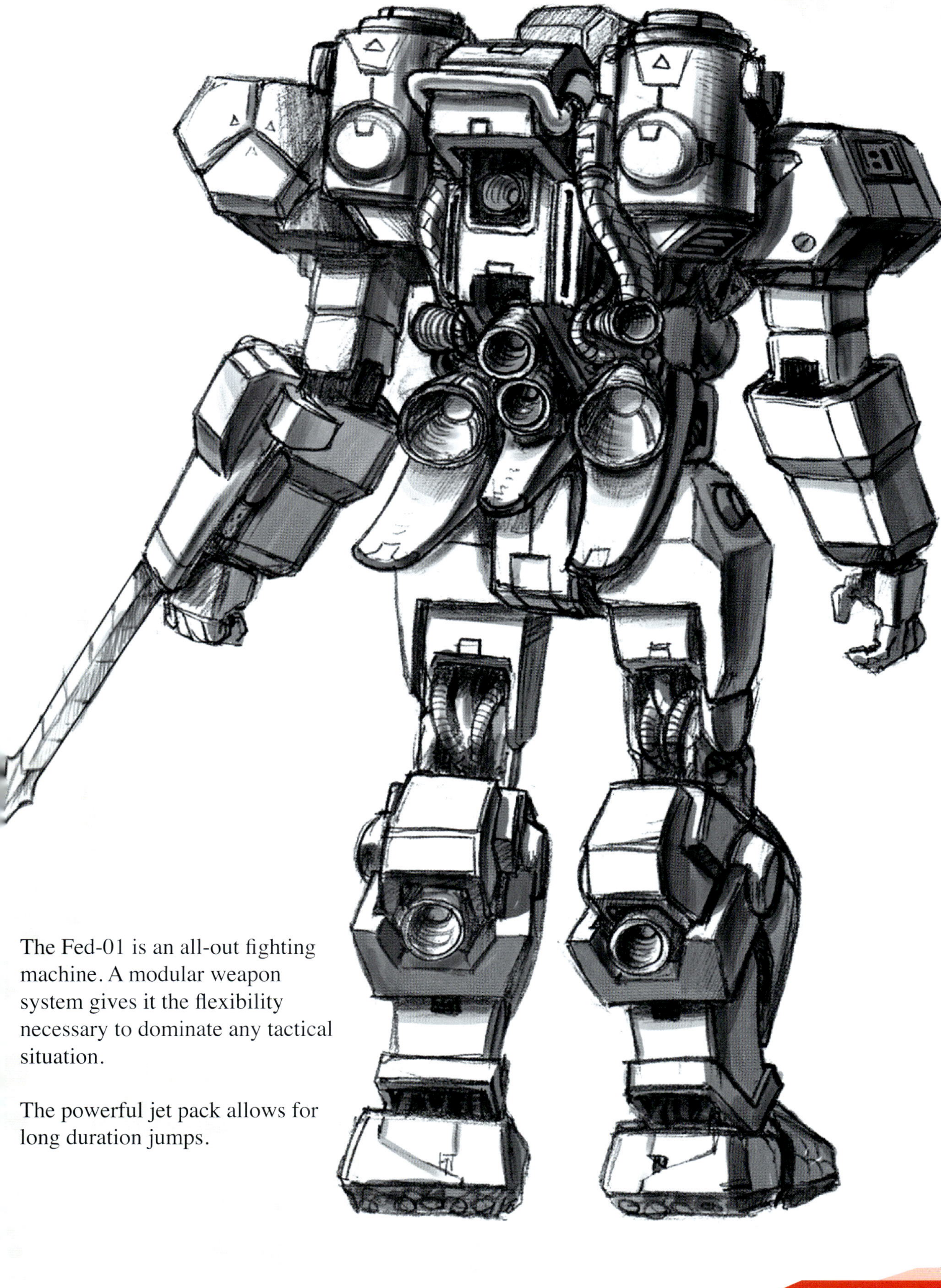

The Fed-01 is an all-out fighting machine. A modular weapon system gives it the flexibility necessary to dominate any tactical situation.

The powerful jet pack allows for long duration jumps.

FED-01

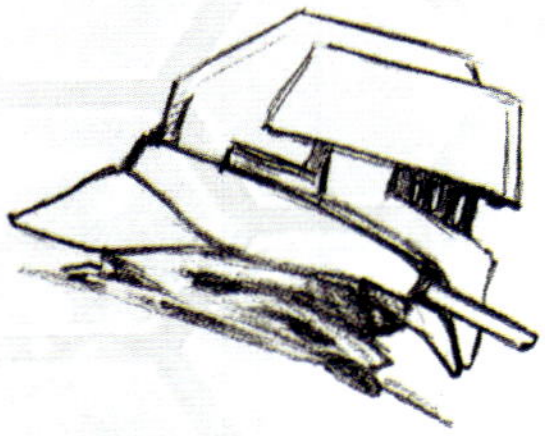

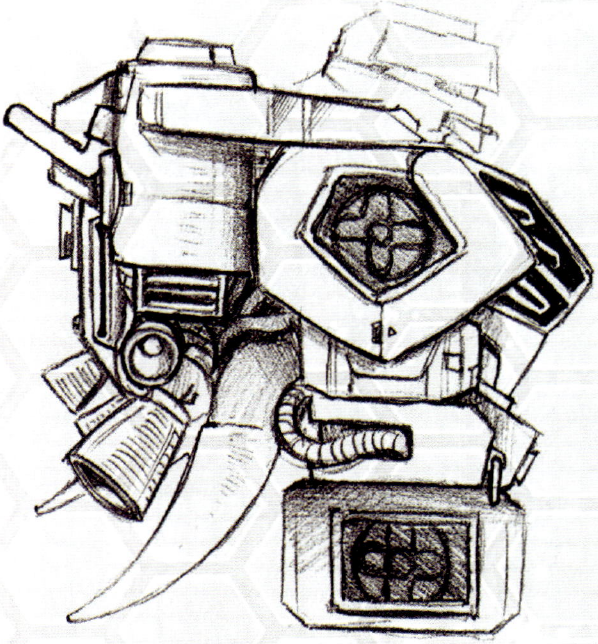

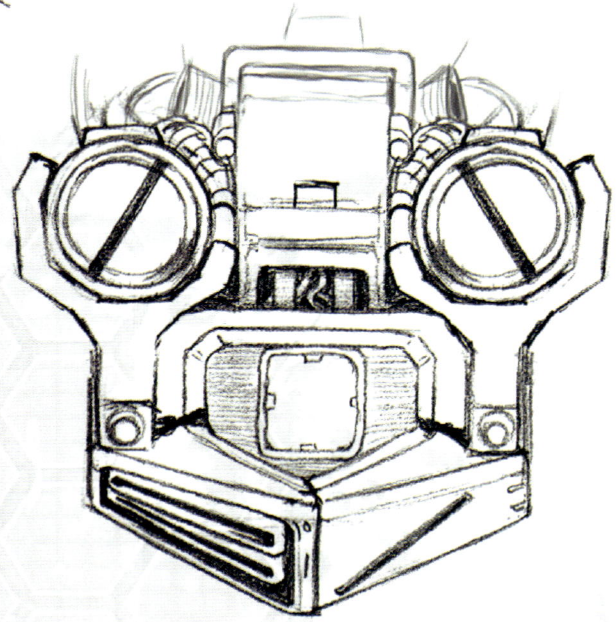

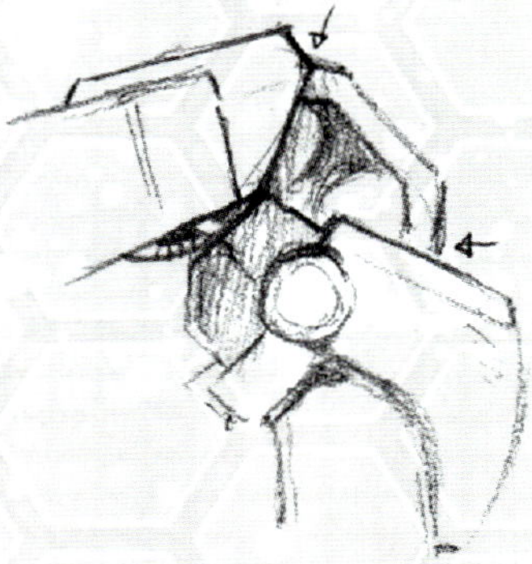

Knee joint detail.

Alternate shoulder weapon.

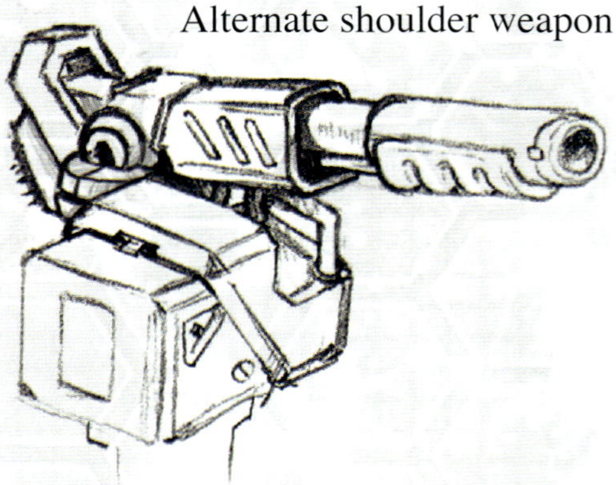

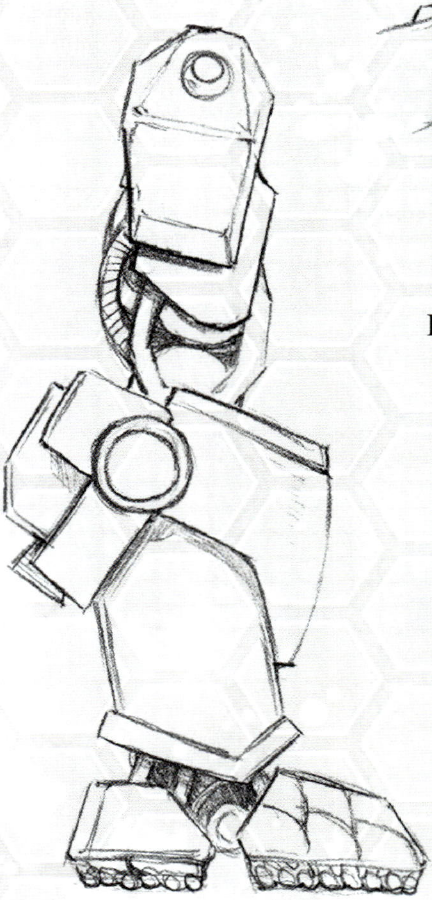

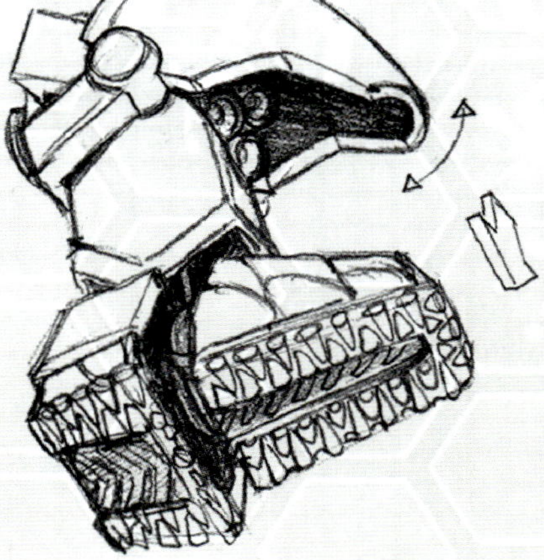

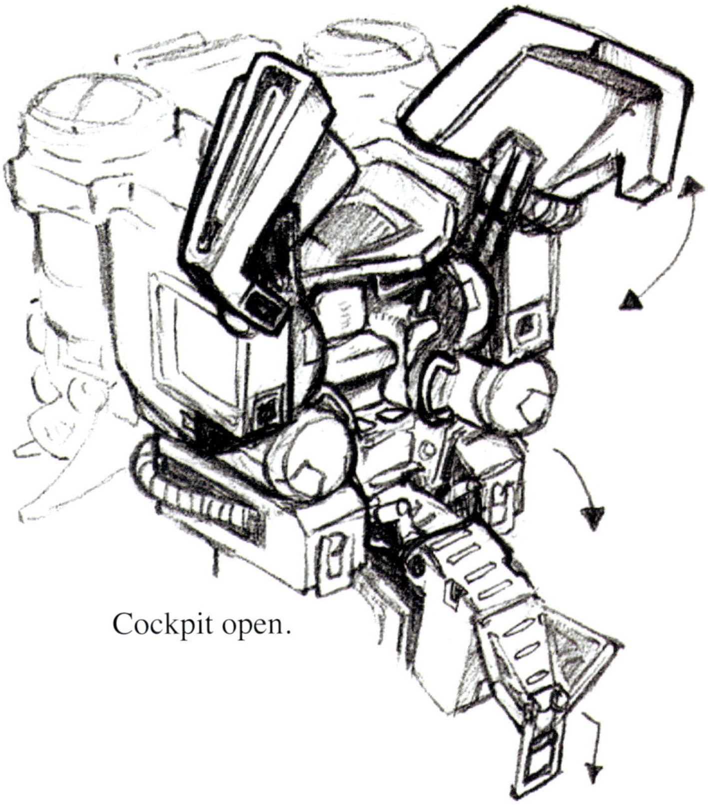

Cockpit open.

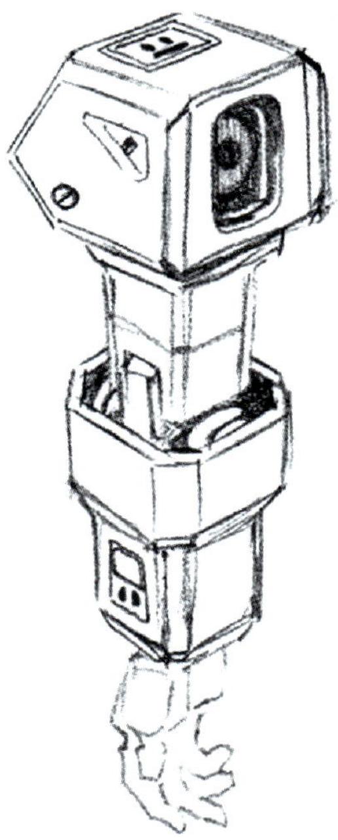

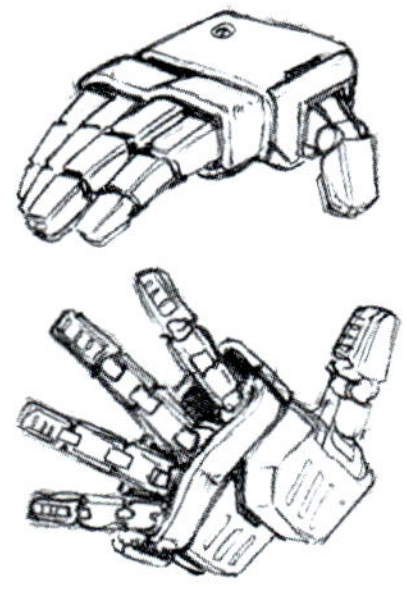

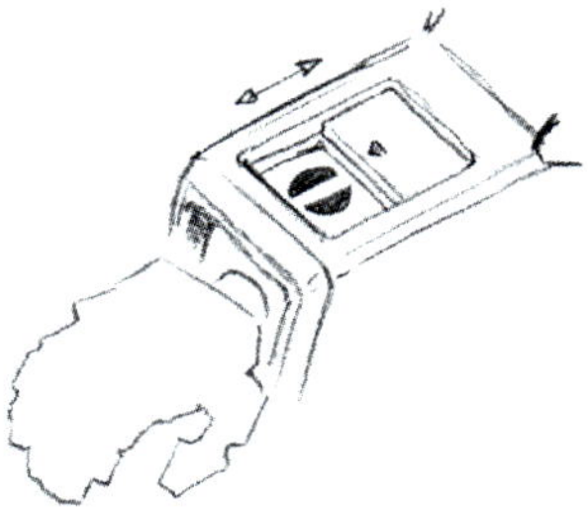

Arm blade.

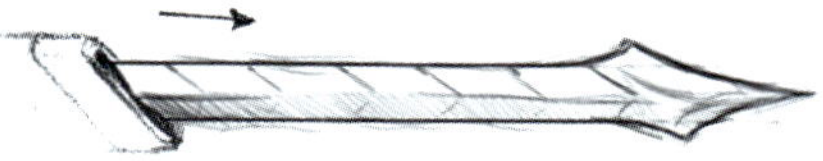

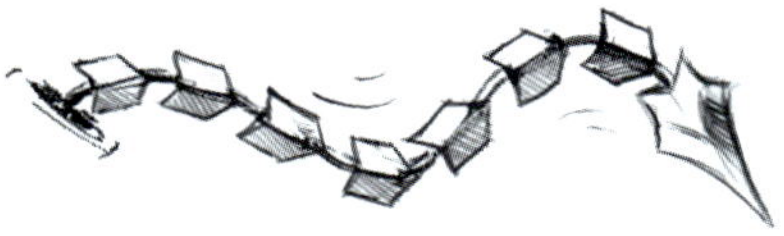

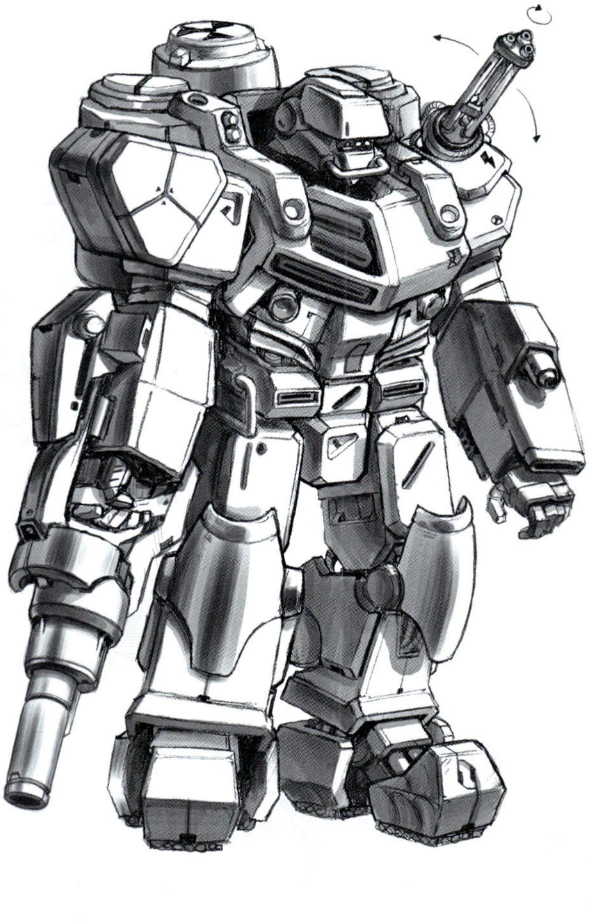

Size comparison.

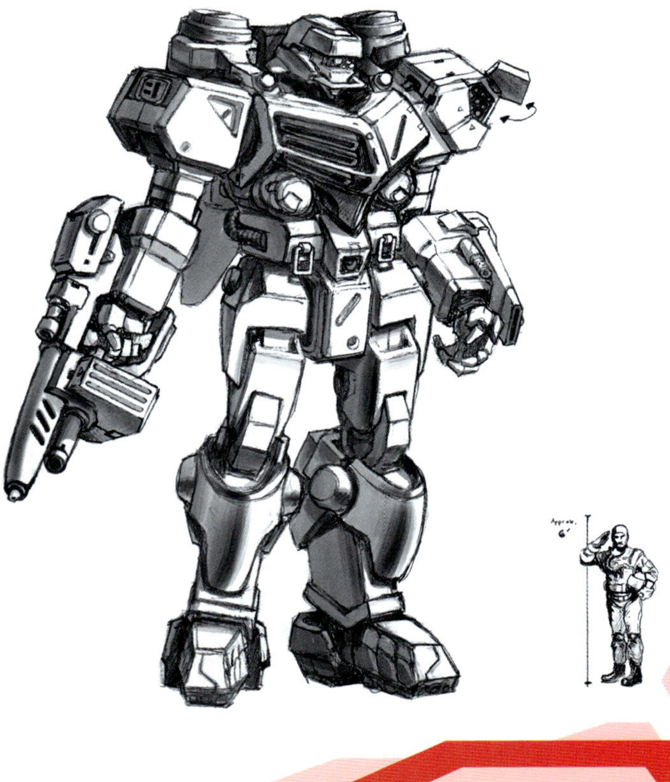

FED-02 HEAVY

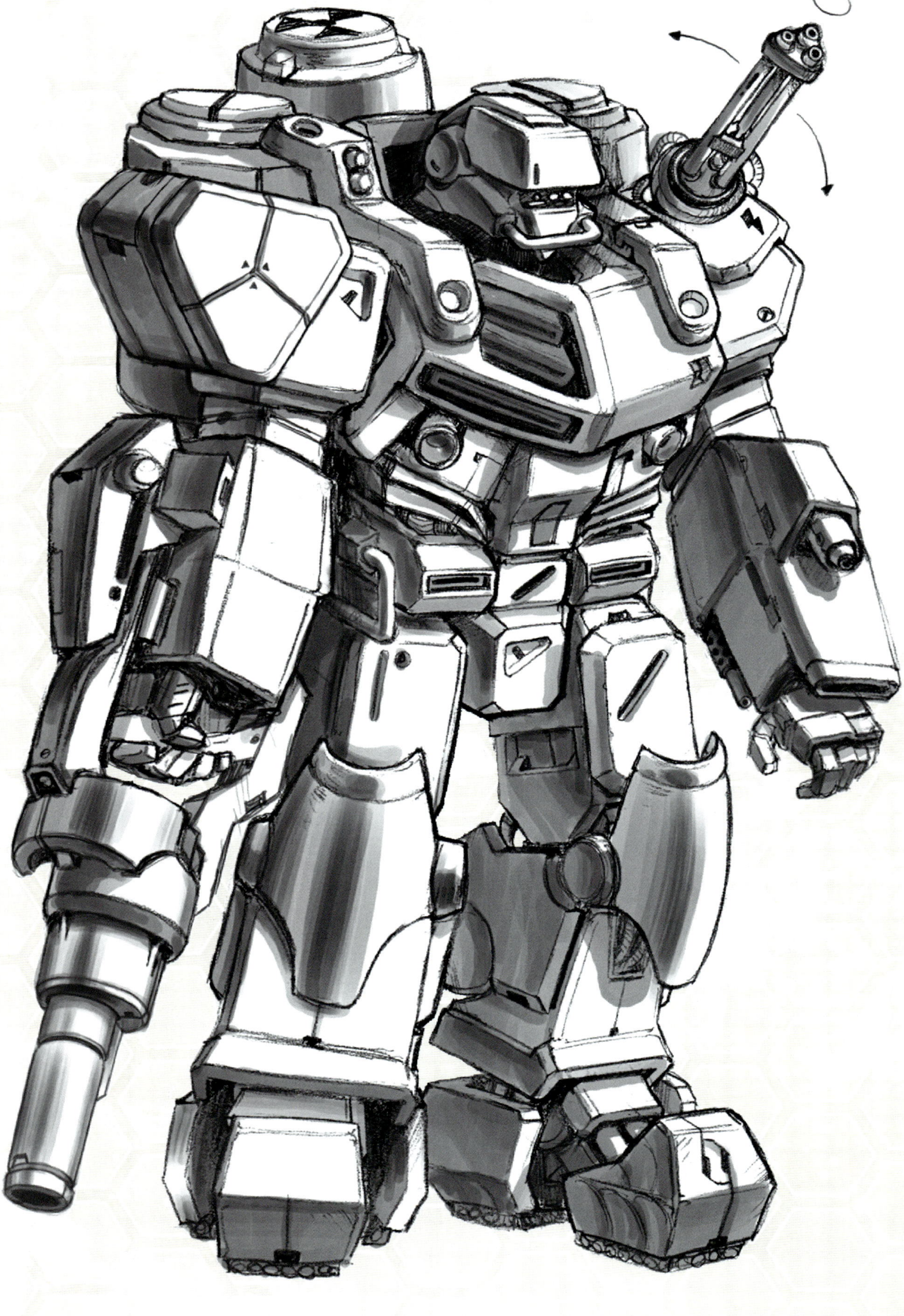

Alternate shoulder weapon.

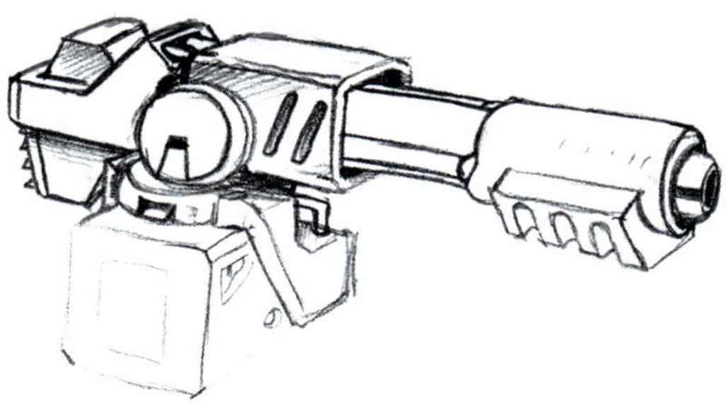

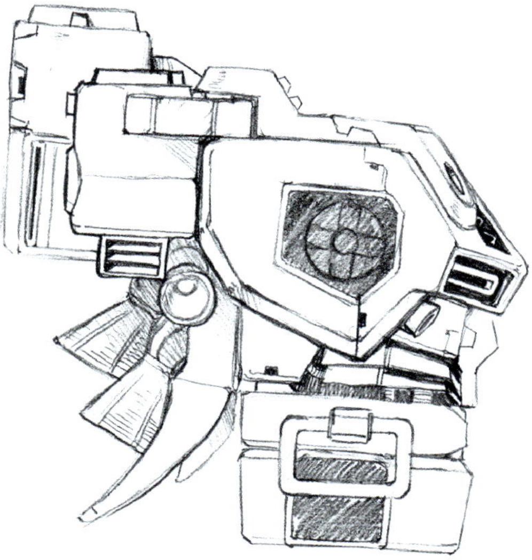

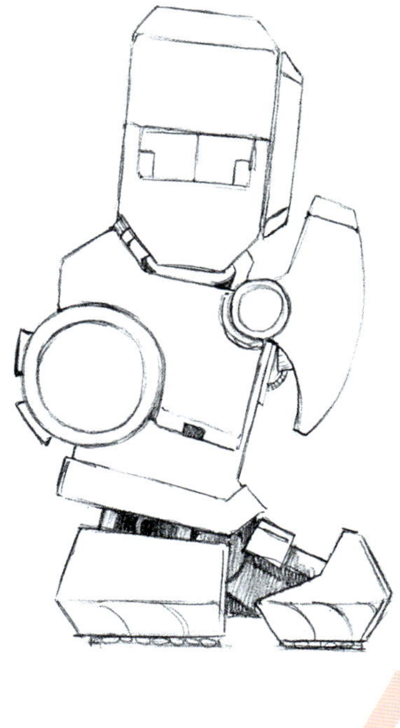

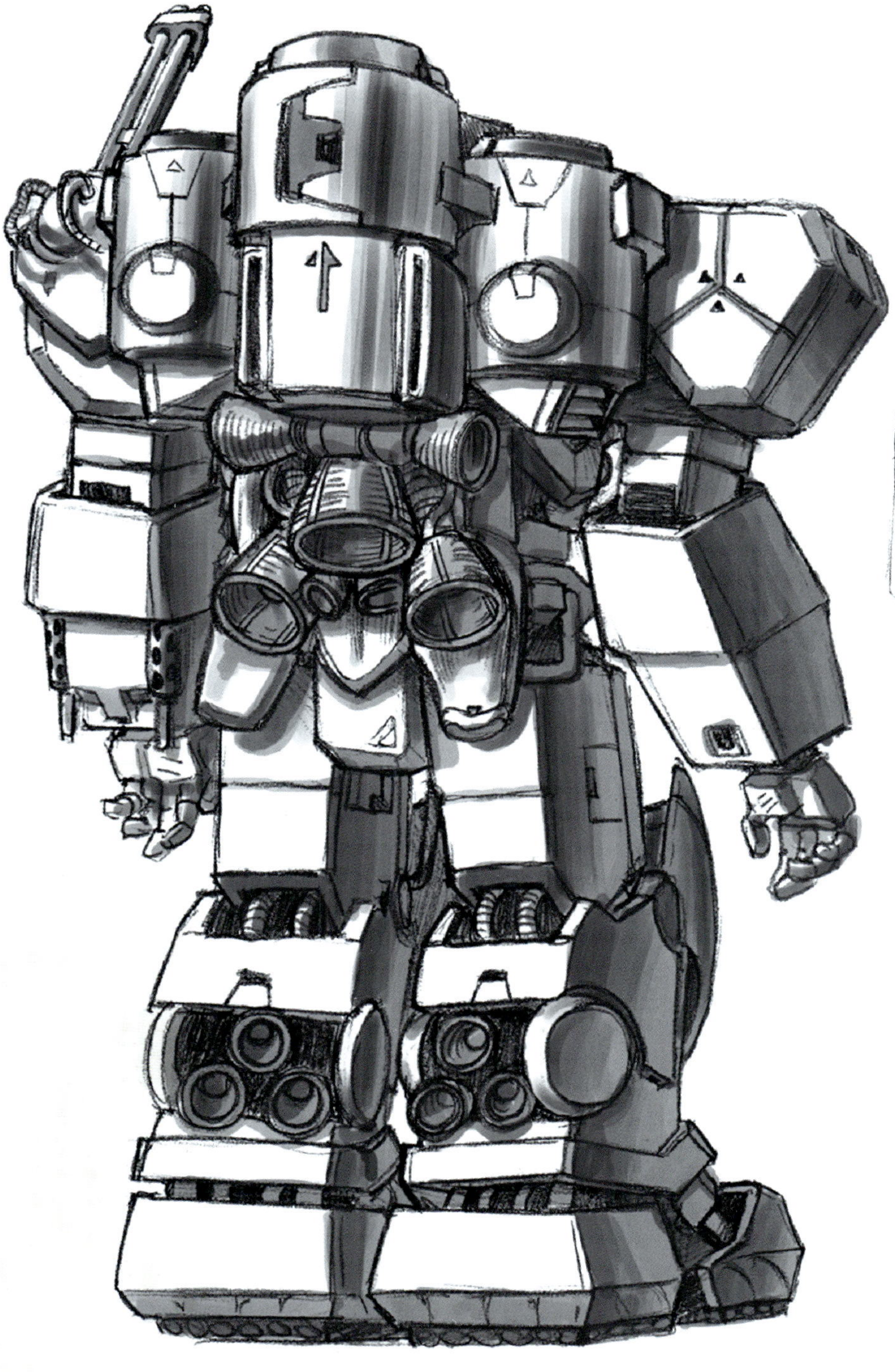

The Fed-02 uses the same skeleton as the Fed-01, but adds more armor and a larger power reactor. It sacrifices speed for brute power.

EU-01

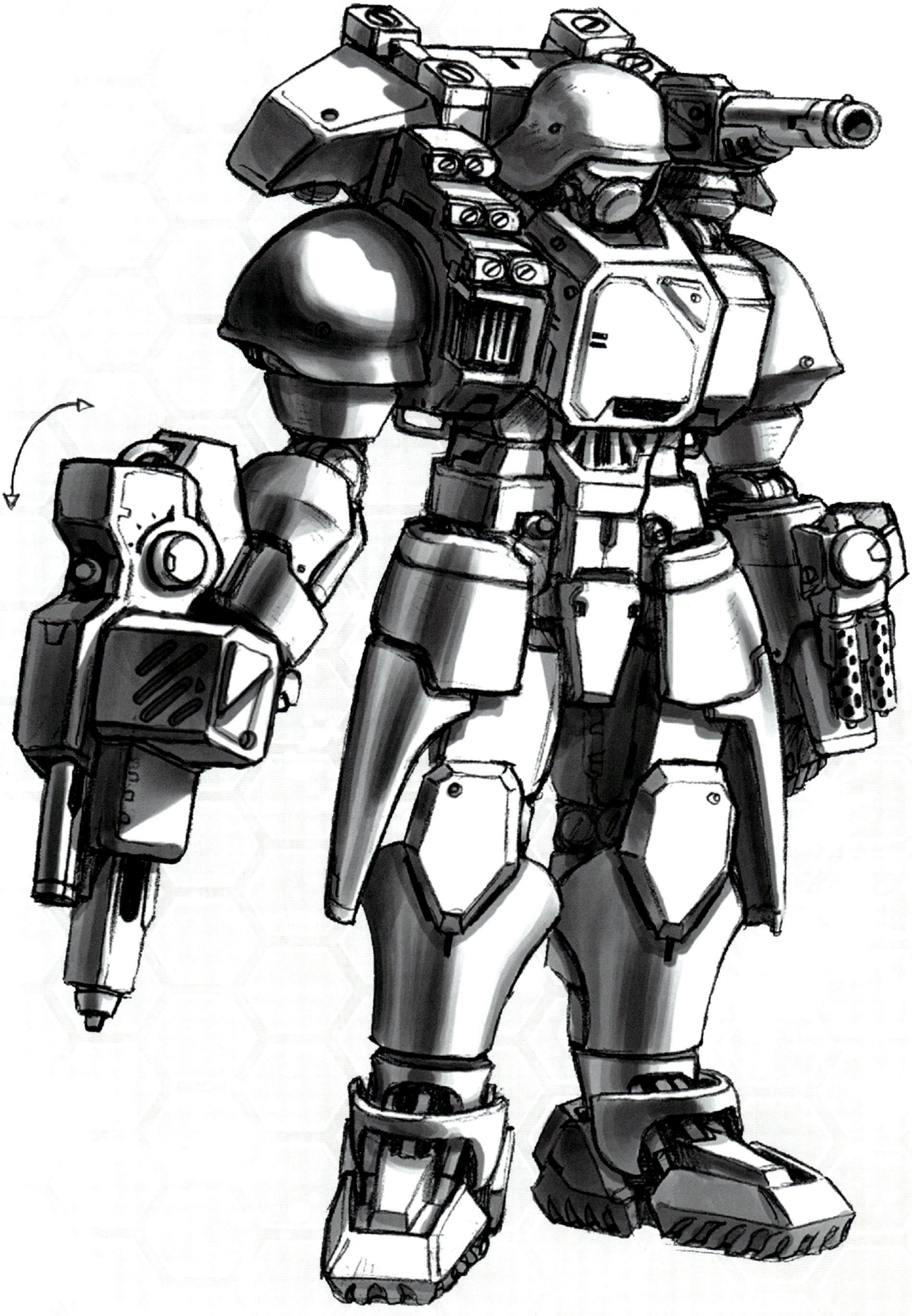

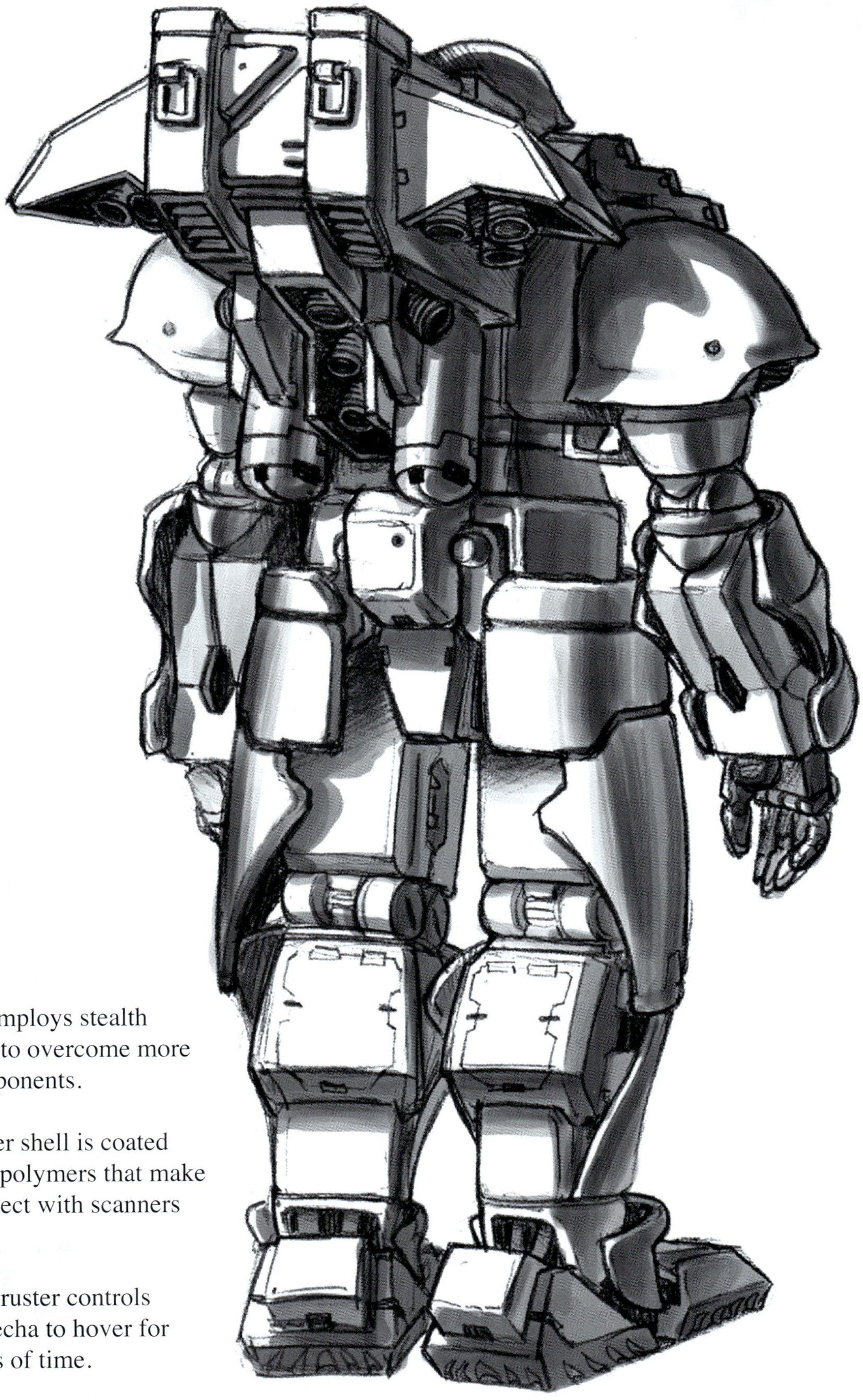

The Eu-01 employs stealth and strategy to overcome more powerful opponents.

Its sleek outer shell is coated with special polymers that make it hard to detect with scanners and radar.

Advanced thruster controls allow the mecha to hover for short periods of time.

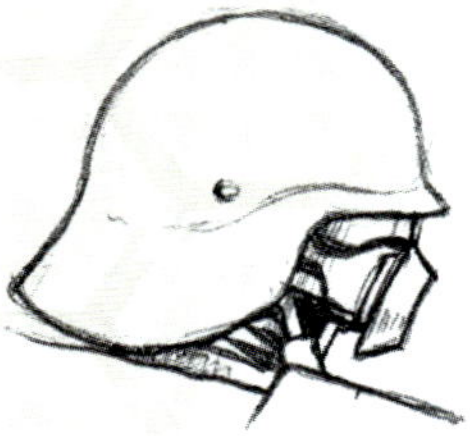

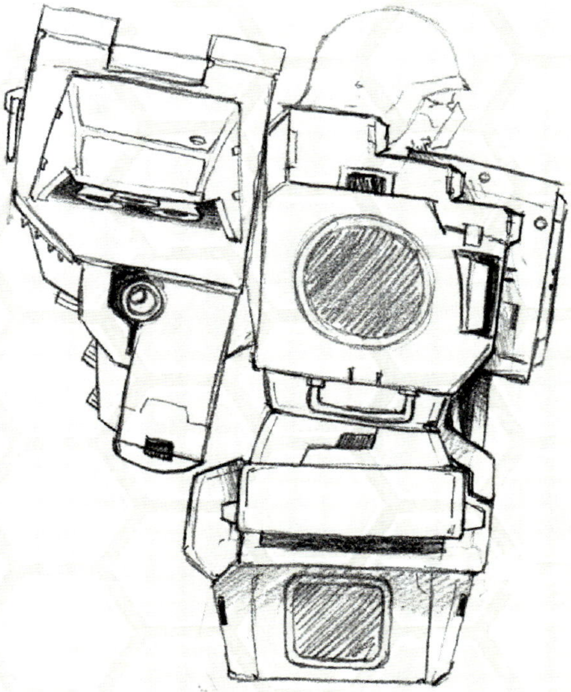

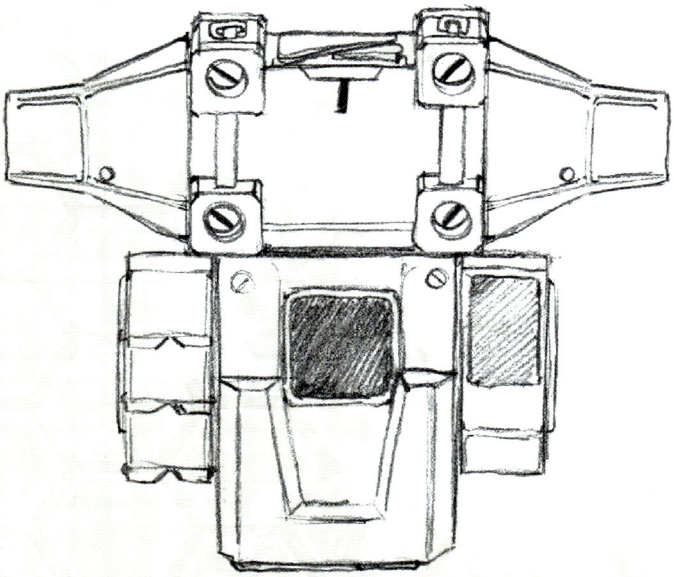

Hip guard.

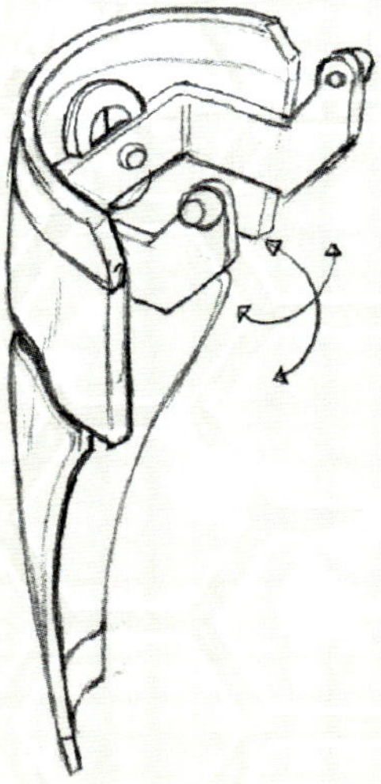

Alternate shoulder weapon.

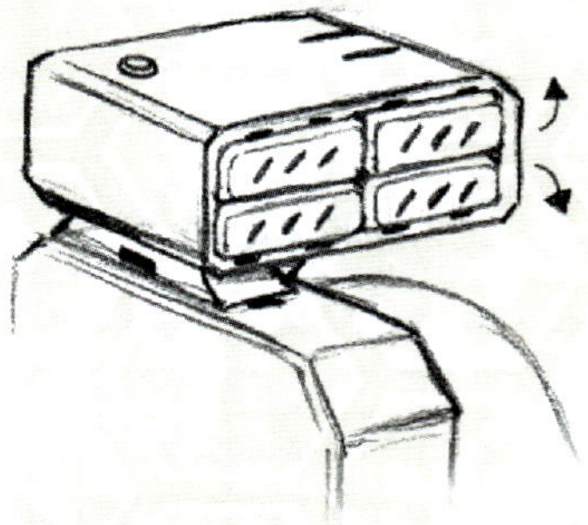

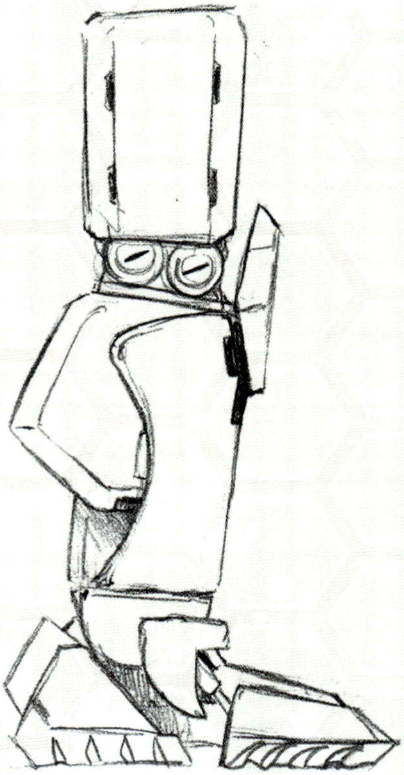

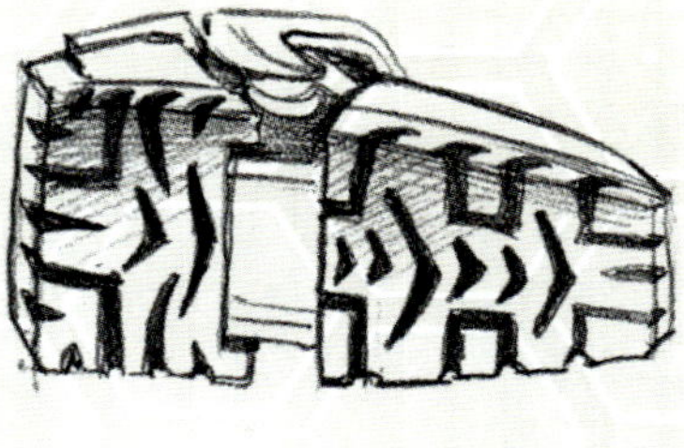

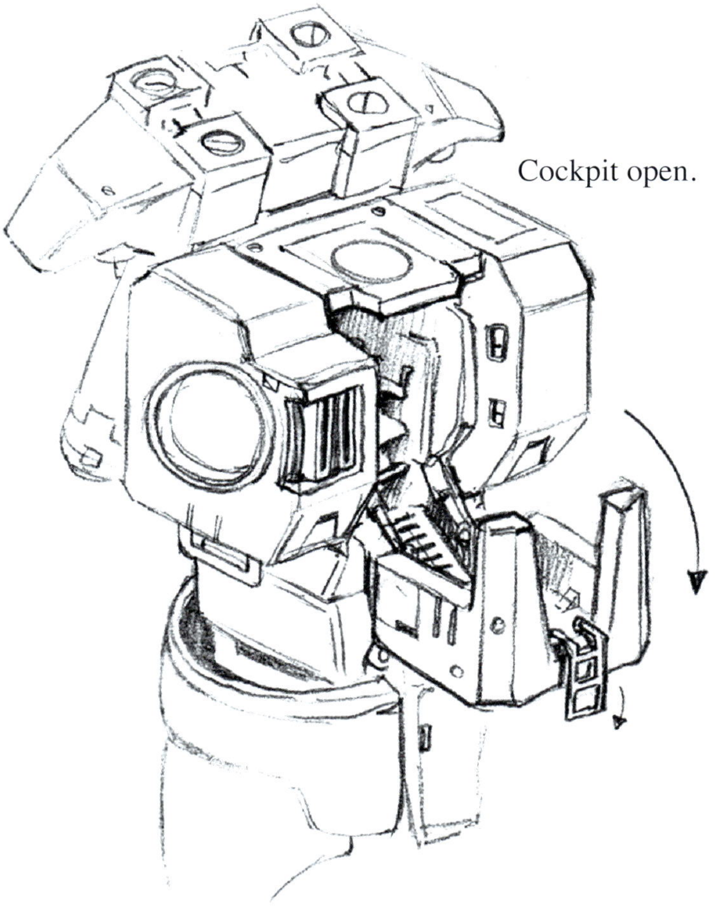

Cockpit open.

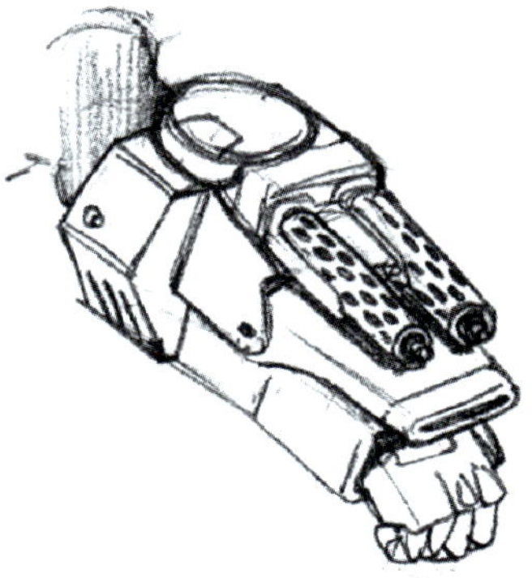

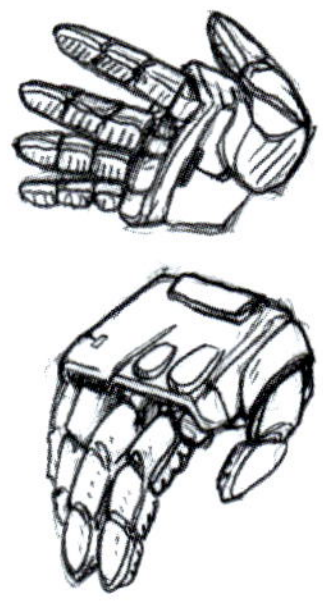

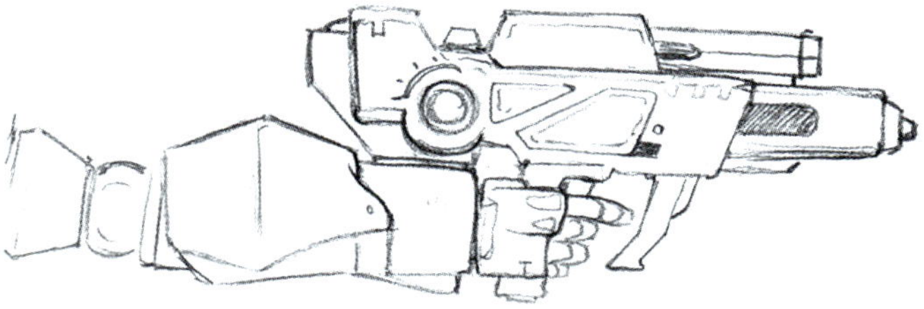

Arm blade.

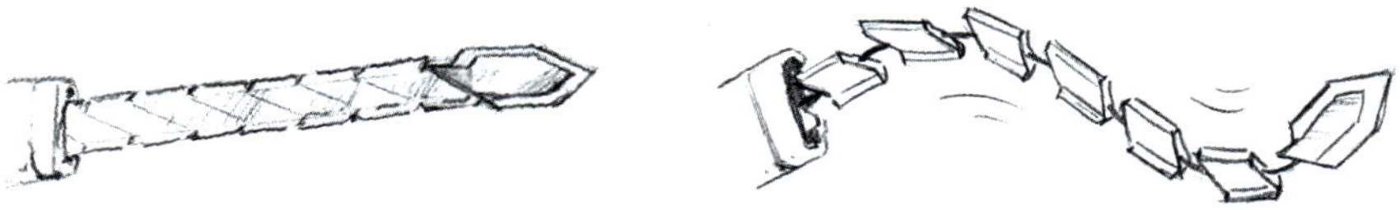

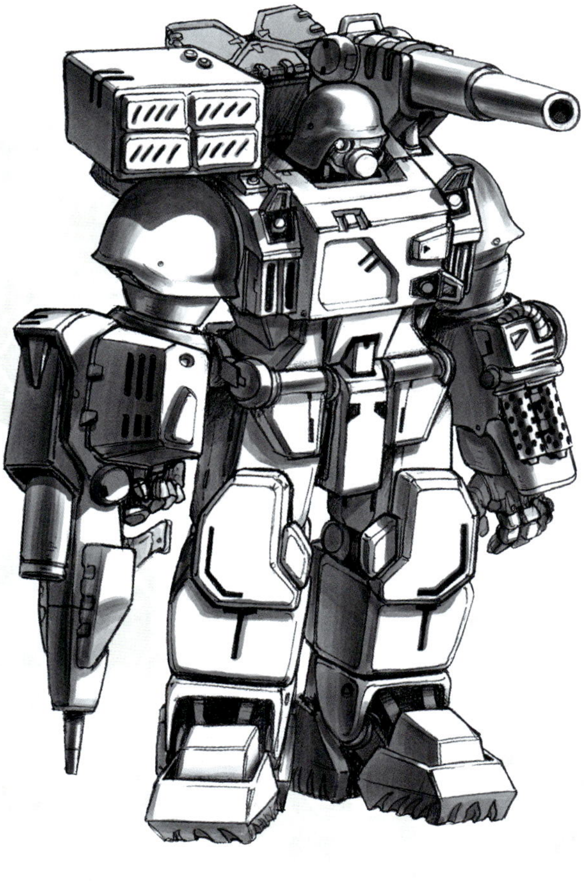

Size comparison.

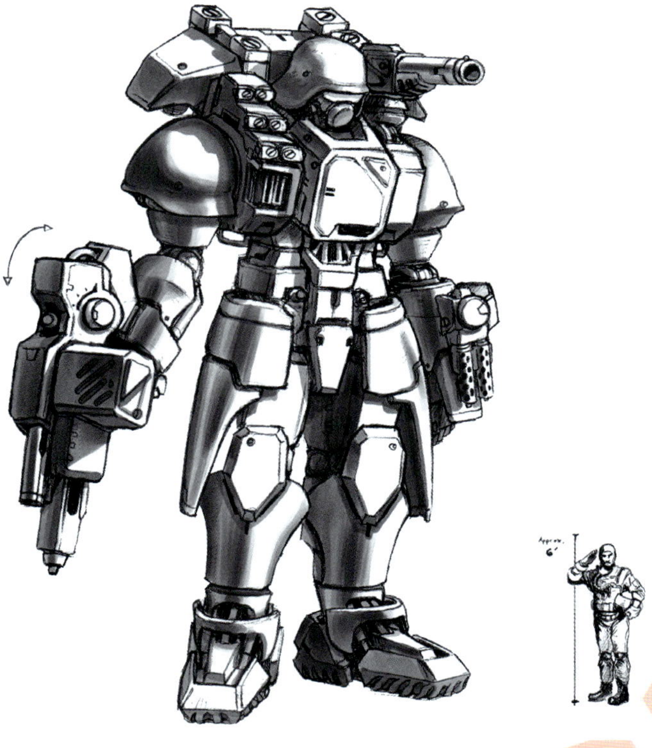

EU-02 HEAVY

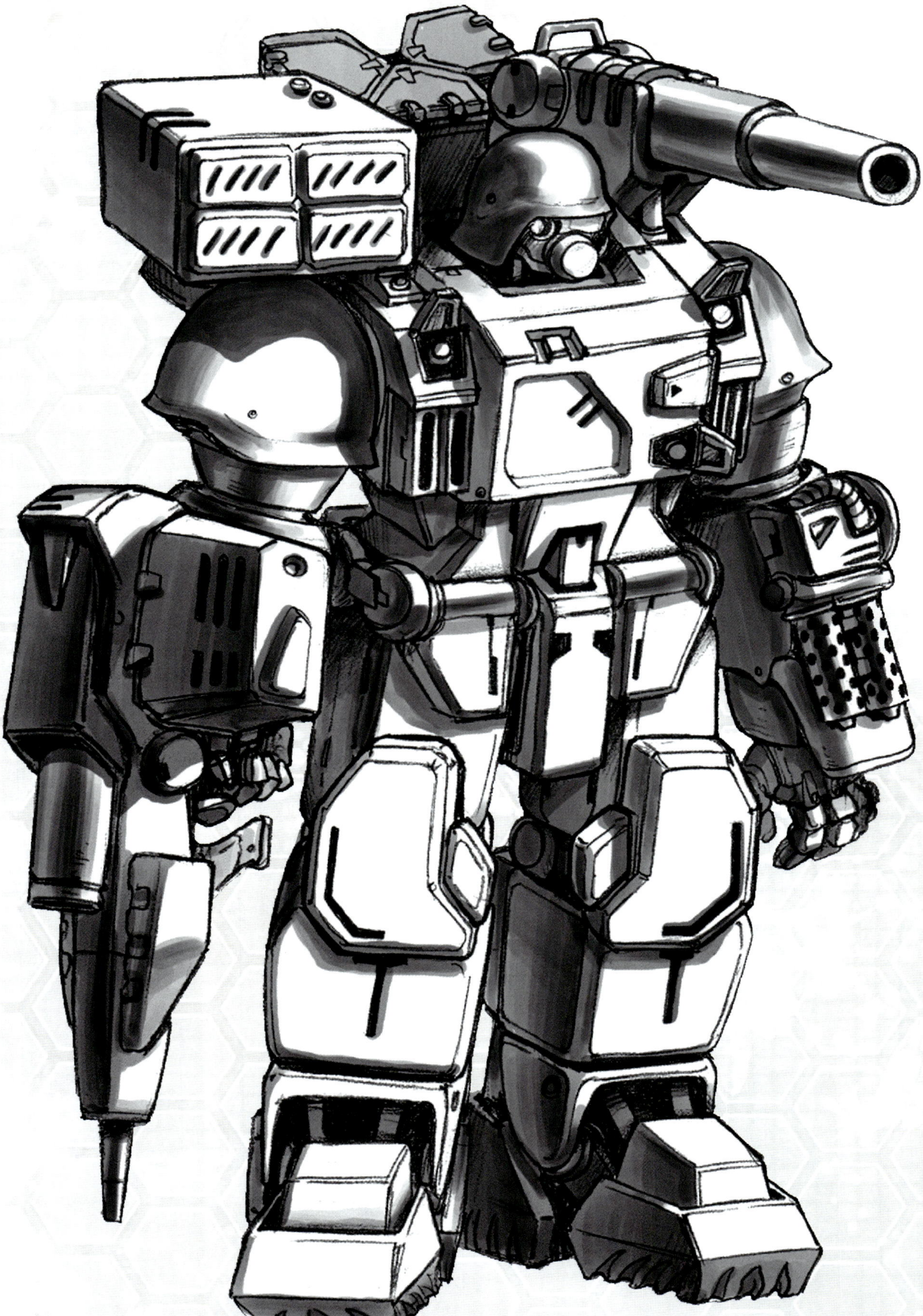

Alternate shoulder weapon.

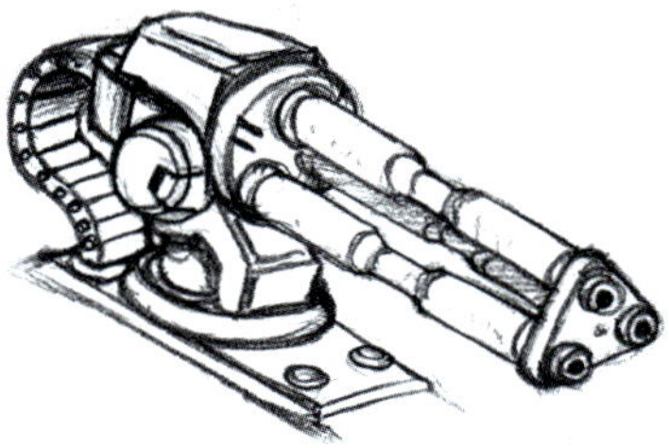

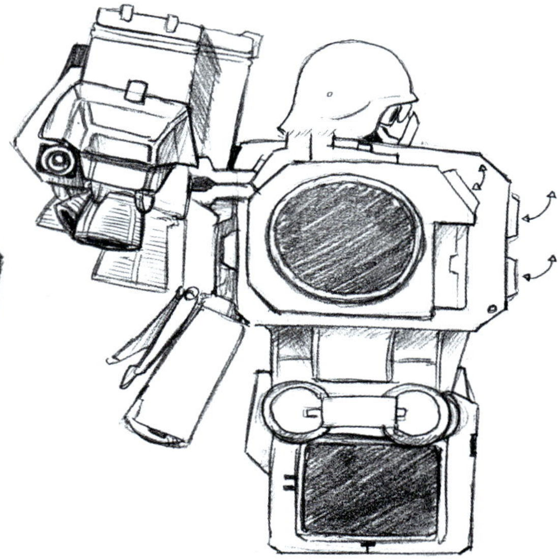

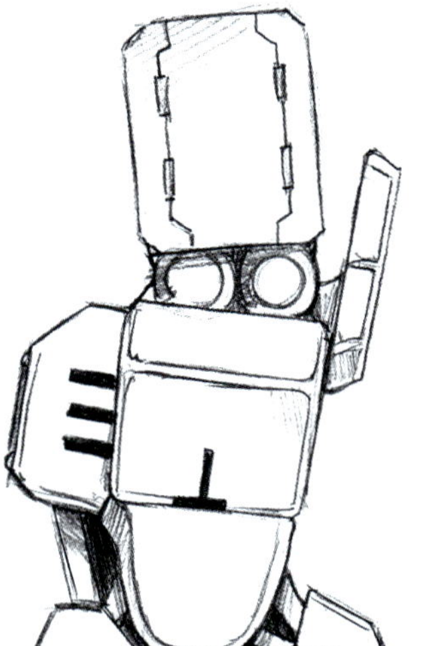

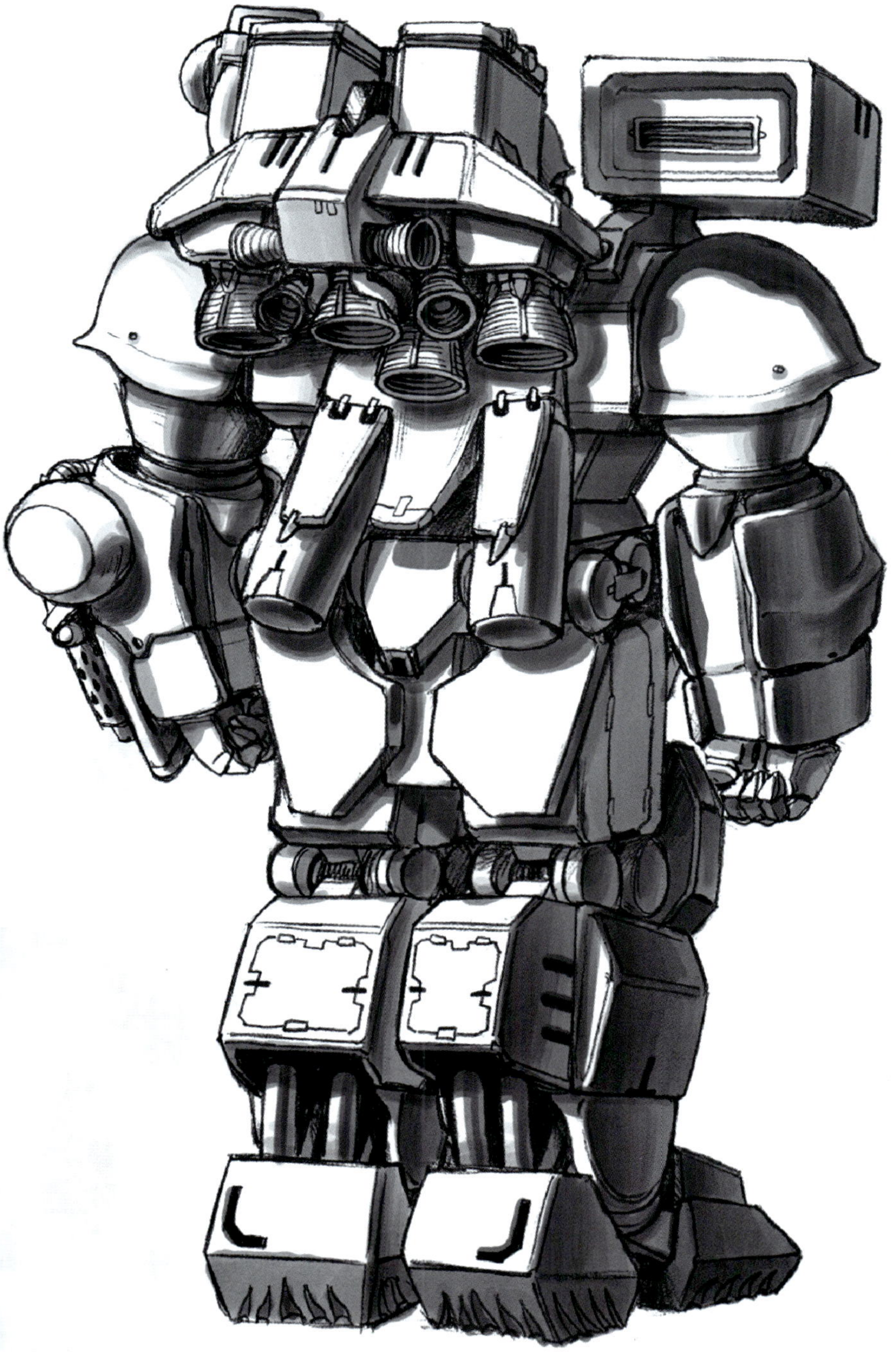

The Eu-02 adds thick armor and extra ammunition storage, but the immense weight reduces the jump-jet capabilities significantly.

CHAPTER 5

Chapter 5 showcases 9 mecha that didn't quite fit into the other chapters. Many of them are older designs created before 1995. Those older mecha may lack the refined finish of my newer work, but I think they still embody my passion for mechanical design. They also provide a good benchmark for my progress as an artist.

Many of these mecha are also more experimental than the designs in the other chapters. Some may say they are weird, but I think they are wonderful. I will leave their stories to your imagination!

SCRAPYARD

Artifact 16

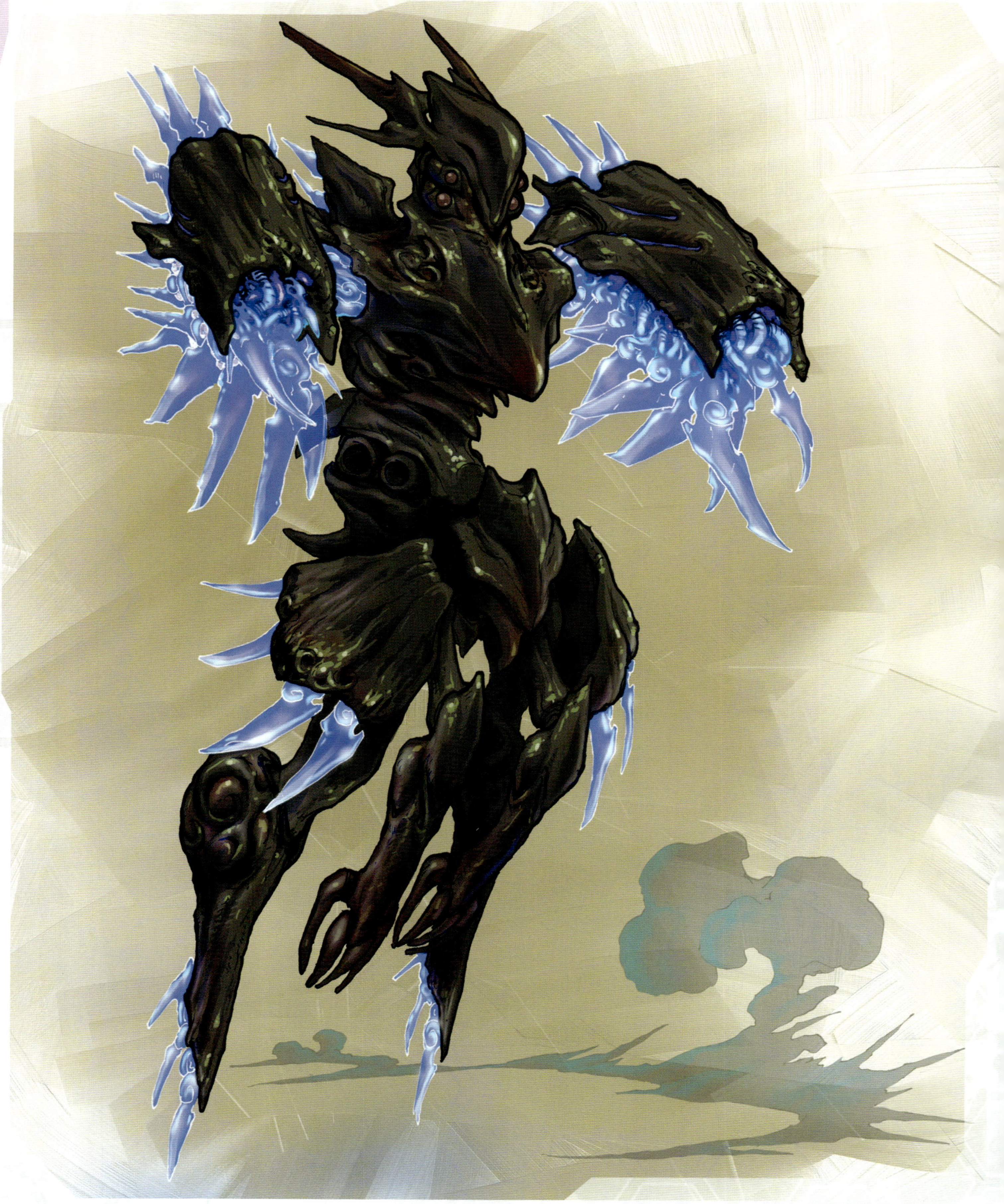

Meridian

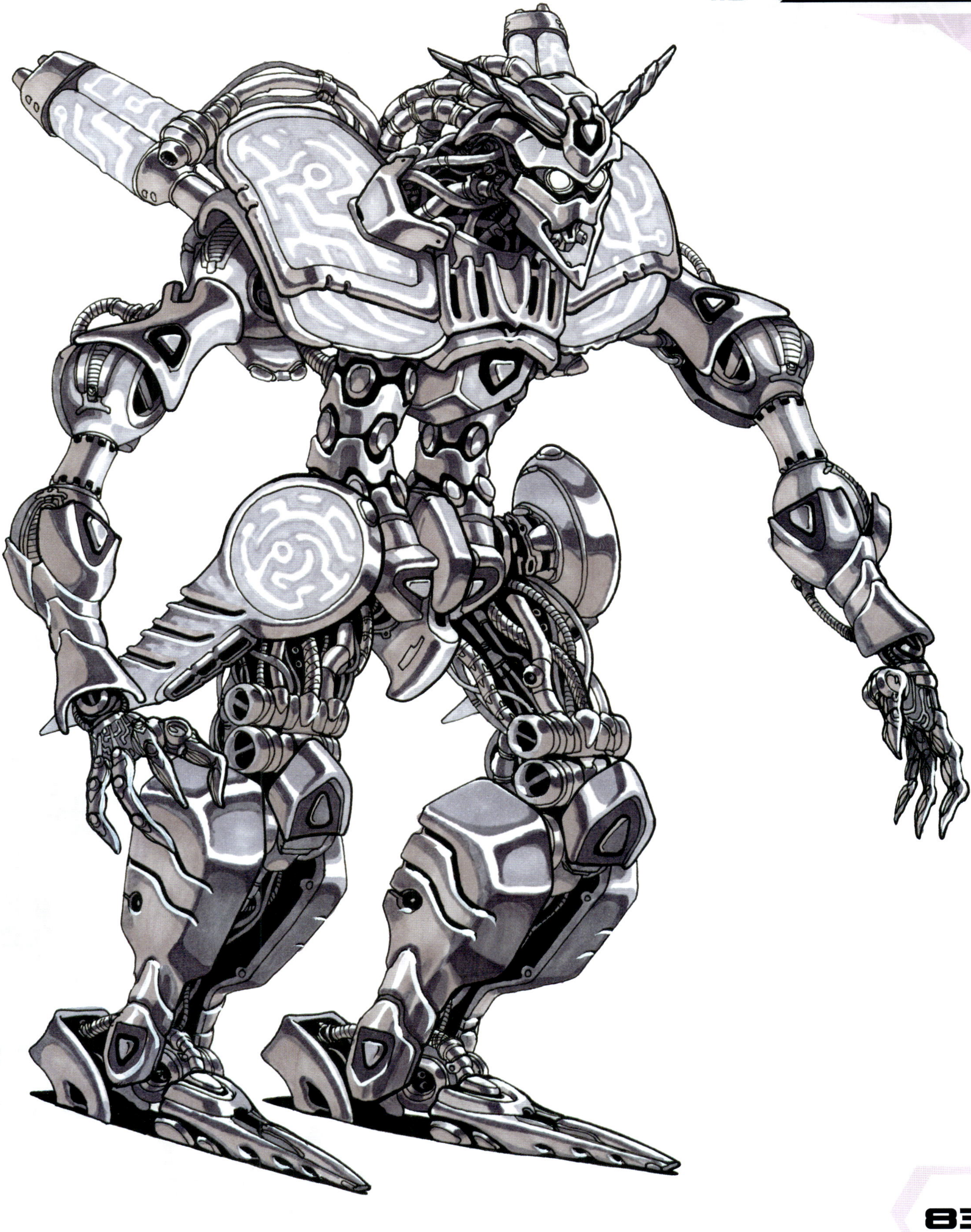

Scout bot

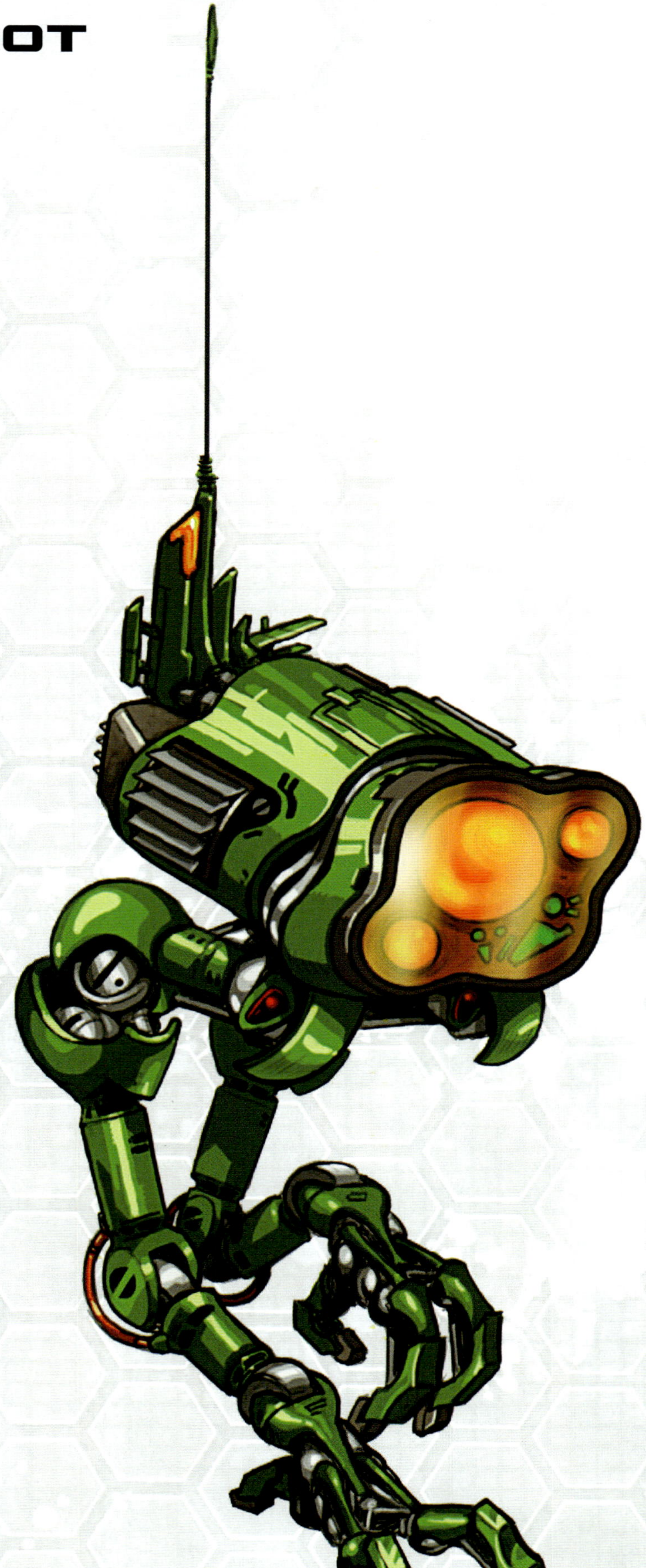

Sylph drone

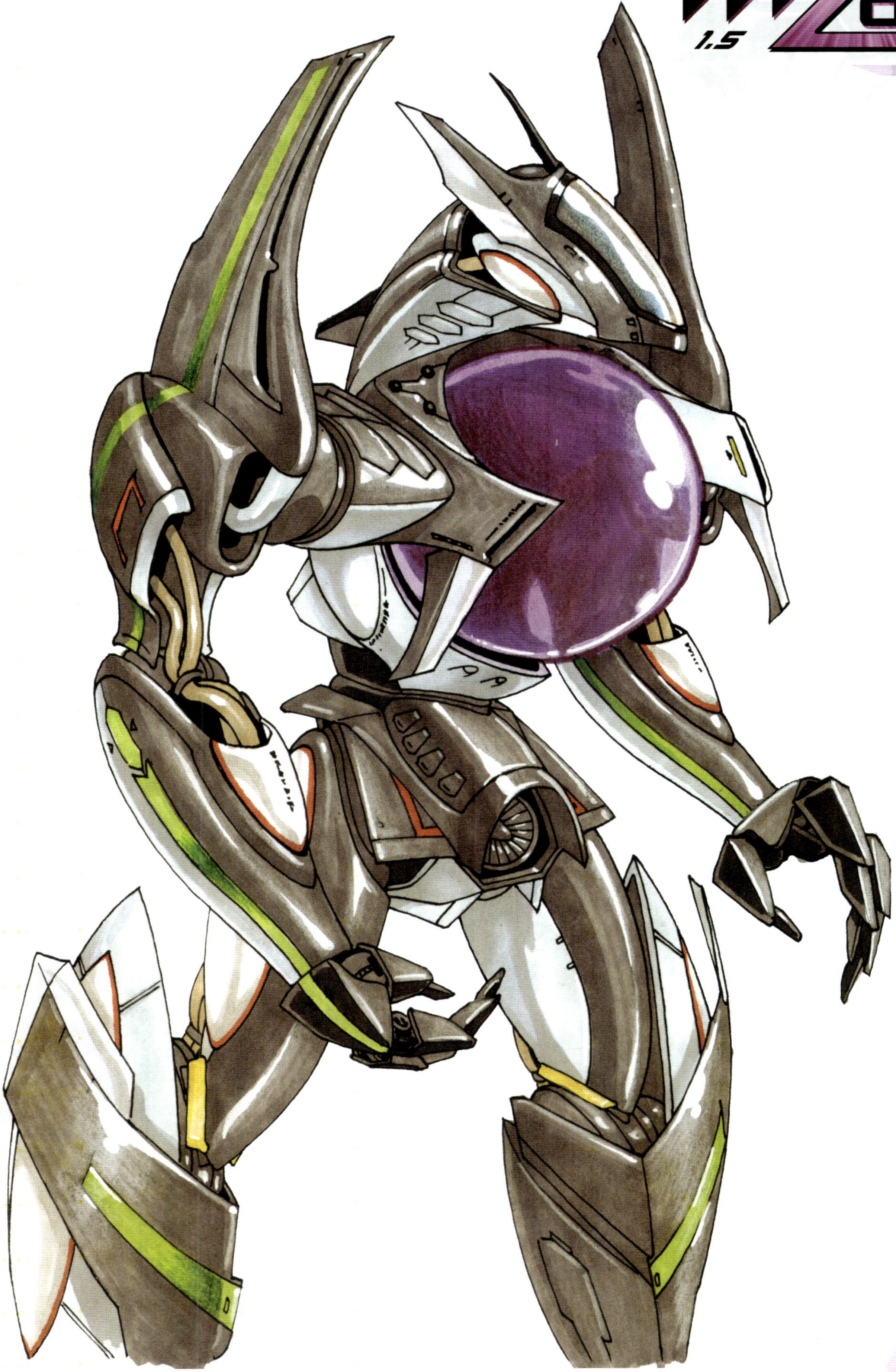

FLOTSAM

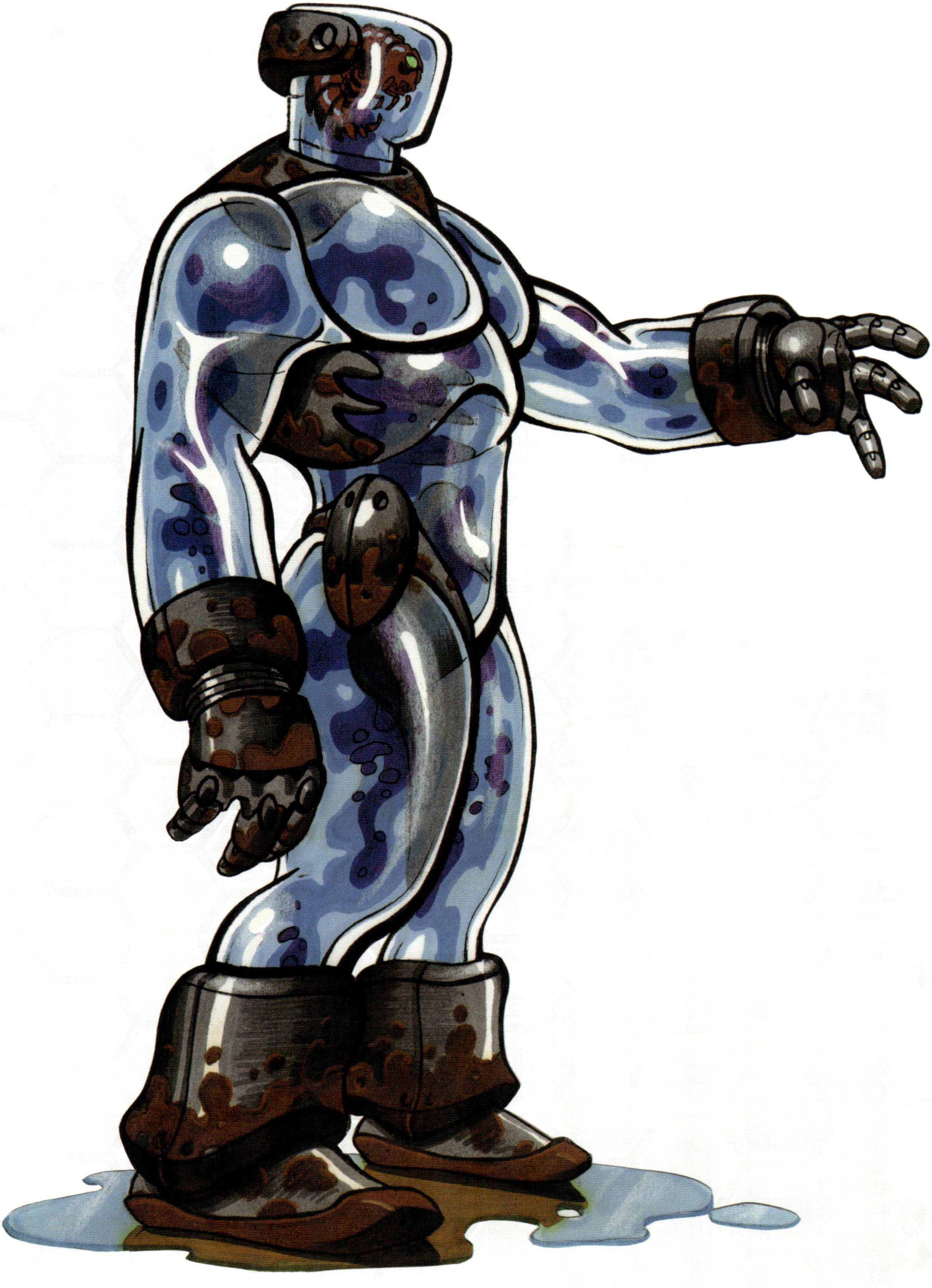

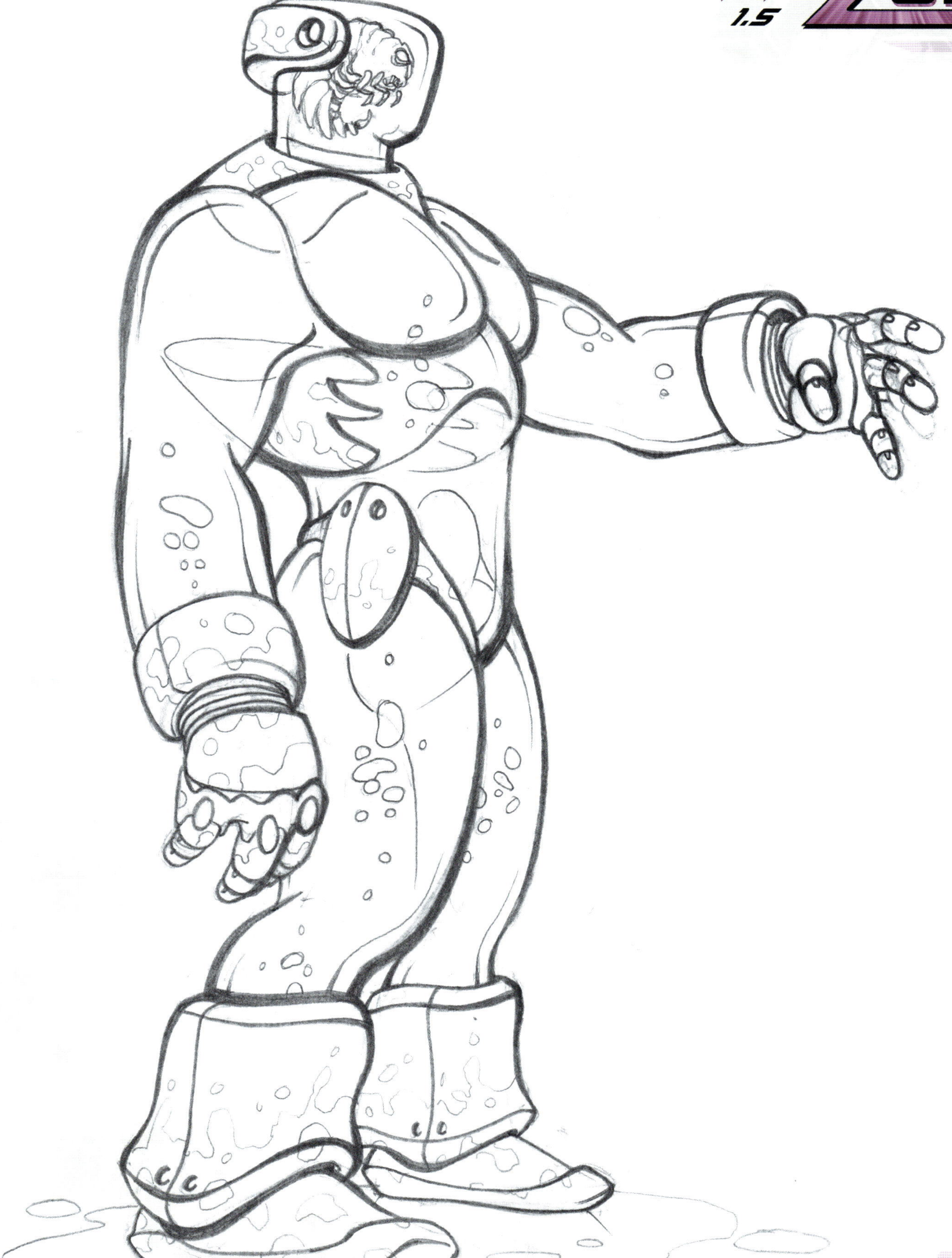

Retro Bot

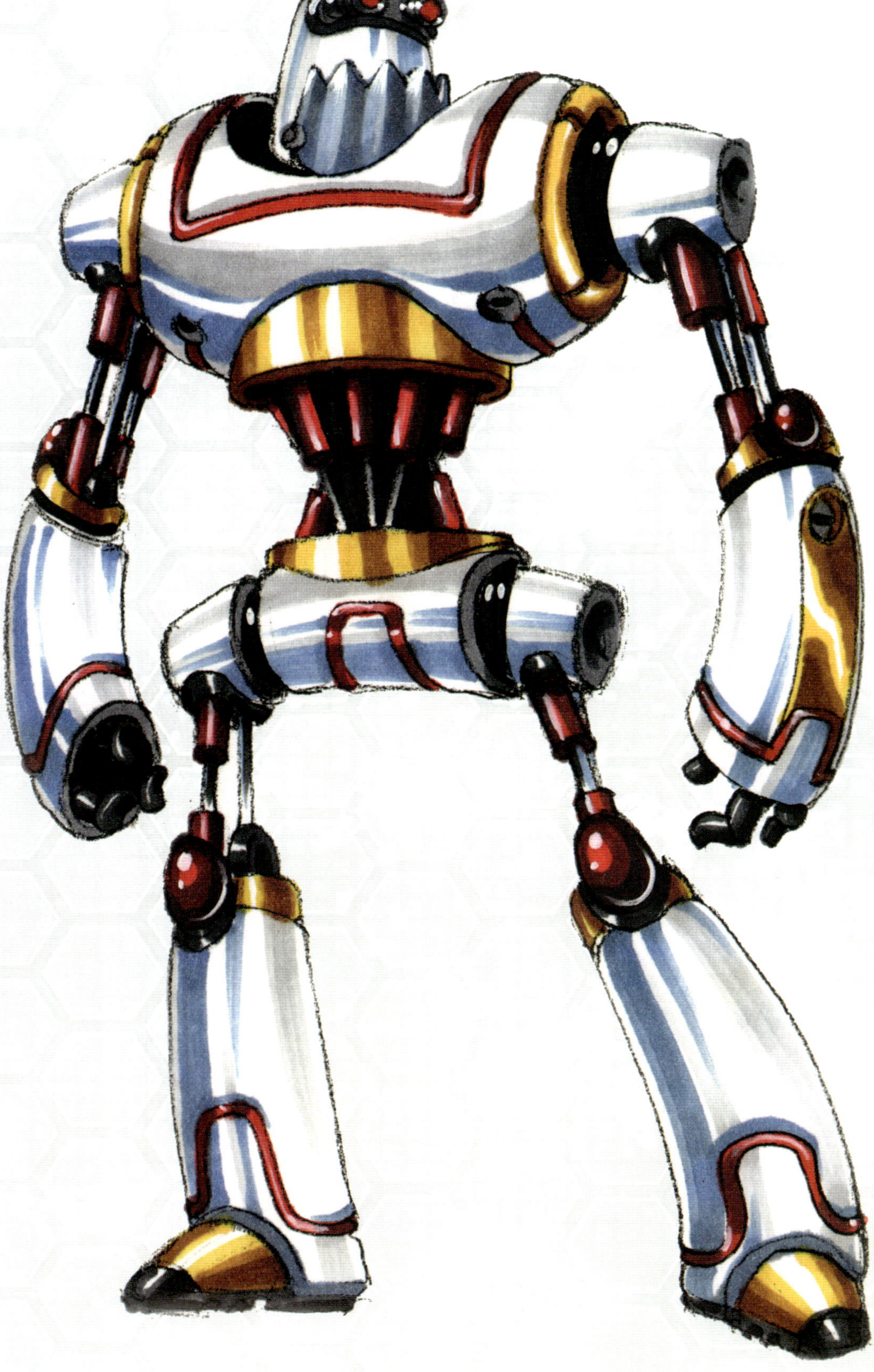

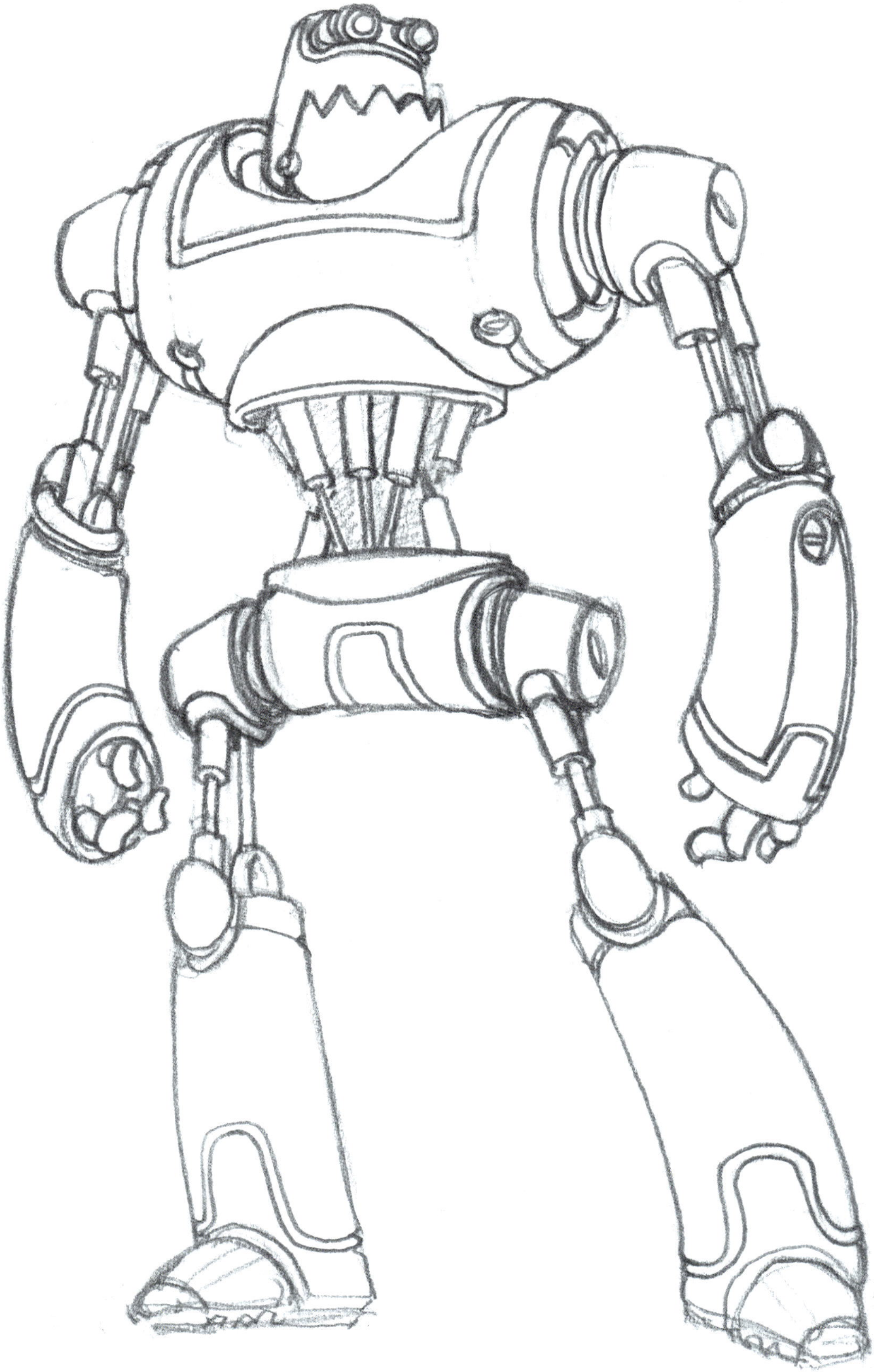

Invader Drone

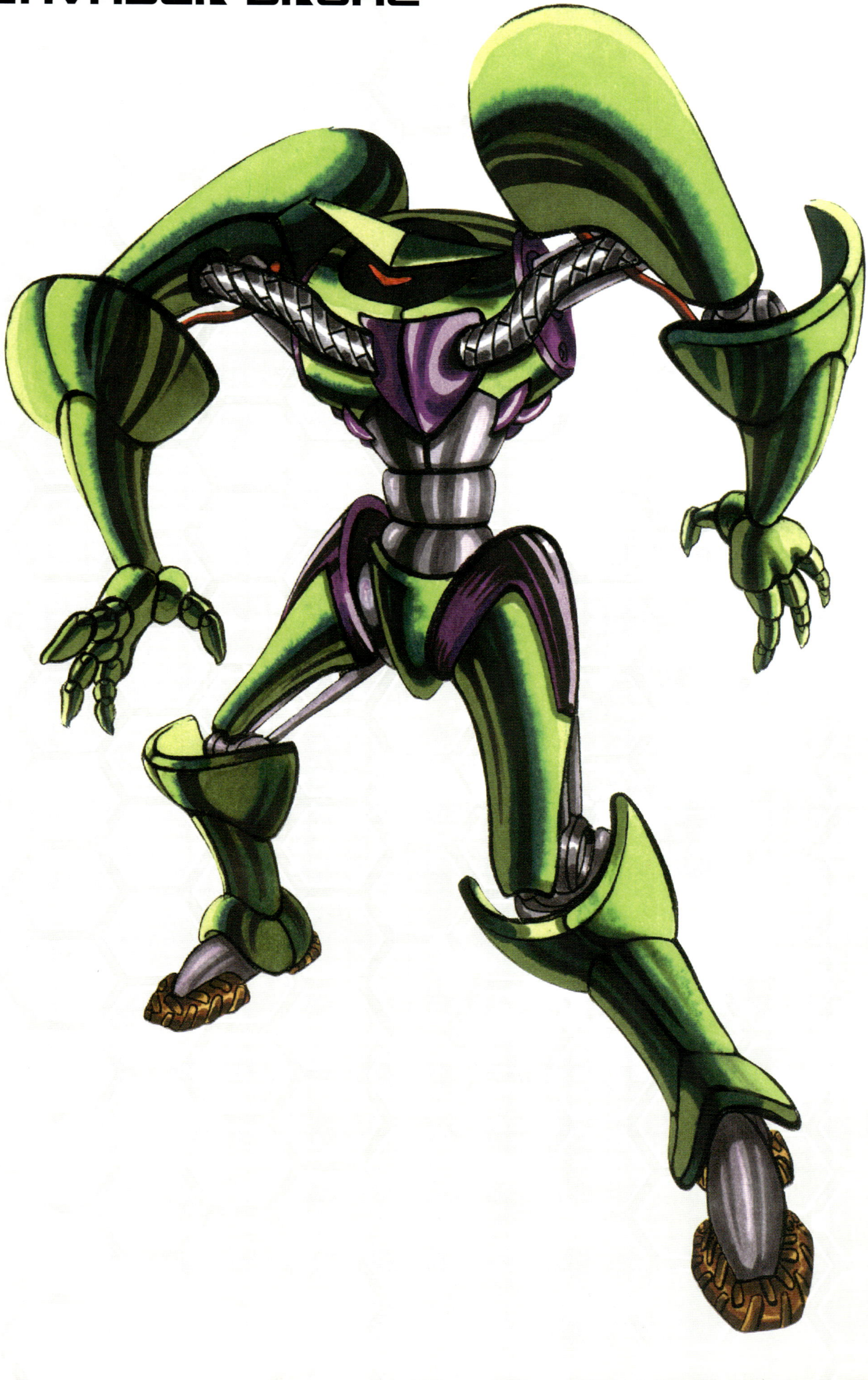

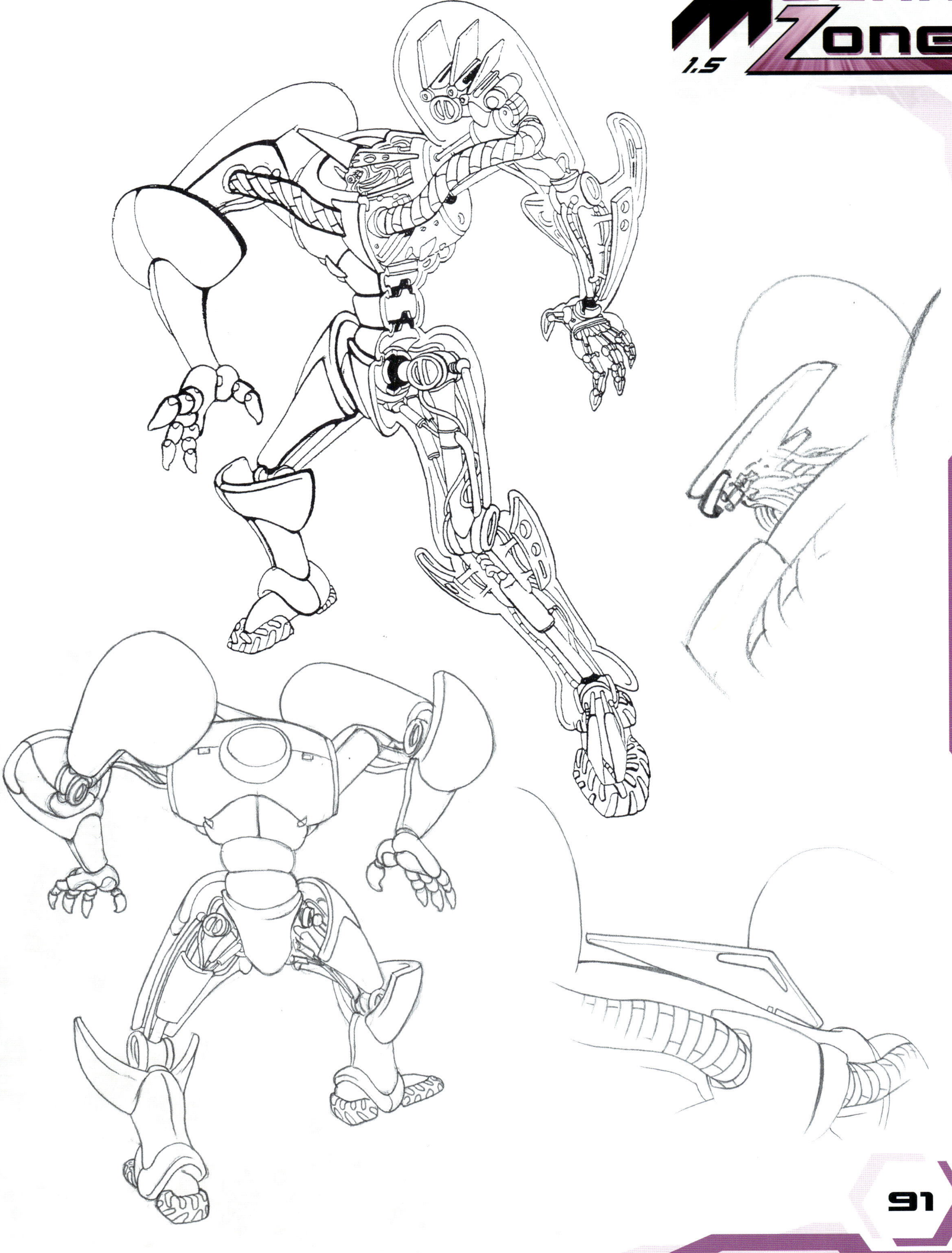

Construction mecha

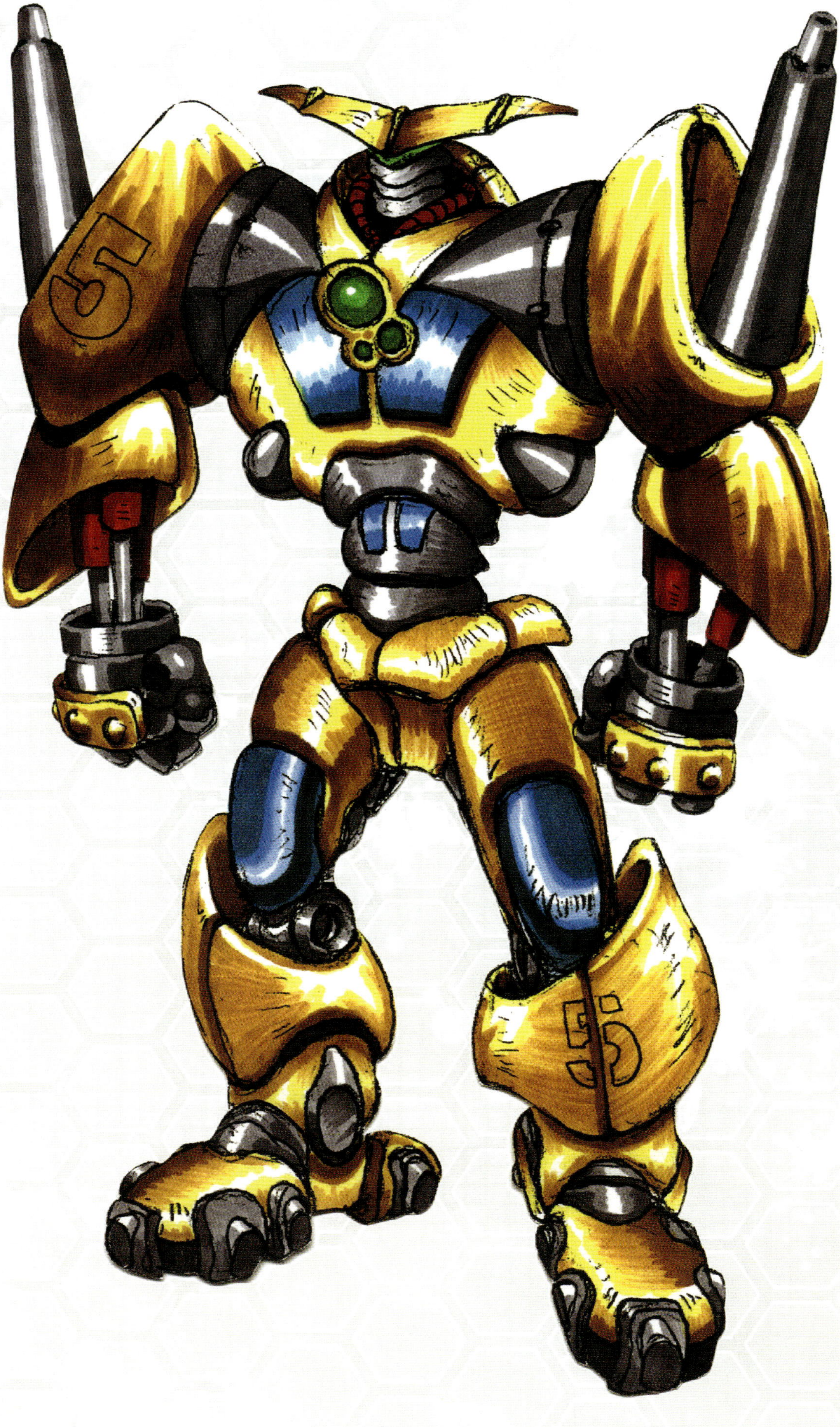

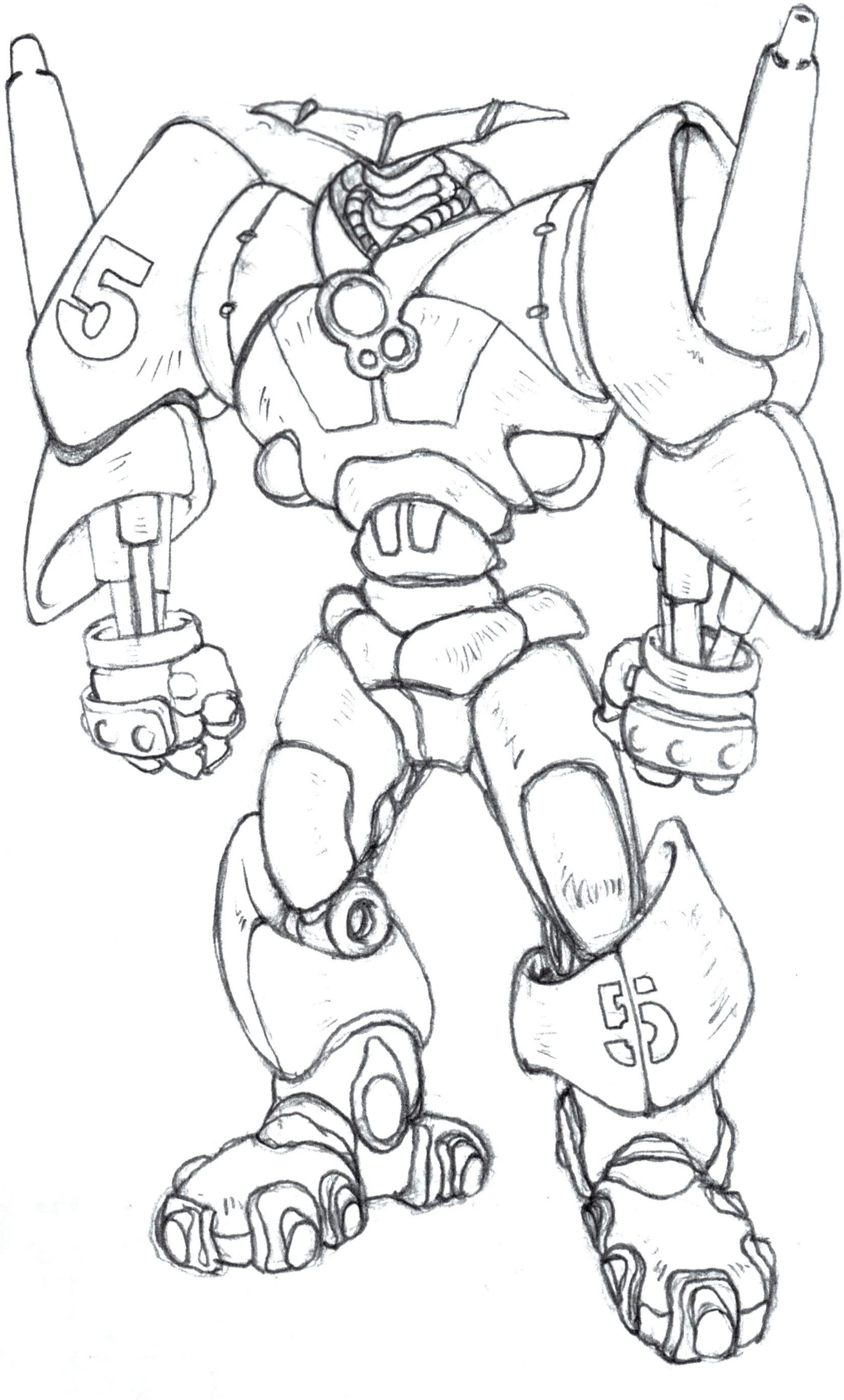

Royal Guard

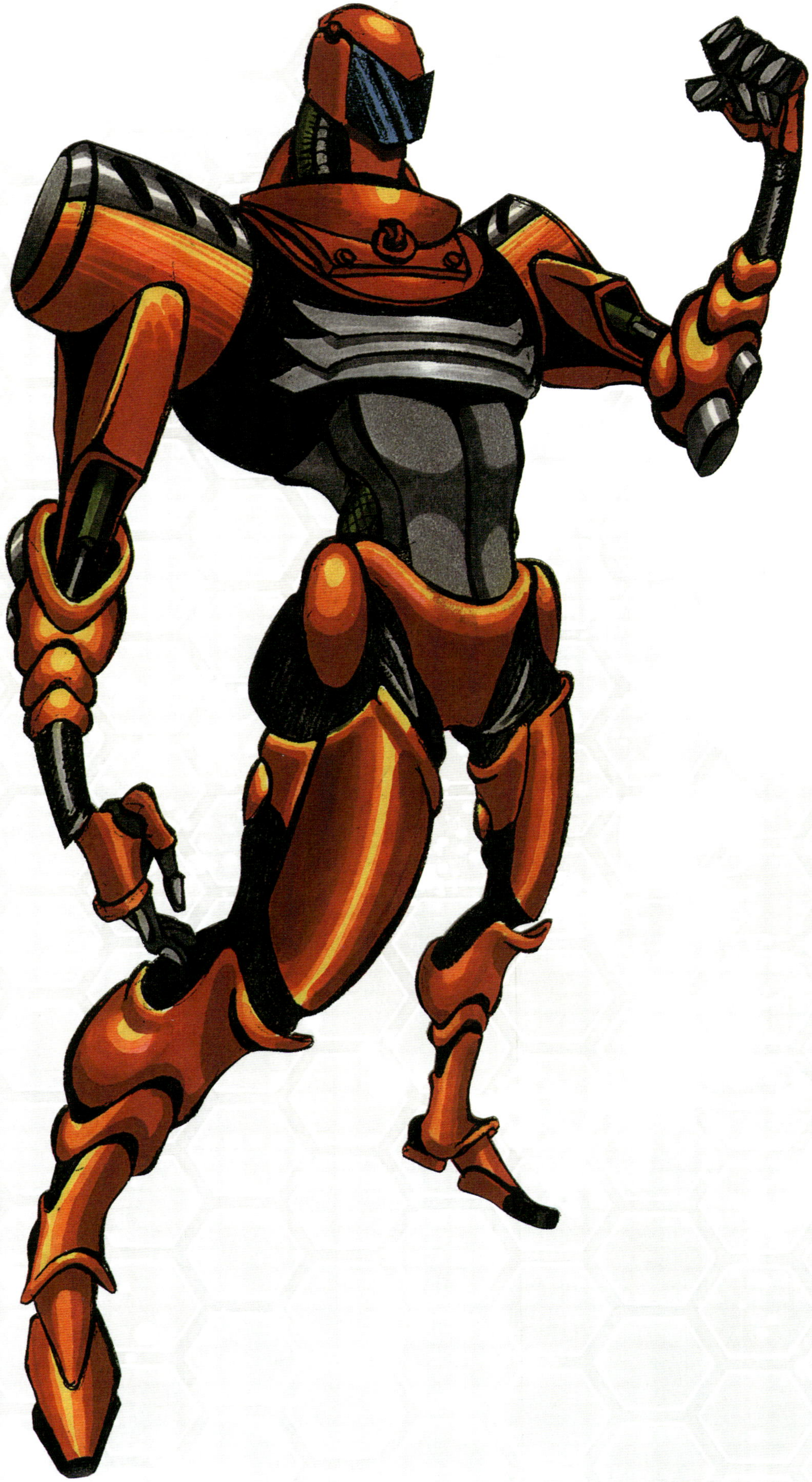

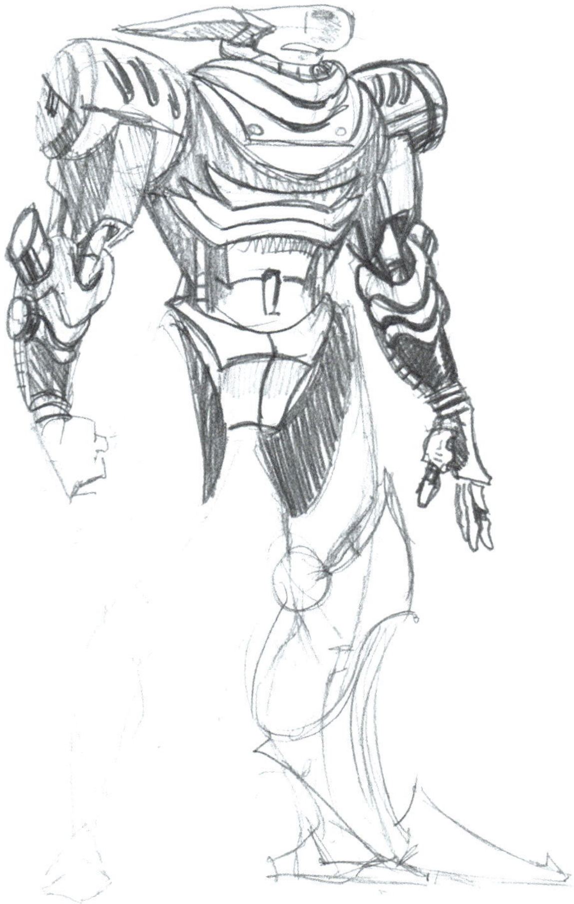

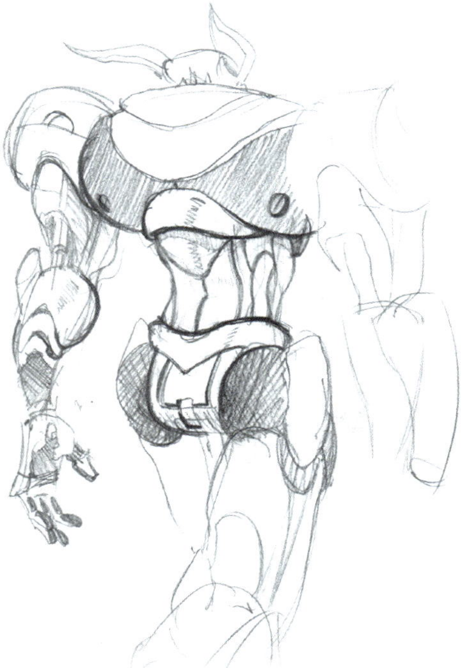

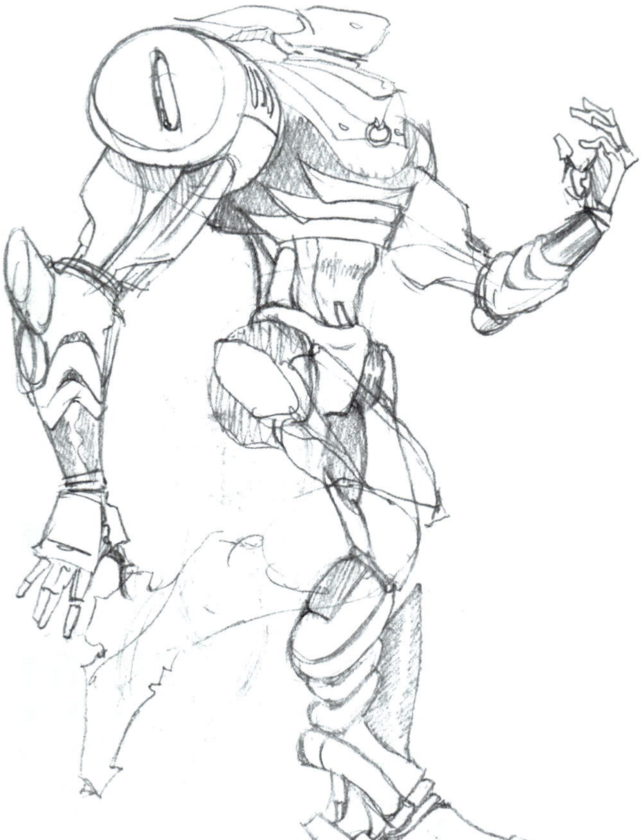

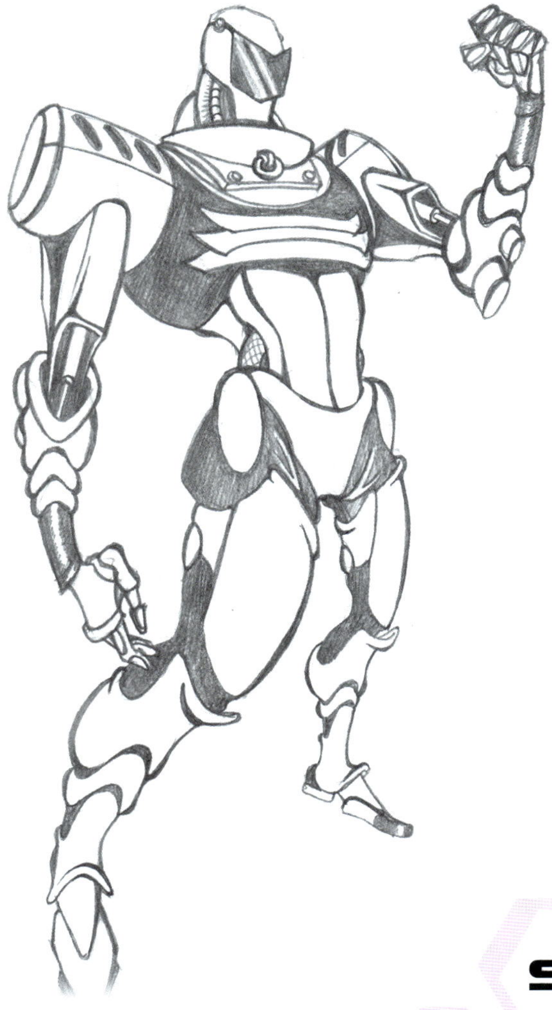

Mecha Zone

1.5

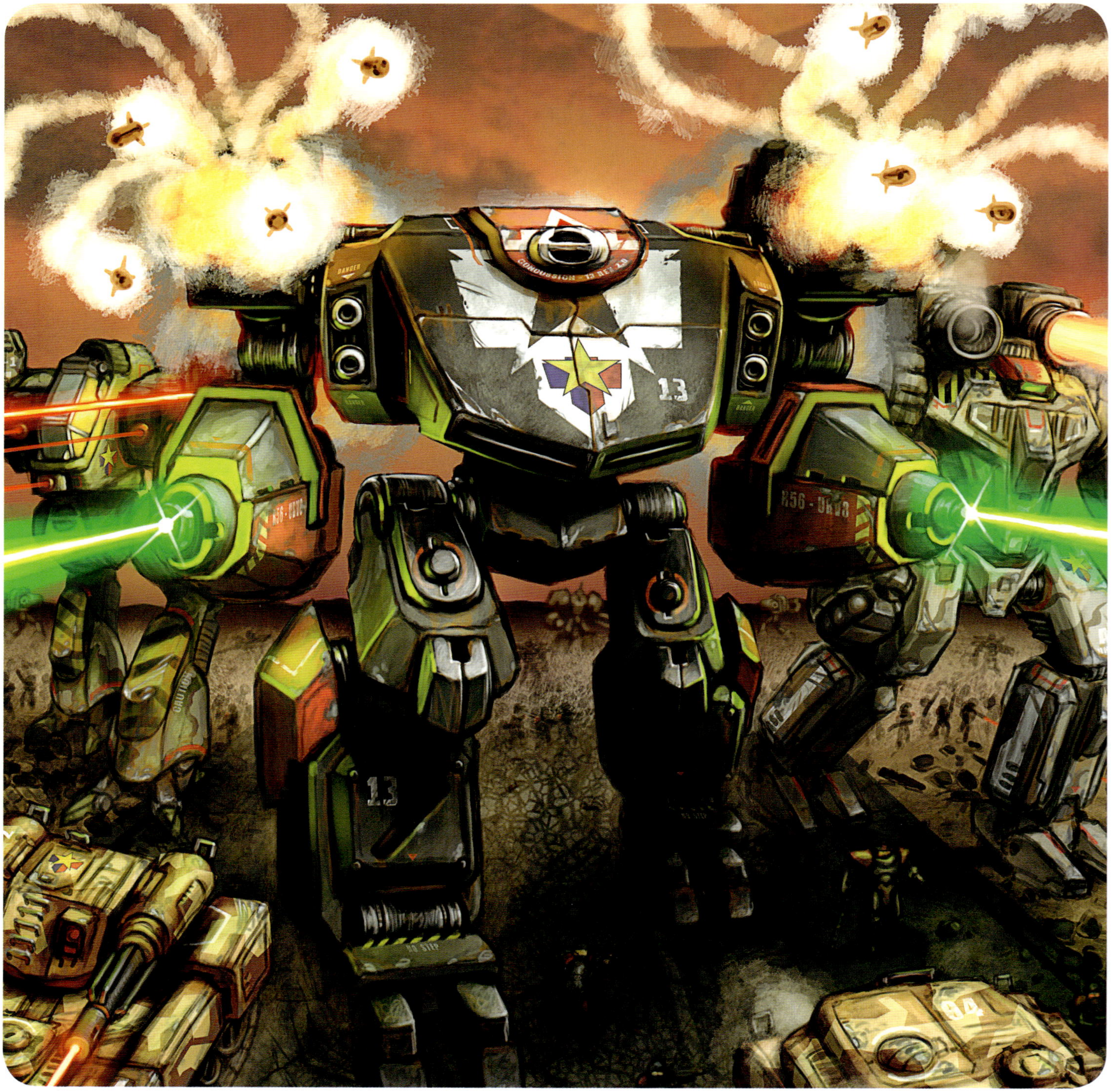

www.mechazone.com